Same-Sex Marriage, Legal Mobilization, & the Politics of Rights

Teaching Texts in Law and Politics

David A. Schultz
General Editor

Vol. 17

PETER LANG
New York • Washington, D.C./Baltimore • Bern
Frankfurt am Main • Berlin • Brussels • Vienna • Oxford

Martin Dupuis

Same-Sex Marriage, Legal Mobilization, & the Politics of Rights

PETER LANG
New York • Washington, D.C./Baltimore • Bern
Frankfurt am Main • Berlin • Brussels • Vienna • Oxford

Library of Congress Cataloging-in-Publication Data
Dupuis, Martin.
Same-sex marriage, legal mobilization,
and the politics of rights / Martin Dupuis.
p. cm. — (Teaching texts in law and politics; vol. 17)
Includes bibliographical references and index.
1. Same-sex marriage—Political aspects—United States. 2. Same-sex marriage—
Law and legislation—United States. 3. Gay rights—Political aspects—
United States. 4. Gay rights—Law and legislation—United States.
5. United States—Politics and government—1993–.
6. United States—Social policy—1993–. I. Title. II. Series.
HQ1034.U5 D86   306.84'8—dc21   2001029121
ISBN 0-8204-5560-1
ISSN 1083-3447

Die Deutsche Bibliothek-CIP-Einheitsaufnahme
Dupuis, Martin:
Same-sex marriage, legal mobilization,
and the politics of rights / Martin Dupuis.
–New York; Washington, D.C./Baltimore; Bern;
Frankfurt am Main; Berlin; Brussels; Vienna; Oxford: Lang.
(Teaching texts in law and politics; Vol. 17)
ISBN 0-8204-5560-1

Cover design by Joni Holst

© 2002 Peter Lang Publishing, Inc., New York

All rights reserved.
Reprint or reproduction, even partially, in all forms such as microfilm,
xerography, microfiche, microcard, and offset strictly prohibited.

To
Michael A. Dively
Friend and Mentor

Table of Contents

List of Tables ix

Acknowledgments xi

Introduction: Law and Social Change 1

1 Law and Rights Discourse in the
   Gay and Lesbian Social Movement
   in the United States 13

2 The History of Judicial Rejection
   of Same-Sex Marriage 33

3 Judicial Acceptance of Same-Sex Marriage 49

4 The Political Response to the Courts 71

5 Vermont's Supreme Court Grants Benefits of Marriage 99

6 Comparative Perspectives on the
   Recognition of Same-Sex Relationships 121

7 Conclusion 155

Bibliography 177

Index 195

List of Tables

Table 4.1: Non-Recognition Bills Passed 76

Table 4.2: Executive Orders Banning Same-Sex Marriage 79

Table 4.3: Constitutional Amendments
 to Ban Same-Sex Relationships 81

Table 4.4: Bills to Ban Recognition
 of Same-Sex Marriage Defeated 87

Table 4.5: Bills Introduced
 to Recognize Same-sex Marriage 89

Table 4.6: State-wide Domestic Partnership Laws 89

Table 5.1: Constitutional Theories
 for Recognizing Same-Sex Marriage 111

Table 6.1: Countries Recognizing Same-Sex Relationships 133

Acknowledgments

Research and writing are often solitary endeavors, but a book is the effort and influence of many people. I would like to thank my family for all their love and support. Friends over the years have provided much encouragement, notably Hugh Farrington, Mike Dively, Frank Flores, Chris Cunningham, Greg Drescher, and Dave Thomas. A special note of appreciation goes to Jason Chenoweth, who will always have a special place in my heart.

Professionally, I am indebted to the mentors who have inspired this project. Alison Renteln, Walter Williams, and Mark Blasius, thank you for all the hours of assistance. I am also grateful for my colleagues at Western Illinois University, especially my office mate, Keith Boeckelman, and my chair, Charles Helm.

The people at Peter Lang Publishing provided unparalleled support in editing and improving the text: David Schultz, Jacqueline Pavlovic, and Bernadette Alfaro.

Introduction
Law and Social Change

In the last decade, the civil rights of lesbians and gay men have become a prominent issue on the public agenda. These issues are being addressed in legislatures and courts in many countries and in international forums. Part of this debate challenges the traditional concept of family as the validity of same-sex relationships is asserted. These efforts to expand the definition of family illuminate both the direct and the indirect and symbolic effects of law in society. Legal scholars continue to debate the role law plays in progressive politics,[1] and the examples from the same-sex marriage struggle show how profound an impact law and perceptions of human rights can have on people's lives. The movement for legal recognition of gay and lesbian relationships, in the United States and abroad, demonstrates that law and conceptions of rights are important political resources for creating social change.

This study highlights the legal and political battles in the United States around same-sex marriage. These cases also demonstrate the tension in the U.S. political system between "anti-majoritarian" judicial decisions upholding constitutional rights against the legislative preferences of elected officials. From a comparative perspective, an examination of the issue of same-sex marriage illustrates how other political systems address rights-based challenges to existing social and religious norms.

Claims of rights, whether based on a concept of natural law, human rights, or constitutional authority, have provided the impetus for challenging perceived injustice for many disadvantaged groups. Rights claims might be the only resource available to people who have no other political clout. The same-sex marriage cases illustrate how individuals' understanding of their "rights" can motivate them to use the legal system to challenge state practices that they consider discriminatory. Social movements reflect this reliance on theories of justice, equality, and liberty by often labeling themselves as organizations devoted to securing some type of right for their members. In the 1960s, the civil rights movement captured America's attention. In the 1970s, women's rights and abortion rights were paramount. Reformers since the 1980s have advocated greater rights for the homeless, the physically and mentally disabled, the environment, and animals. The 1990s could well be remembered as the decade for gay and lesbian rights.

Rights claims are not prominent only in Western liberal democracies. Theories of human rights are enshrined in international treaties and have formed the basis for political struggles across the globe. On the transnational level, treaties such as the United Nations Universal Declaration of Human Rights and the European Convention on Human Rights embody widespread agreements on the dignity of every person. Many nation-states have also recently outlined individual rights, including South Africa in its 1995 Constitution and Canada in its 1982 Charter of Rights and Freedoms. The new democracies of eastern Europe, Asia, and Latin America emphasize the rule of law and the establishment of rights.

The legislative process can be used to expand rights, but when the majority in society is not willing to recognize the claims of the minority, the judiciary is called upon to weigh these competing demands. The legitimacy and scope of the court's power of judicial review, striking down the action of the legislative branch when it conflicts with the fundamental law of the Constitution, havebeen questioned since the founding of the U.S. Republic. Alexander Hamilton, in the *Federalist Papers,* explained that the judiciary, "the least dangerous branch" of government, would interpret the law and resolve individual disputes. Courts would be constrained from making policy by legal procedures and by dependence on the other two branches of government for the enforcement of their decrees. Yet, the judiciary was also envisioned as a check on the "tyranny of the majority" and a protector of minority rights. These dual roles of the judicial system place courts in the middle of disputes between citizens and the government, and courts are called upon to decide the allocation of resources and responsibilities; in other words, politics.

The circumstances under which courts exercise the power of judicial review and the capacity of courts to make effective social policy have been highly contested. Robert Dahl in 1957 analyzed cases where the U.S. Supreme Court declared federal legislation unconstitutional and concluded that the Court is part of the ruling national coalition.[2] Supreme Court decisions rarely deviate too much from the views of elected representatives because the justices are selected by a majority of lawmakers. The Senate will not confirm someone with radically different political views, and the elite group of people who office in any branch of the national government are socialized by similar interests and influences. Consequently, the Court is not the distinguished protector of minority rights as commonly thought. Dahl outlines the Court's main policy-making function:

> The main task of the Court is to confer legitimacy on the fundamental policies of the successful coalition. There are times when the coalition is unstable with respect to certain key policies; at very great risk to its legitimacy powers, the Court can intervene in such cases and may even succeed in establishing policy. Probably in such cases it can succeed only if its action conforms to and reinforces a widespread set of explicit or implicit norms held by the political leadership; norms which are not strong enough or are not distributed in such a way as to insure the existence of an effective lawmaking majority but are, nonetheless, sufficiently powerful to prevent any successful attack on the legitimacy powers of the Court. This is probably the explanation for the relatively successful work of the Court in enlarging the freedom of Negroes to vote during the past three decades and in its famous school integration decisions (294).

Dahl's assessment was written before the Warren Court's expansion of rights in the 1960s.

Jonathan Casper expanded Dahl's research to include Supreme Court decisions addressing statutory interpretation and constitutional issues arising from state and local cases. Casper found a much greater policy-making role for the courts. Rather than just reviewing which policy outcome prevailed, the Court's role in setting an agenda, mobilizing resources, attracting support, providing an alternative of access points to the political system, and legitimizing minority viewpoints also need to be considered.[3]

The debate around the institutional capacity of the courts to make policy has been forcefully articulated by Abram Chayes and Donald Horowitz. Chayes[4] emphasized that judges are insulated from interest groups and political parties, and that they strive for neutral, objective decision making. Adjudication allows a high degree of participation through "friend of the court" briefs, *amicus curiai*, and through expert testimony while the poor and unorganized are often excluded from the legislative process. Our adversarial system encourages attorneys to present all relevant information. Finally, the courts cannot avoid confronting the difficult social issues. Elected officials in the legislature often focus on favored policies that generate political benefits.

Horowitz[5] argued that adjudication is ineffective for making social policy because lawsuits represent narrow, specific complaints that do not reflect larger social concerns. Judges are removed from social and political organizations and may be insensitive to the broader consequences of their decisions. They do not develop an expertise in policy areas as legislators and bureaucrats do. Courts lack the feedback and follow-up procedures to ensure that the desired result is being enforced. Courts are also restricted to assessing the relief requested by the parties to the case and generally cannot consider the costs and benefits of various possible solutions to the general problem. Policymaking, therefore, is best left to the politics of the legislative process.

The notion of politics suggests that groups compete and bargain for policy outcomes. In making a rights claim, there is an attempt to transcend politics. Ronald Dworkin notes that rights are "political trumps."[6] If the members of a group can secure access to a right, they receive the entitlement, treatment, or status desired even if a majority of the population would not grant it. Rights are instrumental for self-definition and for defining relationships with others.[7]

The efficacy of rights-based litigation strategies for social change, however, has been challenged by activists and academics. From the 1950s through the mid-1970s, the courts seemed responsive to protecting minority rights and to supporting liberal social policies. This view was challenged as the Supreme Court under Warren Burger curbed the expansion of rights discourse. Stuart Scheingold in his seminal book, *The Politics of Rights*, and a work that inspired the title of this study, reported that social activists had developed a naive faith in the "myth of rights."[8] This myth suggested that rights affirmed by the Supreme Court are self-implementing and are beyond the constraints of political power. However, litigation as a tool for social change is restrained by ideological, organizational, and financial limitations. Scheingold recognized that courts can play a minimal role in affecting social change by giving prominence to issues and placing them on the public agenda. Stephen Halpern echoed this view and stated that courts act on the margins of social policy.

Three main schools of thought have emerged to examine whether courts can be a vehicle of social change. The critical, structuralist critique emphasizes the systemic, hegemonic attributes of law,[9] and the neo-realist analysis considers "the lure of litigation" a "hollow hope."[10] The constitutive approach, however, argues that law does make a difference in terms of social change, but that the impact can be indirect. These approaches differ in their understanding of the symbolic aspects of law, notions of causality and power, and the criteria of "significant" social change.[11]

Structuralist and Critical Legal Studies Perspectives

Structuralists argue that litigation causes a significant drain on financial and personnel resources, and they emphasize the organizational costs of legal tactics that constrain social movements. Since judicial victories may yield only small gains and the risk of losing the litigation is always present, these costs are not usually justifiable. Furthermore, litigation draws resources and energy away from other more productive or more radical grassroots tactics and privileges the status of lawyers who favor litigation. Finally, litigation "atomizes" movements by fragmenting issues into individual disputes between particular parties, diverts the focus from system-wide injustices, and hinders efforts at broad-based movement building.

Critical legal scholars have also argued that ideological biases pervade the legal system and that these attitudes inherently shape the arguments and decisions of attorneys and judges. Thus, truly progressive change cannot emerge from a legal system which typically serves political and economic elites and supports the status quo. The development of a critical legal consciousness among citizens is impeded by the internalization of existing, dominant, hegemonic legal norms.[12] Law is viewed in static, monolithic, functionalist terms and necessarily serves fundamental systemic roles and interests.[13] Legal rights, therefore, offer only empty "illusions" of social change and a "masquerade" of justice for those disadvantaged citizens who deploy them.[14]

Neo-realists' Perspectives

Much of the neo-realist analysis focuses on the discrepancies between legal victories and behavioral modification. Judicial impact studies have typically found an "expectation gap" between favorable court decisions and social change. Litigation is deemed to be a waste of time and resources because courts lack independence from other branches of government and do not have the institutional capacity to implement and administer reform policies. In addition, neither elites nor the mass of the public follow or understand judicial edicts.[15]

Gerald Rosenberg, in his seminal work, *The Hollow Hope: Can Courts Bring about Social Change*, argues that courts are institutionally constrained by the limitations of precedent, by lack of independence from other branches of government and public opinion, and by their inability to enforce their decisions.[16] Thus, courts are unable to effect social change unless these three constraints can be overcome. This occurs when there is case law supporting bold judicial action or when there is support for the change from legislative and executive officials. To counter the court's weak implementation capacity, there must be citizen support, or at least only a low level of opposition. In addition, some incentive or cost to induce compliance, the opportunity for implementation in the marketplace, or a willingness among extrajudicial actors to use the court's decision as a tool for action is needed.

The Constitutive Perspective

The constitutive theory adopts an interactive, culturally based view of law and analyzes how legal norms and appeals to claims of rights are invoked as a form of political activity. Frances Zemans explains that "Law is ... mobilized when a desire or want is translated into a demand or an assertion of one's rights."[17] Whereas the conventional view is that law is a determinate set of rules that citizens simply obey, the constitutive approach emphasizes the indirect, "radiating" effects of litigation strategies over time. The cultural meaning of law communicates symbols, expectations, legitimacy, and stigmas.[18] Michael McCann, one of the foremost proponents of this theory, states that the goal is "to analyze the constitutive role of legal rights both as a strategic resource and as a constraint for collective efforts to transform or 'reconstitute' relationships among social groups."[19] This approach argues that "law is better appreciated as a continuously contested terrain of relational power among citizens." Constitutive analysis "begins with specific disputes and relations among social groups—rather than with a judicial decision or text—and then inquires about how different legal norms, texts, institutions, and tactics do or do not shape interaction over time."[20] This framework shifts the focus of analysis to the social struggle itself rather than the actions of state officials.

The constitutive theory adopts a "decentered" or dispute-centered perspective. The primary emphasis, McCann explains, is on "nonjudicial actors [who] are viewed as practical legal agents rather than as simply reactors to judicial commands."[21] Legal actions begin with the framing of demands in ongoing social relations rather than with official court decisions. Since judicial intervention is rarely utilized, courts are viewed as to an extent peripheral to most forms of legal action. The neo-realists isolate the courts from the other branches of government and place them in a competitive relationship with other institutions trying to distinguish the power of one from the other.

While structuralists and neo-realists view the legal order as monolithic, the constitutive approach views law in a pluralistic framework. Neo-realists and structuralists are correct in that landmark court decisions by themselves rarely change behavior or personal values. However, these approaches "discount the reciprocal, interactive, relational terms of law's constitutive power" and obscure "the subtle but significant ways that judicial actions shape the strategic landscape within which citizens (including elites) negotiate relations with each other as legal subjects."[22] Judicial proclamations have more impact on "reshaping perceptions of when and how particular values are realistically actionable as claims of legal right" than in altering the substantive values of most citizens through moral persuasion.[23]

Legal conventions, including rights discourse, are shaped by, and in turn are factors in shaping, practical social relations and activities.[24] One's understanding of these conventions, or "legal consciousness,"[25] constructs what is deemed possible and what is just, and may vary depending on the time frame, social space, and institutional site of the legal actor.[26] The primary legal convention in a liberal democracy is a rights discourse. Ronald Dworkin points out that "the language of rights now dominates political debate in the United States."[27] Neo-realists are correct that rights are socially constructed and that their specific substantive content is unstable over time. However, they ignore the fact that rights are "invested with meaning by cultural practices themselves, by the repeated acts of citizens using those conventions to negotiate material relations with each other."[28]

This malleability does not make rights claims an ineffective resource for social change, as neo-realists argue, but rather is the basis for its power. Disadvantaged groups may not accept the official interpretation of a legal norm, and the socio-political consequences of rejecting this definition might be to unite those affected and possibly to cause a further contestation of the law. A practical understanding of the dynamic nature of legal discourse undermines the structuralist argument that invoking legal rights results in the reification of these precepts. The constraints stemming from rights claims are based more on the actual experiences of those trying to invoke a legal right rather than on an ideological mystification or acceptance of the law.[29] McCann concludes that "if realists underestimate law's constitutive power, then structuralist arguments greatly over-determine law's ideological grip on the experience of citizens."[30]

The constitutive approach does not dismiss the structuralist claim that law as an aggregate reinforces the positions of those in power. For the most part, law acts as a constraint and sustains the hegemonic order. Established legal conventions usually favor some people and disadvantage others, and the various resources of groups and individuals allow unequal access to the courts. Legal norms, which are ideally considered to be egalitarian, indirectly reinforce domination of some citizens by others and powerlessness among the members of the dominated group. However, McCann argues that "broadly cast claims about the inherent futility of litigation strategies for social movements are not warranted or illuminating about the politics of law in practice."[31]

Invoking rights converts a desire into a more legitimate claim and summons an "equality of attention" in public debate.[32] Rights discourse is valuable for those with few other political and cultural resources at their disposal. McCann states, "Given the overwhelming systemic inequalities and scarcities in basic resources that oppress subordinate groups, even limited, contingent, uncertain resources such as our legal traditions offer should be appreciated."[33] Key conventions may have a common public meaning, but they can also take on particular conceptions as these are advanced through changing social relations. Rights discourse can be a seed of resistance. Legal tactics may also generate indirect effects which support a movement's efforts, such as mobilizing groups, building group alliances, generating public support, and providing leverage to supplement other political tactics. These indirect effects may be more important for advancing social change than whether the plaintiffs' succeed in court.

Structuralists contemplate social movement resources from a theoretical perspective where one tactic can be substituted for another without recognizing the practical limitations that might exist. Some groups may not be positioned in such a way as to successfully generate grassroots activism, compete with well-financed lobbyists, or wield influence in elections.

Contrary to those critics who argue that litigation is a limiting and constraining tactic, legal defense fund organizations can attract support from middle-class and corporate contributors who would be unlikely to support more radical or disruptive types of activity. Instead of being a drain on resources, legal tactics can generate income through fund raising and the awarding of attorneys' fees. Litigation can be slow or cause delay, but it can also be the impetus for progress. Various types of political tactics should not be viewed as competitive, zero-sum options but rather in concert.

Social movements usually evolve incrementally through local struggles over time rather than through radical, comprehensive, structural change. The constitutive approach, with its emphasis on cultural context, suggests the value of analyzing the impact of law on collective action in terms of the development or evolution of the social movement itself. Legal mobilization may contribute in different ways and with different impacts at various points in the struggle. Legal discourse can contribute to creating social change by shaping the overall structure of opportunities facing movements and by proposing various legal resources to parties struggling for position. By analyzing the litigation strategies and the indirect influences of law and rights discourse employed by the gay and lesbian social movement as it develops, a more thorough and sophisticated understanding of the role of law in society can be achieved.

Notes

1. For an overview of this debate, see volume 3 of this series, Teaching Texts in Law and Politics, David A. Schultz, ed., *Leveraging the Law: Using the Courts to Achieve Social Change* (New York: Peter Lang, 1998).

2. Robert Dahl, "Decision-Making in a Democracy: The Supreme Court as a National Policy-Maker," *Journal of Public Law* 6 (Fall 1957): 279-295.

3. Jonathan D. Casper, "The Supreme Court and National Policy Making," *American Political Science Review* 70 (1976): 50-63.

4. Abram Chayes, "The Role of the Judge in Public Law Litigation," *Harvard Law Review* 89 (1976): 1281.

5. Donald L. Horowitz, *The Courts and Social Policy* (Washington, D.C.: Brookings Institute, 1977).

6. Ronald Dworkin, *Taking Rights Seriously* (Cambridge: Harvard University Press, 1977), xi.

7. Wendy Brown, "Rights and Identity in Late Modernity: Revisiting the 'Jewish Question,'" in Austin Sarat and Thomas R. Kearns, eds., *Identity, Politics, and Rights* (Ann Arbor, Mich.: University of Michigan Press, 1995), 85-130; and Morris B. Kaplan, *Sexual Justice: Democratic Citizenship and the Politics of Desire* (New York: Routledge, 1997).

8. Stuart A. Scheingold, *The Politics of Rights* (New Haven, Conn.: Yale University Press, 1974).

9. Mark Kelman, *A Guide to Critical Legal Studies* (Cambridge: Harvard University Press, 1987).

10. Gerald N. Rosenberg, *The Hollow Hope: Can Courts Bring about Social Change* (Chicago: University of Chicago Press, 1991).

11. Michael W. McCann, "Reform Litigation on Trial," *Law and Social Inquiry* 18 (1993): 1101.

12. Alan Hunt, "Rights and Social Movements: Counter-Hegemonic Strategies," *Journal of Law and Society* 17 (1990): 309-342.

13. Kimberle Williams Crenshaw, "Race, Reform and Retrenchment: Transformation and Legitimation in Antidiscrimination Law," *Harvard Law Review* 101 (1988): 1331-1402.

14. Marc Tushnet, "An Essay on Rights," *Texas Law Review* 62 (1984): 1363-1412.

15. Horowitz, *The Courts and Social Policy*.

16. Rosenberg, *The Hollow Hope*.

17. Frances Zemans, "Legal Mobilization: The Neglected Role of Law in the Political System" *American Political Science Review* 77 (1983): 690-703, 700.

18. Marc Galanter, "The Radiating Effects of Courts," in Keith D. Boyum and Lynn Mather, eds., *Empirical Theories of Courts* (New York: Longman, 1983), 117-142.

19. Michael W. McCann, "Legal Mobilization and Social Reform Movements," *Studies in Law, Politics, and Society* 11 (1991): 225-254, 228.

20. Michael W. McCann, *Rights at Work: Pay Equity Reform and the Politics of Legal Mobilization* (Chicago: University of Chicago Press, 1994), 283.

21. McCann, "Reform Litigation on Trial," *Law and Social Inquiry* 17 (1992): 715-743, 731.

22. McCann, *Rights at Work*, 291.

23. McCann, "Reform Litigation," 732.

24. Susan Silbey, "Making a Place for Cultural Analyses of Law," *Law and Social Inquiry* 17 (1992).

25. Sally Engle Merry, *Getting Justice and Getting Even: Legal Consciousness among Working-Class Americans* (Chicago: University of Chicago Press, 1990).

26. Christine Harrington and Barbara Yngvesson, "Interpretive Sociolegal Research," *Law and Social Inquiry* 15 (1990): 135-158; Austin Sarat, "The Law Is All Over: Power, Resistance, and the Legal Consciousness of Welfare Poor," *Yale Journal of Law and the Humanities* 2 (1990): 343-392.

27. Dworkin, *Taking Rights Seriously*, 184.

28. McCann, *Rights at Work*, 297.

29. Martha Minow, *Making All the Difference: Inclusion, Exclusion, and American Law* (Ithaca, N.Y.: Cornell University Press, 1990).

30. McCann, *Rights at Work*, 301.

31. Ibid., 292.

32. Minow, *Making All the Difference*, 297.

33. McCann, *Rights at Work*, 309.

Chapter One
Law and Rights Discourse in the Gay and Lesbian Social Movement in the United States

In 1991, one gay and two lesbian couples in Honolulu, Hawaii, created one of the most contentious debates on sexuality and the institution of marriage by suing for the right to wed.[1] The Hawaii same-sex marriage case began when a handful of citizens, who happen to be gay and lesbian, acted on their own behalf against the political system, based on a sense of a perceived injustice against them. After they succeeded at the appellate level of the lawsuit, many actors in the political system responded, including the national gay and lesbian organizations, the religious right, Congress, the president, and every state legislature.

The Hawaii Supreme Court rejected the legal reasoning that state courts had followed for the past twenty-five years by holding that the denial of marriage licenses to same-sex couples may violate the equal protection clause of the state constitution.[2] The court found that denying same-sex couples the right to marry constituted a type of sex discrimination and that the definition of marriage need not be sexually biased. The case was remanded to the lower court to determine if there was a "compelling state interest," the most difficult constitutional standard to meet, in prohibiting same-sex marriage. This unexpected judicial victory propelled same-sex marriage to the forefront of the gay and lesbian movement's agenda. Without this favorable court ruling, the issue of same-sex marriage would not even have been seen as a priority, or even a possibility, by the leadership of the national gay and lesbian organizations.

This case generated an enormous political backlash. By 1997, forty-eight states had considered legislation to restrict the recognition of any potential same-sex marriages from Hawaii, even though the courts had not even resolved the issue. These measures were beaten back in twenty-three states. Congress, in a rare act of insertion of the federal government into marriage, fearing the ramifications of same-sex marriage, passed the Defense of Marriage Act (DOMA)[3], which President Clinton signed, despite calling the act "gay-baiting."[4] DOMA raises a number of constitutional issues with regard to federalism, nondiscrimination, and respect for lawful marriage that will also probably be addressed in the federal courts. In 1997, three Vermont same-sex couples sued for the right to wed, and the state high court directed the legislature to devise a method for providing them all the rights of marriage.

Before discussing the issues surrounding the same-sex marriage debate, it is necessary to provide an overview of how the contemporary gay and lesbian social movement has used the law to advance its causes in the United States over the last fifty years. Litigation and its indirect effects were significant in the early stages of the movement, especially when a legal claim could be anchored to a well-established right. Without these legal victories and the resulting political mobilization, the movement might have waned.

Law and Movement Building

The Mattachine Society, the first public gay organization of the contemporary social movement, was formed in Los Angeles, California, in 1951.[5] The founders of the Mattachine Society had been involved with the Communist Party or other left-wing organizations. However, the Soviet Communist Party under Stalin had reversed its tolerance of homosexuality, and the American party echoed this position. Many of the Mattachine Society leaders had given up their party work in order to focus on homosexual issues. At this time, the political organizing by homosexuals was not even allowed in communist circles or in other organizations supporting systemic change in the United States.[6]

The Mattachine Society was a secret organization that had been formed to provide discussion groups for homosexual men. Initially, many people used pseudonyms in order to retain their anonymity. The discussion groups had two goals: sharing personal experiences and developing a theoretical understanding of the oppression of homosexuals. This concern for understanding oppression stemmed from their communist views of the systemic structure of social relations and the lack of interest within the Communist Party itself in exploring the issue.[7] Over time, the discussions expanded to debate such topics as whether homosexuals constituted a minority group, the notion of a "homosexual culture," and the forms, if any, that political action should take.

Some of the leaders wanted to take more political action, but they did not know where to begin. It is important to understand the cultural and political climate at the time. Senator McCarthy's attack on "subversives" included homosexuals as well as Communists, which added to the pressure to remain anonymous. It was common knowledge that federal and state governmental agencies were investigating communist organizations. Less publicized in the media was the repression of sexuality. Public officials attacked behavior they considered deviant, and the United States Senate released a report on "sexual perverts." The founding members of the Mattachine Society had sound reasons to fear persecution based on their communist politics as well as their sexual orientation. For example, Chuck Rowland had lost his job with the federal government because of his involvement in communist politics. Dale Jennings knew first hand the threat of internment from his involvement with Japanese Americans in California in the 1940s. Harry Hay was aware, due to his music teaching career, of the scrutiny of the entertainment industry.

At this time, homosexuals themselves were not sure whether their condition was an illness. Consequently, the strategy for dealing with the larger society was to enroll sympathetic religious leaders, doctors, psychiatrists, educators, and lawyers to provide expert studies on the consequences of same-sex attraction. The notion was that these experts would then be able to educate others.

In February 1952, the issue of police harassment motivated the leadership of the Mattachine Society to take more political action. Dale Jennings, one of the founding members of Mattachine, had been arrested by a plainclothes police officer in a Los Angeles park. Jennings claimed that the officer accosted him and that he was therefore a victim of police entrapment. Indeed, police harassment was commonplace at this time. Newspapers frequently published the names, addresses, and even employers of those who were simply arrested on "lewd and dissolute behavior" charges. Those who were arrested often lost their jobs. Jennings wrote that "[t]o be accused is to be guilty."[8]

After much debate, the leadership of the Mattachine Society agreed to fight the charges. The case would be used to challenge unjust treatment by the police, and the discussion groups became mobilized around a political issue. Since the Mattachine Society wanted to remain a secret organization, an *ad hoc* Citizens Committee to Outlaw Entrapment was created. Press releases and letters to the mainstream media failed to generate much response, so flyers were distributed through the informal networks of the homosexual male subculture to publicize the trial.[9] These leaflets generated an outpouring of moral support and offers of assistance, including financial contributions toward legal fees. In addition, two fundraisers were held for the cause; these were the first benefits for a gay and lesbian civil rights issue in the United States.

The trial began on 23 June 1952. Jennings admitted that he was a homosexual but denied that he was guilty of the charges. Historian John D'Emilio notes, "It was a courageous, and dangerous, stand to take."[10] After thirty-six hours of deliberation, the jury was deadlocked with one juror holding out for a guilty verdict. The district attorney decided to drop the charges. The outcome was considered a significant accomplishment given the prevalent attitudes toward "sexual deviance." A flyer announcing "a GREAT VICTORY for the homosexual minority" was distributed throughout the areas of the city frequented by homosexuals.

This 1952 case was historically significant because it was one of the first times that a gay man was willing to publicly acknowledge his homosexuality and assert a claim of legal rights. The more common practice was for gay men to plead guilty to an offense, despite police complicity. Legal victories in criminal courts over alleged sexual offenses began the process of challenging existing norms, claiming "rights," gaining visibility and revealing the weaknesses of an oppressive and intolerant society.[11]

The circulation of Citizens Committee flyers and the open defense of the right to be homosexual sparked considerable interest and growth in the Mattachine Society. Chuck Rowland recalled that after Jennings' victory, "Mattachine really took off....We moved into a broad sunlit upland filled with whole legions of eager gays. Mattachine was suddenly in! No combination of people in our limited leadership could handle them."[12] Mattachine membership grew significantly and the organization established chapters throughout southern California. In May 1953, Mattachine leaders estimated the membership at more than 2,000 with nearly one hundred discussion groups.

In addition to increased organizing and membership expansion, another indirect effect of the Jennings trial was the recognition that the mainstream media were not willing to cover homosexual issues, unless perhaps there was some scandalous activity involved. Members of the Mattachine Society decided to publish their own magazine, called *ONE*, which premiered in January 1953. *ONE* was intended to be a forum for gays and lesbians to present their views to the public and to each other.

The success of the *ad hoc* Citizens Committee to Outlaw Entrapment inspired the Mattachine Society leadership to take another public step. While it was important for the society itself to remain a confidential group in order to protect its members from persecution, the value of an open organization for reaching out to public officials, professionals, and heterosexual allies was recognized. The Mattachine Foundation was incorporated in the fall of 1952 as a not-for-profit educational organization. The existence of the foundation also alleviated the fears of a number of members who were concerned that participation in a homosexual organization was illegal.

Even with these advances, the leadership of Mattachine was unwilling to undertake more direct legal and political activities. When the Los Angeles chapter voted to take on entrapment cases and other cases "of significance to the whole minority" and "to fight the charges aggressively," the Coordinating Council vetoed the chapter's decision.[13] The Mattachine Society's new attorney advised that

> the very existence of a Legal Chapter, if publicized to society at large, would intimidate and anger heterosexual society.... It would be detrimental to the [Mattachine] Society to let the public know of the existence and activities of the Legal Chapter, and it would probably bring more pressure on the Society if the heterosexual felt that the homosexual, whom he hates, was trying to change the laws to suit himself.[14]

The leadership accepted this position, arguing that Mattachine had to "consider what the outside society feels toward us at this time." The Coordinating Council warned members to be "realistic" and to recognize that the organization was "not yet strong enough" to undertake an "aggressive program."[15] Entrapment cases were referred to reputable, sympathetic lawyers.

Based on similar reasoning, the leadership decided not to pursue penal code reform or the repeal of sodomy statutes. As an August 1953 pamphlet stated, "Any organized pressure on lawmakers by members of the

Mattachine Society as a group would only serve to prejudice the position of the Society.... It would provide an abundant source of hysterical propaganda with which to foment an ignorant, fear-inspired anti-homosexual campaign."[16] Individual members were encouraged to become familiar with pertinent legislation and institute individual action.

The leadership accepted the prevalent evaluation of gays, and this resulted in the retreat from collective action. Kenneth Burns, an officer of the Mattachine Society, states, "We didn't have much confidence at that time. We felt we had to work through people ... who could better present what [homosexuality] was all about, better than ourselves....[We made] a definite decision that by working through research projects and people in education and religion that we would get acceptance."[17] D'Emilio explains, "In sum, accommodation to social norms replaced the affirmation of a distinctive gay identity, collective effort gave way to individual action, and confidence in the ability of gay men and lesbians to interpret their own experience yielded to the wisdom of experts."[18]

Other legal action continued to force people involved with the gay and lesbian social movement to make rights claims and to assert a legal identity. Often, litigation strategies were used successfully to overturn some state action aimed at suppressing gays and lesbians. These claims were anchored in constitutional rights that were firmly established in the legal culture, so that the issue was not the creation or expansion of a new right, but whether existing rights would be extended to gay and lesbian citizens.

The First Amendment's prohibition of government action that abridges speech, the press, and the right of people to assemble was the fundamental argument relied on as a defense against efforts to limit early organizing. In the initial years of the gay rights movement, courts were used to protect the ability of gay bars to serve their customers. In 1951, the owners of a San Francisco bar, the Black Cat, asserted the right to serve gay customers in *Stoumen v. Reilly*,[19] a case that went to the California Supreme Court. The state supreme court held that under the Unruh Civil Rights Act proprietors were required to make their premises available to all classes of persons, including homosexuals. The court also ruled that the mere presence of homosexuals in a public bar did not threaten "public welfare and morals." This position was considered very enlightened for its time.

The courts protected the right of gays and lesbians to assemble, thus permitting public meetings and social interaction and providing space for the development of a "community" identity. Patricia Cain points out, however, that the case did not recognize any rights for homosexuals. Rather, "the constitutional rights at stake were those of the bar owners who could not be arbitrarily and capriciously denied their property rights in their liquor license."[20]

The state liquor commission attempted to eliminate gay social space again in 1955 by enacting laws that denied liquor licenses to "resorts for sexual perverts." The California Supreme Court interpreted this provision as requiring some activity beyond just the congregating of gay or lesbian clients.[21] This activity was not defined, resulting in many arrests for a variety of offenses such as dancing, inappropriate touching by persons of the same sex, publicly announcing a gay or lesbian relationship, and failing to dress in conformity with gender role.

Such cases created the legal distinction between status and conduct which still shapes much of the jurisprudence around gay and lesbian issues. It did not take long for public policy arguments to link personal or group status with a likelihood of conduct which was illegal. The Florida courts upheld a Miami ordinance prohibiting the sale of liquor by a homosexual and preventing two or more homosexuals from congregating on premises where alcohol was served. This law was considered a rational exercise of legislative power to protect the public health, morals, and safety of the citizens. The court stated, "The object of the ordinance is to prevent the congregation at liquor establishments of persons likely to prey upon the public by attempting to recruit other persons for acts which have been declared illegal."[22] The law connects identity or status to activity deemed criminal, specifically sexual activity, and then abridges the liberties of those with that identity on the basis that they may at some point engage in criminal conduct.

Police harassment continued with a focus on gay and lesbian bars and social events across the country. Gay and lesbian rights organizations were being established on the East and West coasts. They were divided over the proper extent of political activism and also over whether to adopt assimilationist tactics or take more militant actions. The Society for Individual Rights (SIR) was formed in San Francisco in 1964 with militant inclinations and "quickly became the largest pre-Stonewall gay rights organization in the country" with 1,000 members by 1966.[23] SIR had helped establish the Council on Religion and the Homosexual (CRH), a group of liberal Protestant ministers who opposed the persecution of homosexuals. SIR's lawyers were arrested at a New Year's Day ball on 1 January 1965 for obstructing the police who were trying to enter the premises without a search warrant or evidence of criminal activity. The CRH ministers were "treated to the most lavish display of police harassment known in recent times," and in response, they held a press conference outlining police abuses, which added legitimacy to their accusations. The ACLU agreed to represent the arrested attorneys because the police action was seen as an attempt "to intimidate attorneys who represent unpopular groups."[24]

The charges were ultimately dismissed but the organization's leaders stated that "the resulting publicity of the event and the new willingness of people to stand up in support of lesbian and gay rights created a turning point for gay rights organizations on the West Coast."[25] In addition, the case substantiated the record of ongoing police harassment. The media and the public could not simply dismiss the complaints of homosexuals now that clergymen and the ACLU had added their voices to the complaints.

The United States Post Office in 1954 banned the mailing of Mattachine's *ONE* magazine, the first homophile magazine to be distributed publicly, on the grounds that it was obscene. After Mattachine had lost at both the trial and appellate levels, the U.S. Supreme Court ruled in 1958 that the ban violated rights to free speech under the First Amendment.[26] This decision set the stage for the rise of a gay and lesbian press, which was crucial for the development of a movement. The courts also upheld the recognition and funding of gay and lesbian student groups on university campuses using First Amendment arguments.[27]

The gay and lesbian movement's response to the legal system was useful in the initial organizing as it provided publicity and created a sense of empowerment and legitimacy. The First Amendment was particularly important for ensuring the ability to meet in groups, to disseminate information to interested parties, and to educate the larger society. At a time when other political resources were unavailable, litigation provided a crucial tool in fighting discrimination and in creating a collective political identity.

Law and Policy Negotiation

Law can be used as a symbolic club or a source of leverage against recalcitrant opponents. Victory in court is not even necessary for political leveraging because the indirect effects of litigation, usually resulting from a rights discourse, can exert significant pressure on the targeted party. This type of strategy includes appealing to the conscience of dominant groups, generating support from additional groups, and creating public pressure on, and negative publicity for, the targeted party. According to Michael McCann, "[I]t is primarily the symbolic manifestations of law, as both a source of moral right and threat of potential outside intervention, that imbues rights discourse with its fundamental social power."[28] These indirect influences are still more powerful when combined with other political tactics such as lobbying, negotiations, or mass demonstrations.

Litigation can provide a powerful means for "expanding the scope of conflict"[29] in ways that enhance the negotiating positions of disadvantaged groups, especially when appeals to widely accepted rights claims are involved. The transactional costs and time required for litigation often encourage settlements. Legal tactics are used to achieve placement on the public agenda by forcing attention to demands and compelling at least some policy concessions from state officials. The main areas of public policy challenged by the gay and lesbian communities have been public employment discrimination, sodomy statutes, lack of opportunities for military service, lack of AIDS/HIV treatment and care, state statutes barring antidiscrimination provisions, and relationship issues. Much research has been done on all these important matters. In order to demonstrate the role law can play in policy negotiation, the legal struggles in two arenas will be highlighted: public employment discrimination and sodomy laws.

Public Employment Discrimination

Gays and lesbians in government employment were considered security risks simply because of their sexual orientation. Congressional findings pronouncing gays and lesbians unfit and of weak moral fiber justified police harassment and the military's purge of homosexuals. Despite due process requirements for dismissing civil servants, courts usually upheld the removal of gays and lesbians for unspecified homosexual acts committed before or during government service.

There were occasional litigation victories requiring specific conduct to be alleged[30] and imposing a rational-basis test for making applicants answer particular questions, thereby recognizing certain rights of privacy.[31] In *Norton v. Macy*,[32] the court demanded some causal connection between the homosexual conduct at issue and unfitness for service. The court required the government to demonstrate an "ascertainable deleterious effect on the efficiency of the service" before terminating an employee for an immoral act.

Attention then turned to what type of conduct was grounds for termination. Positions requiring a security clearance could still be denied because homosexual conduct might invite blackmail. If the homosexual conduct could be used as evidence of an unstable personality or of causing a negative relationship with other employees, then dismissal was defended. In *McConnell v. Anderson*, applying for a license to marry someone of the same gender was deemed to be grounds for dismissal when the application generated some publicity.[33] Cain concludes, "The lesson of *McConnell* and other post-*Norton* cases was that secret homosexual conduct might not be sufficient grounds for job termination. The more public the conduct, however, the more likely an employer would be found justified in terminating the employee" (1579).

On this front, litigation was just one political tactic used in conjunction with public protests and with efforts to seek the support of other groups. On many occasions the White House, the Civil Service Commission building, the State Department, the Pentagon and Independence Hall in Philadelphia were picketed. While these demonstrations were small, with the largest consisting of just forty-five people, their impact was valuable for a number of reasons. They revealed the growing number of people openly avowing their homosexuality. They also generated both print and television media attention for the movement. The picketing also raised a question from a reporter to Secretary of State Dean Rusk regarding the employment of homosexuals, and the Civil Service Commission finally agreed to meet with representatives of the Mattachine Society.[34] The National Capital Area Civil Liberties Union also agreed to fight the Civil Service Commission's exclusion of homosexuals.[35] Thus, litigation was used as a political tactic in concert with other forms of collective action.

Sodomy Statute Repeal

The effort to repeal state sodomy statutes is considered instrumental in eliminating the legal bias against gays and lesbians. While sodomy laws are rarely enforced, they provide the justification for social discrimination. Once a person's sexual orientation becomes known, he or she can be stigmatized as a criminal.

In 1975, the federal district court in Virginia upheld the state's sodomy statute in *Doe v. Commonwealth's Attorney*.[36] The court rejected the arguments made by a number of gay men that the statute as applied to private, consensual homosexual conduct violated their right to privacy under the First and Ninth Amendments, their due process rights under the Fifth and Fourteenth Amendments, their First Amendment right to freedom of expression, and the Eighth Amendment's prohibition of cruel and unusual punishment. This case was not orchestrated as a test case by any of the national gay organizations. The Lambda Legal Defense and Education Fund, established in 1973, two years before the case, did file an *amicus* brief with the Supreme Court requesting a reconsideration, which was denied.[37]

Interestingly, the response of the gay and lesbian community to this landmark case has been ignored in most analyses of the movement. The decision itself did not generate any immediate collective action. It appears, however, that repealing state sodomy laws became more of a theme in gay pride events and in demonstrations at the Democratic National Convention held in New York shortly after the ruling.[38] Law enforcement officials indicated that the Supreme Court decision would have little effect as prosecuting sex crimes would remain a low priority. Gay activists, however, feared that the determination of state legislators to repeal sodomy statutes might be undermined by the case.[39]

The precedential value of the *Doe* decision was not clear since the United States Supreme Court simply summarily affirmed the lower court decision. Some jurisdictions used the case to uphold sodomy laws but other states struck down these laws as violations of the federal Constitution. *Doe* was also cited to support other instances of antigay discrimination, once again conflating status and conduct.

The United States Supreme Court ruled directly on the constitutionality of state sodomy laws in *Bowers v. Hardwick*,[40] the single greatest judicial setback to the gay and lesbian rights movement in the United States. The *Hardwick* case was brought with the encouragement and assistance of the American Civil Liberties Union. Movement leaders thought the facts of the case were suitable to support the expansion of the privacy doctrine to include homosexual sexual intimacy between consenting adults. After all, the police were in Michael Hardwick's bedroom only to serve a summons for failing to appear in court on an open liquor ordinance violation.

A five-to-four majority in the Court held that there was no constitutional right to homosexual sodomy even though the sodomy statute applied to both homosexual and heterosexual conduct. The majority relied on the "ancient roots" of disdain for homosexual sexuality and community standards of morality. The dissent argued that the issue had been misconstrued by the majority as it should have dealt with the fundamental right to be free from governmental interference, especially in controlling the nature of intimate associations. Georgia's claim, the dissent argued, amounted to nothing more than "habitual dislike . . . or ignorance."[41] Much has been written about this decision. In fact, some say only *Roe v. Wade* has generated as much scholarly commentary.[42]

The *Hardwick* case generated days of protests across the country mobilizing the gay and lesbian community.[43] An estimated six hundred men and women denounced the decision on the steps of the Supreme Court on the day it was handed down; hundreds were arrested by police in riot gear and rubber gloves during the massive demonstration of civil disobedience. Activist and author David Deitcher states:

> News of the *Hardwick* decision was enough to awaken the radical in most apolitical queers. The timing had been perfect, in a surreal sort of way. The centennial celebration for the newly restored Statue of Liberty was to reach its kitsch climax on July 4, 1986. Four days earlier, the front pages of every major newspaper in the U.S. trumpeted the Court's ruling, triggering a response among gay men and lesbians that had not been witnessed since the days of Anita Bryant. Spontaneous protests erupted in cities across the country as news reached communities in which frustration and rage had been mounting over the loss of lovers and friends, the accelerating rate and intensity of bias-related violence, and the unprecedented challenge to queer social identity that the epidemic posed.[44]

Jeff Levy, executive director of the National Gay and Lesbian Task Force, commented that "[t]here is an incredible anger out there, people are really prepared to come out and fight" and that the decision "had really galvanized people."[45]

On 1 July 1986, more than one thousand gay men and lesbians returned to the site of the Stonewall riots to pack Sheridan Square and Seventh Avenue to protest the *Hardwick* decision. Deitcher comments, "The demographics of this protest represented a mix of queer humanity that had not been seen in a long time. There, among the disheveled youths, old-time activists, and students were conservative-looking men and women in business attire." This action was the impetus for another demonstration on July Fourth which was designed to interrupt the centennial celebration of the Statue of Liberty. The mainstream press did not give this much, if any, time, but these activities "presaged a renewed radicalism and reinvigoration of the lesbian and gay movement," and the protests against the *Hardwick* decision were "catalysts for AIDS activism . . . an opportunity for young activists . . . to meet older activists."[46]

Only ten months after the *Hardwick* decision, the AIDS Coalition to Unleash Power (ACT UP) was formed as a "diverse, nonpartisan group united in anger and committed to direct action to end the AIDS crisis." Filmmaker Gregg Bordowitz considered the creation of ACT UP an important manifestation of activists' desire for self-determination. He explains, "What was interesting about the turn from the early *Hardwick* protests to the early ACT UP meetings was that we went from a defensive position to an offensive position. Instead of just protesting against repression, we built ourselves up and went forward with our own positive agenda."[47] David Deitcher remarks:

> The national mobilization of 1987 marked the attainment of queer mass, an explosive consolidation of political consciousness the causes of which are not as simple to reconstruct as one might think. To say that the activist explosion resulted from the galvanizing horrors of the AIDS epidemic would be to recite a truism about something that was far more complexly determined. The immediate catalyst for queer outrage was the Supreme Court's ruling in *Bowers v. Hardwick* less than a year before the 1987 March on Washington. But the significance of that decision, specifically, the way that its meaning was experienced subjectively by gay men and lesbians across the country, depended upon political and personal circumstances that transformed the Court's majority ruling into a document that read like a declaration of war against us.[48]

The community also turned to making the repeal of sodomy laws a priority. William Rubenstein, director of the ACLU Lesbian and Gay Rights Project, comments, "Despite its harsh outcome, the *Hardwick* decision has not retarded the movement for gay rights. In fact, the decision may have activated many in lesbian/gay communities and solidified support for this fight among many non-gay people."[49] Since the *Hardwick* case, sodomy laws have been declared unconstitutional by courts in nine states, and the legislature has rescinded them in three more. In 1961, every state in the country had a sodomy law; only fifteen did by Spring 2001.

Conclusion

The struggle to end discrimination based on sexual orientation demonstrates the power of law and rights discourse even in the face of judicial rejection of the claims advanced. While litigation strategies have resulted in a variety of advances and setbacks for the gay and lesbian social movement, the prevailing debate still focuses on claims of equal protection, freedom of expression, privacy, and due process. The practical experience of activists and attorneys with the law has shown that some of these arguments are likely to be ineffective in future suits, but losses in the courtroom do not seem to undermine the belief in these claims or to foster an acceptance of the courts' interpretations.

The use of rights claims as a resource is shown in the response to the *Hardwick* case. This case shapes the parameters of future legal claims in significant ways. After the *Hardwick* decision, it seems that a claim for gay and lesbian rights based on a substantive due process argument, such as privacy, will not succeed in the United States. Litigators for gay and lesbian rights will now have to separate homosexual status from homosexual conduct. *Hardwick* allows states to criminalize homosexual conduct with constitutional impunity. Arguments can still be made, however, that states cannot discriminate against homosexuals as a class in areas other than sexual conduct. Most often this type of argument consists of an equal protection claim.

As discussed earlier, this distinction may be problematic. Courts are often reluctant to require a high level of scrutiny under equal protection arguments when the basis of the status is defined as criminal conduct.[50] The Federal Circuit Court explicitly stated the position of gay and lesbian rights during the decade that followed *Hardwick*, "After *Hardwick* it cannot logically be asserted that discrimination against homosexuals is constitutionally infirm."[51] This case seriously set back the quest for gay and lesbian rights, significantly changing the tenor of the constitutional debate. The legal framework for discussing the rights of gays and lesbians was redefined with this decision. As Patricia Cain argues, "The post-*Hardwick* shift in focus by litigators from individual liberty to equal rights mirrors the general shift in the movement away from the original concept of 'gay liberation,' towards a more conservative concept of 'gay rights.'"[52] The U.S. Supreme Court's decision in *Romer v. Evans*,[53] finding unconstitutional Colorado's law prohibiting discrimination claims based on sexual orientation, further modified the terms of the debate and provided some encouragement that discrimination against gays and lesbians will not be tolerated.

Legal tactics have been influential in mobilizing gays and lesbians and in creating political identity and community. The indirect consequences of legal mobilization that McCann emphasizes, such as "dramatic levels of rights consciousness raising, defiant political activity, organizational bonds, and multi-group alliances,"[54] can be found in the gay and lesbian social movement. The increased political activism of the gay and lesbian movement in lobbying, participation in elective politics, and even participation in public protest and civil disobedience has been inspired and shaped by the community's response to judicial actions.

Litigation strategies seemed to confine the debate to a rights discourse embedded in classical liberalism. Much emphasis is on property rights and issues considered to be in the "public" realm. Rarely have legal cases discussed the rights implicated for the gay or lesbian couple.[55] Even the sodomy debate is not defined in the law as an issue of intimacy between two people, as is heterosexual sexual conduct. Overall, litigation strategies have been useful in fighting the denial of established rights but have been less effective in advancing new claims.

The law has protected the right of gays and lesbians to organize and meet, thus allowing the movement to proceed. The First Amendment has proven to be the most effective legal means to protect gay and lesbian rights. This accommodation by the legal system again reflects a liberal restriction on government authority and not a sensitivity to the position of minorities within society. Only in rare instances have substantive legal claims promoting gay and lesbian civil rights been adopted by the courts.

Legal tactics have also been used to defend advocates of change from overt repression by dominant groups and state officials. Courts protect some types of protest and certain types of civil disobedience as political speech, and they provide procedural rights for those committing actions deemed criminal. Legal claims of basic rights have helped to expand the space permitted for social struggle. The experience of the gay and lesbian social movement with the law reveals the capacity of rights discourse to instill a sense of personal and collective empowerment, create group solidarity, and enroll additional support from other individuals and groups. The law has proven to be a significant resource for efforts to secure gay and lesbian civil rights when other political tactics have seemed futile. Litigation has pushed the social movement forward on many issues and has placed gay and lesbian civil rights in the forefront of the public agenda. These indirect and symbolic aspects of litigation and rights discourse demonstrate the importance of law for social movements.

Notes

1. Baehr v. Lewin, 852 P.2d 44, clarified on grant of reconsideration in part, 852 P.2d 74 (Ha. Sup. Ct. 1993).

2. Hawaii Constitution, Article I, Section 5.

3. Defense of Marriage Act, Public Law No. 104-1909, sec. 3(a), 110 Stat. 2419, (1996).

4. Melissa Healy, "Clinton Signals He'd Sign Anti-Gay Marriage Bill," *Los Angeles Times*, 23 May 1996, A15.

5. John D'Emilio, *Sexual Politics, Sexual Communities* (Chicago: University of Chicago Press, 1983).

6. Barry D. Adam, *The Rise of a Gay and Lesbian Movement* (New York: Twayne Publishers, 1995).

7. Stuart Timmons, *The Trouble with Harry Hay: Founder of the Modern Gay Movement* (Boston: Alyson Publications, 1990).

8. Dale Jennings, *ONE*, January 1953, 10-13.

9. Flyers, "An Anonymous Call to Arms," "Now Is the Time to Fight,""An Open Letter," and "VICTORY," Jim Kepner papers, Los Angeles, Calif.

10. D'Emilio, *Sexual Politics*, 71.

11. Patricia A. Cain, "Litigating for Lesbian and Gay Rights: A Legal History," *Virginia Law Review* 79(1993): 1559.

12. Chuck Rowland, interview by John D'Emilio, 17 January 1977, in D'Emilio, *Sexual Politics*, 75.

13. Southern Area Council Newsletter, 2 November 1953 and Coordinating Council Minutes, 23 October 1953, Jim Kepner papers, Los Angeles, Calif.

14. Coordinating Council Minutes, 28 August 1953, Lucas papers, quoted in D'Emilio, *Sexual Politics*, 82.

15. Coordinating Council Minutes, 23 October 1953, Jim Kepner papers, Los Angeles, Calif.

16. San Francisco Area Council, "Mattachine: What's It All About?" August 1953, Jim Kepner papers, Los Angeles, Calif.; D'Emilio, *Sexual Politics*, 83.

17. D'Emilio, *Sexual Politics*, 83.

18. D'Emilio, *Sexual Politics*, 81.

19. Stoumen v. Reilly, 234 P.2d 969 (Cal. 1951).

20. Cain, "Litigating for Lesbian and Gay Rights: A Legal History," 1568.

21. Vallegra v. Dept. of Alcoholic Beverage Control, 347 P.2d 909 (Cal. 1959).

22. Inman v. City of Miami, 197 So.2d 50 (Fla. 1967), cert. denied, 201 So.2d 895 (Fla. 1967), and cert. denied, 389 U.S. 1048 (1968).

23. Martin Duberman, *Stonewall* (New York: Penguin, 1993), 99.

24. *Mattachine Review*, January/February 1965, 8-9.

25. Cain, "Litigating for Lesbian and Gay Rights: A Legal History," 1564; Eric Marcus, *Making History: The Struggle for Gay and Lesbian Equal Rights 1945-1990* (1992), 145-165.

26. One, Inc. v. Olesen, 241 F.2d 772 (9th Cir. 1957), rev'd per curium, 355 U.S. 371 (1958).

27. Wood v. Davison, 351 F. Supp. 543 (N.D. Ga. 1972); Gay Students Organization of the University of New Hampshire v. Bonner, 509 F.2d 652 (1st Cir. 1974); Gay Alliance of Students v. Mathews, 544 F.2d 162 (4th Cir. 1976); Gay Lib v. University of Montana, 558 F.2d 848 (8th Cir. 1977); Gay Activists Alliance v. Board of Regents of University of Oklahoma, 638 P.2d 1116 (Okla. 1981); Gay Student Services v. Texas A&M University, 737 F.2d 1317 (5th Cir. 1984); Student Services for Lesbians/Gays and Friends v. Texas Tech University, 635 F. Supp. 776 (N.D. Tex. 1986); Gay Rights Coalition of Georgetown University Law Center v. Georgetown University, 536 A.2d 1 (D.C. 1987).

28. McCann, "Legal Mobilization," 242.

29. E. E. Schattschneider, *The Semi-Sovereign People* (New York: Holt, Rinehart and Winston, 1960).

30. Scott v. Macy, 349 F.2d 182 (D.C. Cir. 1965), reversing the decision of the Civil Service Commission excluding an applicant solely on the basis that he was a homosexual and had engaged in homosexual conduct although no specific conduct was alleged.

31. Scott v. Macy, 402 F.2d 644 (D.C. Cir. 1968).

32. Norton v. Macy, 417 F.2d 1161 (D.C. Cir. 1969).

33. McConnell v. Anderson, 451 F.2d 193 (8th Cir. 1971).

34. "Homosexuals Stage Protest in Capital," *New York Times*, 30 May 1965, 42.

35. Jack C. Landau, "Unspecific Charge of Homosexuality Held No Bar to Federal Employment," *Washington Post*, 29 August 1965, 3.

36. Doe v. Commonwealth's Attorney, 403 F. Supp. 1199 (E. D. Va. 1975), aff'd, 425 U.S. 901 (1976).

37. Doe v. Commonwealth's Attorney, 425 U.S. 985 (1976).

38. R. W. Apple, Jr., "Carter Promises No. 2 Spot Will Go to 1 of 7 Queried," *New York Times*, 12 July 1976, 21.

39. Grace Lichtenstein, "Ruling on Homosexuality Seems to Have Little Effect," *New York Times*, 9 May 1976, 26.

40. Bowers v. Hardwick, 478 U.S. 186 (1986).

41. Bowers v. Hardwick, 219.

42. Gerard V. Bradley, "Remaking the Constitution: A Critical Reexamination of the *Bowers v. Hardwick* Dissent," *Wake Forest Law Review* 25 (1990): 501-546.

43. William G. Blair, "City's Homosexuals Protest High Court Sodomy Ruling," *New York Times*, 3 July 1986, B5.

44. David Deitcher, *A Question of Equality* (New York: Scribner, 1995), 149.

45. Robert Lindsey, "Homosexuals, Upset by Ruling, Plan Drive to Abolish Anti-Sodomy Laws," *New York Times*, 5 July 1986, 32.

46. Deitcher, *A Question of Equality*, 147.

47. Gregg Bordowitz quoted in Deitcher, *A Question of Equality*, 151.

48. Deitcher, *A Question of Equality*, 140.

49. William B. Rubenstein, "The Stonewall Anniversary: 25 Years of Gay Rights," *Human Rights*, Summer 1994, 18-23.

50. Padula v. Webster, 822 F.2d 97, 103 (D.C. Cir. 1987).

51. Woodward v. United States, 871 F.2d 1068, 1076 (Fed. Cir. 1989), cert. denied, 494 U.S. 1003 (1990).

52. Cain, "Litigating for Lesbian and Gay Rights," 1640.

53. Romer v. Evans, 116 S. Ct. 1620, 134 L. Ed. 2d 855 (1996).

54. McCann, "Legal Mobilization," 249.

55. Mary Anne Case, "Couples and Coupling in the Public Sphere," *Virginia Law Review* 79 (1993): 1643.

Chapter Two
The History of Judicial Rejection of Same-Sex Marriage

The institution of civil marriage gives rise to myriad rights, benefits, entitlements, and burdens for its members. These include "property rights, tax breaks, veterans' and social security benefits, testamentary benefits, recovery for loss of consortium, employment benefits, lower insurance premiums, spousal testimonial privileges, financial support upon separation, and status as next-of-kin to make medical decisions or burial arrangements."[1] A General Accounting Office report requested by Representative Henry Hyde (R-Ill.) at the urging of gay member Steve Gunderson (R-Wis.) indicated 1,049 federal laws that affect benefits, rights, and privileges based on marital status.[2]

Arguments around Same-Sex Relationships

Opponents of same-sex marriage argue that recognizing such relationships would undermine the important role the institution of marriage plays in society. They stress that the concept of marriage has traditional and religious connotations. Others are opposed to same-sex marriage because they think that homosexuality is unnatural, immoral, or sinful. As one opponent said, "The fight is about whether or not the heterosexual family will continue to be the central and favored form of family life or whether we are going to use such a broad definition of the family that it will no longer have any significance."[3] In addition, opponents argue that recognizing gay marriage may assist in the spreading of homosexuality. They also claim that gay marriage will result in an unhealthy, confusing environment for children.

Some people who support many civil rights for gays and lesbians suggest that recognizing same-sex marriage is going too far. These people argue for privacy rights for all, but not social recognition of alternative families. As two law scholars state

> There is ... a difference between decriminalizing private consensual conduct

between homosexuals and affirmatively blessing such relationships through marriage. The former step signifies a removal of hostility and an expression of social tolerance that stops short of approval. The latter requires the state to give elevated and hallowed status to an alternative sexual lifestyle fundamentally at odds with the moral precepts of most Americans.[4]

This argument suggests that people should be able to do what they want as long as they do not "flaunt it."

Within the gay and lesbian communities, there is also disagreement on the level of priority and the amount of resources that should be devoted to this cause.[5] Some gay and lesbian criticisms of marriage are informed by the feminist argument that marriage as an institution is patriarchical and "inherently problematic."[6] The institution of marriage is sexist and inhibits social acceptance of alternative lifestyles. Another argument against marriage suggests that the ideological compromises that the institution requires will force the mainstreaming of the social movement, eliminating the potentially liberating aspects of gender norms and sexual expression that may become available in the movement. Finally, some take the position that the resources required for the judicial and legislative marriage battles would be better spent on securing a more egalitarian distribution of social goods such as health care or on more obtainable, less rhetorically charged goals such as employment nondiscrimination provisions.

Proponents of same-sex marriage contend that the issue is one of privacy. They also suggest that it is discriminatory to deny homosexuals the right to marry. Supporters think they should be free to associate with whomever they wish. Andrew Sullivan, editor of the *New Republic*, supports same-sex marriage and states that without it "their [gay] relationships are given no anchor, no endpoint, no way of integrating them fully into the network of family and friends that make someone a full member of civil society."[7] Alissa Friedman suggests, "Once it is recognized that lesbian and gay family interests are essentially identical to heterosexual family interests, the state's denial of marriage licenses to same-sex couples becomes recognizably invidious and irrational."[8] Stable relationships, it is argued, benefit society as a whole.

Litigating for Marriage Rights

Until 1993, none of the court cases addressing the denial of same-sex marriage rights found any abridgment of state or federal constitutional rights. The rationales these courts used to justify their decisions are noteworthy. The arguments advanced by the plaintiffs and the courts' reasoning are outlined below to show the extent to which social and cultural values have influenced the judicial process.

Baker v. Nelson

The first attempt to establish marriage rights for same-sex couples in the United States came in 1971 in a challenge to the State of Minnesota's refusal to grant a license to two men who had no statutory impediment to a heterosexual marriage license.[9] In *Baker v. Nelson*, the clerk of the county district court refused to issue Mr. Baker and Mr. McConnell a marriage license on the sole ground that they were of the same sex. The district court ruled that the clerk was not required to issue marriage licenses to applicants of the same sex and specifically directed that a license not be issued to them. On appeal, the state supreme court took up the issue of whether a marriage of two persons of the same sex is authorized by state statutes and, if not, whether state authorization is constitutionally compelled.

The court held that there was no legislative intent to allow same-sex marriage and that such marriages are accordingly prohibited. The court looked at the "common usage" of the word "marriage" and its dictionary definitions. Webster's *Third New International Dictionary* was cited. It defines marriage as "the state of being united to a person of the opposite sex as husband and wife."[10] *Black's Law Dictionary* states, "Marriage . . . is the civil status, condition, or relation of one man and one woman united in law for life, for the discharge to each other and the community of the duties legally incumbent on those whose association is founded on the distinction of sex."[11] Minnesota's marriage statute contains references to "husband and wife" and "bride and groom," so the court reasoned that the original drafters of the statute could not have contemplated same-sex marriages.

The plaintiffs then advanced a number of constitutional arguments.[12] First, the prohibition of same-sex marriage is a denial of a fundamental right guaranteed by the Ninth Amendment of the Constitution. Second, this prohibition is a denial of liberty and property without due process and is a denial of equal protection of the laws as guaranteed by the Fourteenth Amendment. The court summarized these arguments as a claim for a "fundamental right" to same-sex marriage and stated that "restricting marriage to only couples of the opposite sex is irrational and invidiously discriminatory."[13]

The United States Supreme Court had already established that the right to marry is a fundamental right protected under the Constitution. In *Loving v. Virginia*, Chief Justice Warren wrote, "Marriage is one of the 'basic civil rights of man,' fundamental to our very existence and survival."[14] The *Loving* case dealt with Virginia's antimiscegenation statute, which prohibited interracial marriages. The U.S. Supreme Court held that the statute was invalid because of its patent racial discrimination.[15]

The plaintiff, Baker, cited the antimiscegenation statute as analogous to the prohibition of same-sex marriage.[16] The Minnesota court dismissed this argument, stating that there is a "clear distinction between a marital restriction based merely upon race and one based upon the fundamental differences in sex."[17] The Fourteenth Amendment, stated the court, does not prohibit the state's classification of persons authorized to marry so long as there is no irrational and invidious discrimination.

The Minnesota court held that marriage is an institution for procreation and the rearing of children and is "as old as the book of Genesis" in the Bible. *Skinner v. Oklahoma*,[18] which invalidated Oklahoma's Habitual Criminal Sterilization Act on equal protection grounds, was cited as evidence of this proposition. The U.S. Supreme Court in *Skinner* stated, "Marriage and procreation are fundamental to the very existence and survival of the race." [19] In *Griswold v. Connecticut*,[20] a statute prohibiting the use of contraceptives by married couples was held to violate the due process clause of the Fourteenth Amendment. The Supreme Court held that the state was prohibited from intruding on the right of privacy inherent in the marital relationship.

Given the history and importance of the institution of marriage, the Minnesota court felt that it could not accept the "contemporary concept of marriage and societal interests" put forward by Baker. The court stated, "The due process clause of the Fourteenth Amendment is not a charter for restructuring it by judicial legislation."[21] Evidently, the Minnesota court felt that the Supreme Court was not engaging in judicial legislation when it found the "historical" definition of marriage as the union of two people of the same race unconstitutional. The Supreme Court dismissed an appeal in *Baker* "for want of a substantial federal question."[22]

Jones v. Hallahan

The next attempt to secure same-sex marriage came in 1973 in *Jones v. Hallahan*[23]; two women in Kentucky were denied a marriage license and sued for its issuance. Upon denial, the plaintiffs appealed on the grounds that the ban "deprived them of three basic constitutional rights, namely, the right to marry; the right of association; and the right to free exercise of religion."[24] They also claimed to be subject to cruel and unusual punishment.

The marriage statute of Kentucky did not define "marriage" and did not specifically prohibit same-sex marriage although male and female references were made. The court once again adopted dictionary and common usage definitions for the term "marriage" and concluded that appellants were prevented from marrying due to their incapacity to enter into a marriage as that term is defined. This court felt that the claim did not involve constitutional issues and that no punishment was being administered. The court in one sentence ruled that a claim of religious freedom cannot be made superior to the law of the land. To extend a professed doctrine above the law would "permit every citizen to become a law unto himself."[25]

Singer v. Hara

In *Singer v. Hara*,[26] two men sought a marriage license in the State of Washington in 1974. They were refused, and the trial court found no *prima facie* showing that Washington law permitted same-sex marriage or that any constitutional rights were abridged by the denial of the license. The Washington Appeals Court held that the legislature never intended to authorize same-sex marriage, even though the marriage statute is gender neutral.

In *Singer*, the appellant's brief devotes nearly forty pages to a discussion of homosexuality and same-sex marriage by sociologists, theologians, scientists, and doctors. Singer contended that "a basic understanding of homosexuals and society is a precondition to an enlightened discussion of the legal grounds raised."[27] The court noted this material in a footnote and stated that while this information was interesting, it did not constitute a legal argument.

Singer then argued that the prohibition against same-sex marriage was unconstitutional as applied. This prohibition violated the Equal Rights Amendment (ERA), which had just become part of Washington's constitution and reads in pertinent part, "Equality of rights and responsibilities under the law shall not be denied or abridged on account of sex."[28] The *Singer* court also discussed the arguments raised in the debate around the Equal Rights Amendment. Part of that debate focused on whether voters intended to allow same-sex marriage when the ERA was approved. The court cited campaign literature, newspaper articles, and public opinion polls in finding no intent by the electorate to permit same-sex marriage.

Singer argued that a state law permitting a man to marry a woman but denying a man the right to marry a man is to construct an unconstitutional classification "on account of sex." The state responded that there was no sex-based discrimination if marriage licenses were denied equally to both male couples and female couples. This same type of argument was raised in *Loving*, when the state of Virginia argued that its antimiscegenation law applied to both races equally. Here the Supreme Court held that equal application does not release the state from the obligation to justify the statute's race-based classification under a compelling state interest test and found that such a classification could not be used to deny interracial couples the "fundamental" right to marry.

The *Singer* court did not agree that there was an analogy between *Loving* and the appellants' case, because the term "marriage" constitutes a relationship between a man and a woman. The court said that it was unnecessary to resort to dictionary definitions because the meaning of the term was so obvious. Therefore, the court reasoned, marriage was not being denied to Singer because of his sex; rather the denial was based on the definition of marriage as a relationship that could be entered into only by two persons of the opposite sex.

In addition, the *Singer* court rejected the appellants' argument that at the time *Loving* was decided the definition of marriage barred interracial unions, and the courts changed that definition through their interpretation of the Fourteenth Amendment. Singer suggested that the Equal Rights Amendment operated in an analogous manner. The court stated that the definition of marriage as the legal union of one man and one woman was not changed in *Loving* and *Perez v. Lippold*,[29] the California case that had found antimiscegenation laws unconstitutional nineteen years before the

United States Supreme Court ruled on the issue. These cases "merely" held that race could not be considered by the state in granting marriage licenses.

Singer next argued that the absolute language of the Equal Rights Amendment prohibits the denial of same-sex marriage. The court held, however, that the ERA does not create any new rights but instead ensures that existing rights and responsibilities are applied without regard to sex. The court stated that marriage was not being denied because of appellants' "status as males" but "based upon the state's recognition that our society as a whole views marriage as the appropriate and desirable forum for procreation and the rearing of children." Since same-sex couples cannot give birth to a child, the court went on to say:

> The fact remains that marriage exists as a protected legal institution primarily because of societal values associated with the propagation of the human race. . . . Thus the refusal of the state to authorize same-sex marriage results from such impossibility of reproduction rather than from an invidious discrimination on account of sex.[30]

Singer claimed the state's failure to grant him a marriage license violated the equal protection clause of the Fourteenth Amendment. He argued that the statute created a classification based upon sex, and that therefore the equal protection clause deems such a classification as "inherently suspect" and requires the state to demonstrate a "compelling state interest" for the statute. Alternatively, the statute creates an inherently suspect classification because it discriminates against homosexuals as a group.

The *Singer* court, in defining what standard of review was required, framed the issue in terms of whether the statutory classification in question, the exclusion of same-sex relationships from the definition of marriage, rests upon a "reasonable basis." The court ruled that there is a rational basis for the state to limit the protection of its marriage laws to one man and one woman but left the legislature to examine the societal values which are involved in this area.

Singer also claimed that the statute as applied violated his right to privacy under the Ninth Amendment and his right to due process under the Fourteenth Amendment. The denial of the marriage license also constituted cruel and unusual punishment, which was prohibited by the Eighth

Amendment. The court found it unnecessary to review these arguments given its conclusion concerning the arguments raised under the equal protection clause. The plaintiffs in *Baker* and *Singer* were dismissed from their jobs for initiating the lawsuits.[31]

Adams v. Howerton

In *Adams v. Howerton*,[32] a federal court in 1980 denied "immediate relative" status for immigration purposes to a male Australian citizen who had gone through a marriage ceremony with a male American citizen. The county clerk in Boulder, Colorado, issued the two men a marriage license. Richard Adams claimed he was the spouse of Anthony Sullivan and therefore met the immediate relative conditions of the Immigration and Naturalization Code. The federal court rejected this claim of marriage under both Colorado and federal statutory law and looked to the Colorado marriage statute, which did not specifically prohibit same-sex marriage. Despite the fact that the county clerk had issued a marriage license, the court once again looked at the definition of marriage and cited the previous cases which had found against a right to same-sex marriage. Also, the Colorado attorney general addressed an informal, unpublished opinion to a state legislator stating that marriages between persons of the same sex had no legal effect.

The court went on to discuss federal law, stating that even if Colorado law recognized same-sex marriage, the court would nevertheless deny "immediate relative" status on the grounds that the Colorado law violated federal public policy. The court said that the underlying societal values for the recognition of marriage needed to be explored to identify the federal public policy. The main value articulated was propagation. The court argued that while some couples marry when they cannot have or choose not to have children, denying same-sex couples marriage rights under this rationale does not constitute illegal discrimination just because the classification of who can marry is over-inclusive. This classification is still valid because the state has a compelling interest in encouraging procreation and stability for child rearing. The court traced the history of marriage law to the English civil law, which was influenced by canon law as administered by the ecclesiastical courts. The court reasoned that canon law in both Christianity and Judaism could not sanction same-sex marriage because of the "vehement condemnation" in the scriptures of all homosexual activity.

The court concluded that same-sex marriage was "unthinkable and, by definition, impossible," and therefore Congress did not intend to permit people of the same sex from becoming a married couple. The court also dismissed a "putative spouse" claim, referring to the scriptural, canonical, and civil law cited and "the prevailing mores and moral concepts of this age."[33]

The constitutional issues were then addressed. The United States Supreme Court's dismissal of the appeal in *Baker v. Nelson* for want of a substantial federal question was interpreted as a rejection by the Court of any due process or equal protection claim for the denial of same-sex marriage rights. The Ninth Circuit reached the same decision on the constitutional issues as the Minnesota Supreme Court did in *Baker*.

De Santo v. Barnsley

The issue was once again before a state court in 1984. In *De Santo v. Barnsley*,[34] a man filed suit for divorce against another man, claiming that they had entered into a common law marriage. De Santo claimed that the trial court did not distinguish between ecclesiastical and common-law marriage. The ecclesiastical courts and church were interested in regulating morality and upholding Judeo-Christian teachings. A common-law marriage, De Santo argued, is a judicial recognition of an oral contract. Common-law marriage protects long-term stable relationships and is equally well served when applied to two people of the opposite sex or of the same sex. The court, however, found that the definition of marriage has the same meaning whether applied to common-law or state statute.

The court took up the question of whether there is any sound reason to expand the concept of common law marriage to include a contract between same-sex couples. The court found that the history of common-law marriage does not support an expanded definition, and common-law marriages should not be encouraged since they are often a source of perjury and fraud. Common-law marriages should be scrutinized carefully, and couples have a heavy burden of proof to establish their existence. The court also found that there was no social policy justification for expanding the concept of common- law marriage. Finally, the court said that it would be abusing judicial power to create a form of common-law marriage for same-sex couples when marriage law prohibited such a union. Such a ruling would in effect amend a state statute, and only the legislature could do that.

The court would not consider the argument that a denial of the validity of common-law marriage to same-sex couples violated the Pennsylvania Equal Rights Amendment, because the issue was not raised at the trial court. The trial court refused to hear expert testimony on "gay lifestyles," but the question whether this evidentiary ruling was an error was not taken up, because no matter what the parties' words and intentions, they could not enter into a common-law marriage as a matter of law.

Dean v. District of Columbia

In 1992, Craig Dean and Patrick Gill sued the District of Columbia for a marriage license.[35] The court rejected the plaintiff's argument that the D.C. Marriage and Divorce Act authorized same-sex marriage. The legislative history, indicating that same-sex marriage had been contemplated but was not included in the act, was reviewed. In addition, the law had contained gender- distinct terminology defining marriage as a union of a man and a woman since the turn of the century. The consanguinity prohibitions demonstrated the legislative recognition of procreation in marriage. The statute referred to "matrimonial incapacity," meaning the inability to consummate the marriage by sexual intercourse. The city council must have had in mind marriage between a man and a woman because "the legislature could hardly have intended that one party to a marriage would be entitled to an annulment unless the other party agreed to 'consummate' it by participating in the commission of the crime of sodomy."[36]

The court explained that it did not have to make any judgments about the morality of same-sex marriage to decide the case. Only the historical definition of the term marriage needed to be determined. The court cited Genesis and other parts of the Bible as evidence of societal recognition of marriage as a union between a man and a woman. The court ruled that the D.C. Human Rights Act, which prohibited discrimination on the basis of sexual orientation, did not apply to the regulation of marital relationships, and even if it did, the denial was not based on sexual orientation but rather on the definition of marriage. If two heterosexuals of the same sex had applied for a marriage license, they would also have been denied.

The plaintiffs appealed and claimed that their due process and equal protection rights under the Fifth Amendment had been violated. The court distinguished the fundamental right to marry from an alleged right for persons of the same sex to marry one another. The latter was not given constitutional protection because it is not "deeply rooted in this nation's history and tradition."[37]

The court also held that sexual orientation is not a suspect or quasi-suspect classification requiring enhanced constitutional protection.[38] The court noted that homosexuals today are not so lacking in political power as to need the greater constitutional safeguards that being designated a suspect class confers. The denial of same-sex marriage is rationally related to two legitimate state interests. The first is procreation. The second is the fact that recognition of same-sex marriage "would constitute tacit state approval of the sexual conduct, to wit, sodomy, commonly associated with homosexual status, conduct deemed by society to be so morally reprehensible as to be a criminal offense." The court noted that "there is no constitutional barrier to legislation having notions of morality as its genesis.[39]

Finally, the court said that its references to the Bible in its earlier opinion were a historical aid and did not offend the Establishment Clause of the First Amendment, prohibiting the governmental advancement of religion. Furthermore, it argued that there are compelling and clear secular purposes for the prohibition of same-sex marriage.

Conclusion

Historically, the demand for same-sex marriage has been dismissed by the courts. These courts narrowed the issue to that of "gay marriage" as opposed to the claim of marriage as a fundamental right advanced by the plaintiffs. By defining the issue as same-sex marriage, courts were able to "simply"look at the definition of marriage, determine that marriage means a relationship between a man and a woman, and reject the claim as incompatible with the definition. With this type of legal reasoning, judges were able to hold that homophobic bias was not an issue and that the result naturally followed from the definition. If the issue had been framed as the question of whether an individual such as an indigent[40] or a prisoner[41] has a fundamental right to marry, the outcome would likely have been different.

The courts relied upon a traditional conceptualization of marriage and family despite the increasing rate of divorce among heterosexual couples and the growing recognition of gay and lesbian relationships that developed from the 1970s to the 1990s. The purpose of marriage continued to be defined as propagation and the raising of children rather than the mutual care of two individuals. Those taking this view ignored the fact that many gays and lesbians had children. Despite the First Amendment's prohibition on governmental action establishing religion, Judeo-Christian definitions and values often seemed to be the underlying rationale for the decision. These courts refused to expand the definition of marriage, or in the case of *De Santos*, the notion of common-law marriage.

The Hawaii court in *Baehr v. Lewin* upholds many of the prior constitutional interpretations of previous same-sex marriage decisions regarding issues of privacy, the fundamental right to marry, and sexual orientation as a suspect classification under the Constitution. However, the reasoning of earlier courts on the issue of sex discrimination has been rejected in Hawaii. The case has captured a national audience.

Notes

1. Mary Patricia Treuthart, "Adopting a More Realistic Definition of 'Family,'" *Gonzaga Law Review* 26 (1990/91): 92.

2. General Accounting Office, GAO/OGC-97-16.

3. William Glaberson, "Ruling Stretches Legal Concept of Family," *New York Times*, 8 July 1989, A25.

4. J. Harvie Wilkinson, III, and G. Edward White, "Constitutional Protection of Personal Lifestyles," *Cornell Law Review* 62 (March 1977): 572.

5. Evan Wolfson, "Crossing the Threshold: Equal Marriage Rights For Lesbians and Gay Men and the Intra-Community Critique," *Review of Law and Social Change* 21 (1994): 567 - 615.

6. Nancy Polikoff, "We Will Get What We Ask For: Why Legalizing Gay and Lesbian Marriage Will Not 'Dismantle the Legal Structure of Gender In Every Marriage'," *Virginia Law Review* 79 (1993): 1535; Nan Hunter, "Marriage, Law, and Gender: A Feminist Legal Inquiry," *Law and Sexuality* 1 (1991): 9.

7. Andrew Sullivan, "The Politics of Homosexuality," *New Republic*, 10 May 1993, 37.

8. Alissa Friedman, "The Necessity for State Recognition of Same-Sex Marriage: Constitutional Requirements and Evolving Notions of Family," *Berkeley Women's Law Journal* 3 (1987/88): 169.

9. Baker v. Nelson, 191 NW 2d. 185 (Minn. 1971).

10. *Webster's Third New International Dictionary* (New York: Simon & Schuster, 1966), 1384, quoted in Baker v. Nelson, 186.

11. Henry Campbell Black, *Black's Law Dictionary*, 4th ed. (St. Paul, Minn.: West Publishing, 1968), 1123, quoted in Baker v. Nelson, 186.

12. The court dismissed without discussion the claims that Minnesota's marriage statute contravenes the First and Eighth Amendments.

13. Baker, 186.

14. Loving v. Virginia, 388 U.S. 1 (1967), 12 (87 S.Ct. 1817, 18 L.Ed.2d. 1010).

15. A 1991 Gallup poll of white Americans found that 45 percent disapprove of interracial marriage, while 44 percent approve. A 1990 General Social Survey of predominantly white respondents, however, found that 65 percent object to a close relative marrying an African American. Lynne Duke, "25 Years after Landmark Decision, Still the Rarest of Wedding Bonds," *Washington Post*, 12 June 1992, A3. A 1991 poll of 1,500 Americans of all races found that one in five whites believed interracial marriage should be illegal. In 1972, two in five whites

held similar beliefs. Barbara Karkabi, "Love, Marriage, Race and Kids," *Houston Chronicle*, 11 October 1992, 1.

16. For additional scholarly arguments comparing the antimiscegenation argument to the prohibition of same-sex marriage, see James Trosino, "American Wedding: Same-Sex Marriage and the Miscegenation Analogy," *Boston University Law Review* 73 (1993): 92-105; and Mark Strasser, "Family, Definitions, and the Antimiscegenation Analogy," *Suffolk University Law Review* 25 (1991): 98-1034.

17. Baker, 187.

18. Skinner v. Oklahoma, 316 U.S. 535, 62 S.Ct. 1110, 86 L.Ed. 1655 (1942).

19. Skinner, 541.

20. Griswold v. Connecticut, 381 U.S. 479, 85 S.Ct. 1678, 14 L.Ed.2d 510 (1965).

21. Baker, 186.

22. Baker v. Nelsen, 409 U.S. 810 (1971), appeal dismissed.

23. Jones v. Hallahan, 501 S.W.2d 588 (Ky. App. 1973).

24. Jones, 589.

25. Jones, 590.

26. Singer v. Hara, 522 P.2d 1187, 11 Wash.App. 247 (1974).

27. Singer, 1189.

28. Washington Equal Rights Amendment, HJR 61, approved 7 November 1972, effective 7 December 1972. Constitutional amendment 61, adding article 31.

29. Perez v. Lippold, 32 Cal.2d 711, 198 P.2d 17 (1948).

30. Singer, 1195.

31. The court of appeals held that the Civil Service Commission's dismissal of Singer, "who openly and purposely flaunted his homosexual way of life and indicated further continuance of such activities while identifying himself as an employee of a federal agency was proper and not arbitrary or capricious and not in violation of employee's First Amendment rights." Singer v. U.S. Civil Service Commission, 530 F.2d 247, 248 (9th Cir. 1976), vacated, 429 U.S. 1034 (1977). The grounds for dismissal were "immoral and notoriously disgraceful conduct." Ibid. In McConnell v. Anderson, 451 F.2d 193 (8th Cir. 1971), cert. denied, 405 U.S. 1046 (1972), the court of appeals held that it was not "arbitrary, unreasonable or capricious" for a university to dismiss an employee who pursued an "activist role in implementing his unconventional ideas" as evidenced by pursuing a marriage license with another man.

32. Adams v. Howerton, 486 F. Supp. 1119 (C.D.Cal. 1980); aff'd, 673 F.2d 1036 (9th Cir. 1982), cert. denied, 458 U.S. 1111, 102 S.Ct. 3494, 73 L.Ed.2d 1373 (1982).

33. Adams, 1123.

34. De Santo v. Barnsley, 476 A.2d. 952 (Pa. Super. Ct 1984).

35. Dean v. District of Columbia, DC Super.Ct., No. 90-13892, 2 June 1992 (on reconsideration of 18 FLR 1141), 18 FLR 1387, 23 June 1992.

36. Dean v. District of Columbia, 18 FLR 1141, 1142, 28 January 1992.

37. Dean, 18 FLR 1387, 23 June 1992, quoting Moore v. City of East Cleveland, 431 U.S. 494, 503 (1977). A similar "narrowing of the issue" approach was employed in Bowers v. Hardwick, 478 U.S. 186 (1986), where the Georgia court said the issue was not the right to privacy, as the plaintiffs contended, but "whether the Federal Constitution confers a fundamental right upon homosexuals to engage in sodomy."

38. The Supreme Court has recognized only three classifications as suspect: race, alienage, and national origin. Gender and illegitimacy are considered quasi-suspect classifications.

39. Dean, 18 FLR 1387, 1388.

40. Zablocki v. Redhail, 434 U.S. 374 (1978).

41. Turner v. Safely, 482 U.S. 78 (1978).

Chapter Three
Judicial Acceptance of Same-Sex Marriage

Hawaii Court Recognizes Same-Sex Marriage

In 1991, three same-sex couples applied for marriage licenses in Hawaii and were denied solely because they were of the same sex. Bill Woods, a controversial Honolulu gay activist, initiated the idea of a legal challenge to the state's marriage laws and introduced the three couples, Ninia Baehr and Genora Dancel, Joseph Melillo and Patrick Logan, and Tammy Rodrigues and Antoinette Pregil, to each other. When the marriage applications were rejected, Woods sought the assistance of the American Civil Liberties Union (ACLU) and the Lambda Legal Defense and Education Fund. Both organizations declined to support the case, fearing the creation of additional bad precedents on the issue as well as a conservative backlash. No prior arrangements had been made for financing the litigation, either. Woods "pulled out for the good of the project,"[1] and the plaintiffs approached attorney Daniel Foley for representation.

Foley, a married, heterosexual man with two children, had worked for the Hawaii ACLU but had only handled one gay rights case since his practice consisted mostly of personal-injury and criminal defense work. Foley took the case despite thinking it was a "loser," because he felt that people were entitled to their day in court and that no couples should be denied the option to marry. The Hawaii Supreme Court had never heard a gay rights case up to that time, and he felt it would be interesting to bring the first one before it. Foley felt that "possibly something good could come from the case in the area of enunciating some principles in the area of privacy, due process, equal protection, and gender and/or sexual orientation."[2]

The gay and lesbian couples recognized the economic advantages of marriage, mentioning specifically the inclusion of partners in health insurance and pension benefits. Joseph Melillo commented, "You meet someone you love, you get married and you grow old together."[3] They also expressed the romantic, symbolic value of marriage. The sense of being discriminated against was also a significant motivating factor. Ninia Baehr remarked, "I wanted equal rights."[4]

None of the plaintiffs had been working in the gay and lesbian social movement prior to the case, and their political mobilization was in response to the injustice they perceived. Their lack of practical political experience contributed to their naivete about the likely outcome of their case. At the time the litigation commenced, most of the leaders within the gay and lesbian communities considered the issue premature, doomed to failure, or a low priority. Baehr rejected this emphasis on practical objectives over principle: "For me, the politics are not lets go for what we can win, but let's go for what we want. And what I really wanted was to marry Genora."[5] Dan Foley observed of the plaintiffs, "They were all politically out of step, naive.... Politically correct people would not have tried this."[6]

They filed suit in the case of *Baehr v. Lewin*,[7] and two years later the Hawaii Supreme Court held that marriage is defined by sex-based classifications requiring strict scrutiny of the statute. In procedural holdings, the court stated that the plaintiffs factual allegations must be considered as true. Appellate courts view the facts in the complaint in the light most favorable to the plaintiffs in order to determine whether any alternative grounds warrant relief. The plaintiffs' pleadings claimed a number of factual issues relating to social attitudes, for example, (1) the argument that Hawaiis' marriage statute infringed on a person's right to individual expression and right to make basic lifestyle decisions, and (2) the contention that homosexuals had faced discrimination. The absence of any record of discovery addressing these issues was detrimental to the Department of Health, the defendant state agency.

The court then went on to hold that the right of privacy does not include a basic right to same-sex marriage. The court stated that it is well established that implicit in the United States Constitution is a "guarantee of certain areas or zones of privacy.[8] The Hawaii Constitution explicitly expands this concept and states "the right of the people to privacy is recognized and shall not be infringed without the showing of a compelling state interest,"[9] and the framers of Hawaii's constitution declared that privacy is to be "treated as a fundamental right."[10] However, the Hawaii court looked to the United States Supreme Court's decisions to determine the parameters of the right to privacy. While the right to marry has been established, it has always been defined in terms of a man and a woman and linked to the fundamental rights of procreation, childbirth, abortion, and childrearing. To determine whether there is a constitutional right of same-sex marriage, the court looked at the standard defined in *Griswold v. Connecticut*,[11] to ascertain whether the right is so "rooted in the traditions and conscience of our people that failure to recognize it would violate the fundamental principles of liberty and justice that lie at the base of all our civil and political institutions" or "is implicit in the concept of ordered liberty." The Hawaii Supreme Court found that the right of same-sex marriage could not pass this test, and thus there is no right to same-sex marriage under Article I, section 6, of the Hawaii Constitution.

The plaintiffs argued that the Hawaii statute as applied denies them the right to equal protection by the laws. They argued that the right of the state to regulate marriage is well established,[12] and the State of Hawaii has guarded this right so carefully that common law marriages were banned in 1920. This state right, however, is subject to constitutional limitations, and the right to marry can only be denied for compelling reasons. The Hawaii equal protection clause is more elaborate than that contained in the United States Constitution and provides that "No person shall . . . be denied the enjoyment of the person's civil rights or be discriminated against in the exercise thereof because of race, religion, sex, or ancestry."[13] The court found that the Department of Health's argument, that the right of same-sex couples to marry does not exist because marriage, by definition and usage, means a special relationship between a man and a woman, was circular and unpersuasive.

The Hawaii court distinguished the *Baker* case because no state constitutional issues were raised in it. The *Baker* court concluded that the United States Constitution does not include the right of same-sex couples to marry. In *De Santo*, the equal protection argument was not raised at trial. The *Jones* court, likewise, did not have to address an equal protection claim. The Hawaii court argued that the U.S. Supreme Court's reasoning in *Loving* unmasks the tautological and circular reasoning of *Jones* and the defendant's argument. In *Loving*, the U.S. Supreme Court said that applying the anti-miscegenation statute to both Caucasians and African Americans on an "equal basis" still constituted racial discrimination and that the definition of marriage could not be racially biased.[14] By analogy, prohibiting men and women from marrying members of the same sex on an equal basis constitutes a type of sex discrimination, and the court held that the definition of marriage need not be sexually biased. The Hawaii court said it rejected "the tortured and conclusory sophistry" in *Singer* and *Jones*.[15]

Due to the court's finding that the Hawaii marriage statute regulates access to the marital status and its concomitant rights and benefits on the basis of the applicant's sex, a suspect classification, the state was required to show a compelling state interest for the distinction and to show that the statute is narrowly drawn to avoid unnecessary abridgement of constitutional rights. The court remanded the case to the trial court and ordered this lower court to resolve the problem.

The Hawaii Supreme Court was careful to distinguish a number of issues. First, the court did not hold that homosexuality constitutes a suspect class. In fact, the court drew a distinction between homosexuals and same-sex couples, suggesting that in fact the two classifications were not inclusive. Also, the Hawaii court noted that the United States Supreme Court has not defined "sex" as a suspect class but has used an intermediary classification. However, the Hawaii court based its classification on the Hawaii Constitution, which contains an equal protection clause specifically enumerating sex as a basis for suspect classification.

A concurring opinion by Judge James S. Burns raised the issue of the causation of homosexuality. He suggested that if sexual orientation is biologically caused, then the word "sex" includes these variances as it does the male/female difference, and the equal protection clause should be invoked. If sexual orientation is not biological, then the state may encourage heterosexuality and restrict marriage to opposite-sex couples. His concurring opinion relies heavily on sociological evidence but only to demonstrate that the question of the cause of homosexuality is controversial and scientifically unresolved. His opinion also cites newspaper articles discussing the biological versus environmental debate as to the cause of homosexuality.

The dissenting judge in this case took a position similar to that of the rationale suggested by the *Singer* court and said that the legislature is authorized to address these questions of public policy. The State of Hawaii requested an order clarifying the scope of the remand, and with the addition of a new justice, Paula Nakayama, a majority of the court then adopted the plurality's approach of sex discrimination and ordered the lower court to determine whether the "different-sex restriction" can survive "strict scrutiny."[16]

Thirteen *amicus* briefs were filed in the case on remand. Seven supported same-sex marriage, and six opposed it. A group called Na Mamo O Hawaii, which represents native Hawaiian traditions, indicated that the concept of *ohana*, or extended family, embraces same-sex marriage. Within this concept of the extended family, nonbiological parents often raise children. There is also a tradition of recognizing same-sex relationships in the state. The brief states that "In traditional Hawaii culture, same-gender relationships were not considered sins; there were no *kapu* [taboos] against such behavior."[17]

The American Friends Service Committee, an organization associated with the Quakers, argued that denying same-sex marriage hurts children and denies them and their parents the equal protection of the law. Two groups of scholars in child and family psychology also submitted briefs in support of same-sex marriage. The ACLU supported the plaintiffs, as did a coalition consisting of the New England organization, Gay and Lesbian Advocates and Defenders, the National Center for Lesbian Rights, and the National Organization for Women. Finally, the Hawaii Women Lawyers, an affiliate of the Hawaii State Bar Association, reinforced the equal protection claim.

On the opposing side, Hawaii's Future Today (HFT) argued that banning same-sex marriage is necessary to ensure the strength of traditional notions of marriage. Marriage between a man and a woman is at the heart of society, and, the brief claims, "protecting it becomes a compelling government interest in and of itself." Debi Hartman, chairwoman of HFT, said the group represents the opinions of about 75 percent of the people in the state, based on newspaper polls. She remarked that "The fundamental structure of Hawaiian society is marriage and children and any major change in this structure will ultimately harm us all," and that marriage is marriage only because it includes a man and a woman. The Hawaii Catholic Conference argued that marriage between a man and a woman "helps to humanize and civilize society." The Mormon Church also urged the court to reject same-sex marriage. A brief filed on behalf of many conservative groups, such as the American Family Association Law Center, the Christian Family Network, and the Traditional Values Coalition, claimed that same-sex marriage was not consistent with the laws of nature or of God and was harmful to society. The American Center for Law and Justice submitted its own brief, as did a group of state legislators.

The trial in the circuit court lasted ten days, and on 3 December 1996, Hawaii Circuit Judge Kevin S. C. Chang ruled that the state had failed to show a compelling interest in denying marriage licenses to same-sex couples. Chang is a former prosecutor and corporate lawyer and is known as a middle-of-the-road judge. One commentator observed, "He had to operate, however, within the narrow confines of a 1993 state Supreme Court ruling in the case and the evidence presented at trial."[18]

Deputy Attorney General Rick J. Eichor argued the case for the state and based his argument on the issue of parenting and childrearing. Children, it was argued, deserve to be raised by both their mother and their father, and same-sex couples offer at most only one biological parent. Children do best in intact families with male and female role models, and the marriage laws merely seek to support children in these relationships. Many expert witnesses were called to support the argument that the traditional family structure of the biological mother and father was the best for raising children, and that protecting that family unit for the sake of the children was the compelling state interest. However, the attorneys for the plaintiffs argued that when this structure breaks down or is not available there is no inherent disadvantage to gays and lesbians bringing up children.

Judge Chang noted instances where the expert testimony produced by the state actually supported the plaintiffs' case. In the forty-six-page opinion, he acknowledged that there is a benefit to children from being raised by their mother and father in an united and relatively stress-free home. There is, however, a diversity in the structure of families, which include single parents, step-parents, adoptive parents, and gay and lesbian parents. The evidence presented establishes that "the single most important factor in the development of a happy, healthy and well-adjusted child is the nurturing relationship between parent and child." Same-sex couples who choose to have children prove to be just as fit as parents in more traditional families. Judge Chang concluded that "[The] defendant has failed to establish a causal link between allowing same-sex marriage and adverse effects upon the optimal development of children."[19] He went on to reason that allowing same-sex marriage might actually help children now being raised by gay and lesbian couples by giving them the protection and benefits of marriage.

Chang also rebuked Eichor for failing to introduce evidence on the benefits of traditional marriage to society or on the implications of nonrecognition of Hawaii's marriages by other states. These issues were raised in the states pleadings but were not argued in court.

Eichor appealed the decision to the Hawaii Supreme Court, which at this time still included three of the five justices who had originally remanded the case to the circuit court. Eichor commented, "I will admit to the court the likelihood of success is not tremendous in this case.... He [Chang] didn't just disagree with us in that opinion, he buried us."[20] While the gay and lesbian community hailed the decision, no marriage licenses would be issued because Judge Chang agreed to suspend his order until the Supreme Court had heard the state's appeal. Allowing same-sex marriages only to have the high court later reverse them "would be unfair and prejudicial to both sides.... Given the long history and importance of the issues in this case, I believe the receipt of a final decision from the Hawaii Supreme Court is in order."[21] Foley said he would ask for an expedited appeal.

Matt Coles, director of the ACLU Lesbian and Gay Rights Project, stated, "This is the first court in the United States that has ever said it is unconstitutional to deny gay men and lesbians the right to marry. It's the first time a respected, important institution has . . . acknowledged that lesbian and gay relationships are functionally the equivalent of heterosexual relationships. We have a long way to go to get the rest of the country to see that. But this is an important first step." Conservative opponents of same-sex marriage expressed strong disapproval of the court for its activist decision. Robert H. Knight, director of cultural studies at the Family Research Council in Washington, remarked, "This is a slap in the face of the Hawaiian people and Americans everywhere. Once again an activist judge has flouted public opinion and a perfectly reasonable law and imposed his own agenda."[22]

Dan Foley, attorney for the gay and lesbian couples, suggested that the constitutional amendment allowing the legislature to limit marriage to opposite-sex couples passed by voters in 1998 can be reconciled with the court's previous ruling. He claimed that the rights and benefits of the institution of marriage should be granted to same-sex couples under a different name. The court could expand the existing statewide domestic partnership program to include all the civil rights of marriage. The Hawaii Attorney General's Office filed a brief arguing that the "new amendment undermines the argument that the Hawaii Constitutions equal protection clause prohibits a ban on same-sex marriage." The prior decisions allowing same-sex marriage "must be overturned, since voters approved a constitutional amendment giving the Legislature power to limit marriage to opposite-sex couples."[23]

Distinguishing *Baehr*

During the litigation, the makeup of the Hawaii Supreme Court changed drastically. Younger, more liberal jurists replaced older judges on the five-person tribunal. The court that originally heard the case included two new permanent members and three temporary substitutes filling spots that were vacant or held by a judge who had disqualified himself. Chief Justice Ronald Moon, fifty-two at the time of the trial, is the grandson of turn-of-the-century Korean immigrants to Hawaii and is "seen as a moderate who is sensitive to bias allegations." Justice Steven Levinson, forty-six at the time of the trial, came to the state to serve as a clerk to his uncle, Hawaii Supreme Court Justice Bernard Levinson. Bernard Levinson was a legendary justice "known for his cutting-edge opinions of individual rights."[24] Dan Foley, commenting on the change in the court from older justices to "baby-boomers" posited that "As we all know, attitudes towards gay and lesbians and their relationships, there's certainly a correlation with age, the older being more prejudiced, the younger being the more tolerant."[25]

The Hawaii Supreme Court case departs from the legal rationale developed over the last twenty years. This case relies on the state constitution with its specific equal rights provision. However, this alone does not explain the differences in the various courts' rationales. The State of Washington also has an equal rights amendment, and yet the court did not find unconstitutional discrimination in *Singer*. The *Singer* court held that sex-based discrimination did not exist if the prohibition applied to both sexes on an equal basis. As previously discussed, this same logic had been used to deny interracial marriage. The Hawaii court could have chosen to apply the legal standards articulated in the earlier cases but instead chose to define the issue anew. The Hawaii Supreme Courts level of analysis focused on the sex of the person desired for a spouse, and the court found sex-based discrimination if a person could not marry another on account of the sex of the desired spouse.

The *Baehr* court defined the issue as one of gender discrimination. Daniel Foley, the Honolulu attorney who represented the plaintiffs, said this reasoning was presented in a footnote in the briefs he filed. He said the court ignored the two more common arguments used in gay rights cases: that the right to privacy protects same-sex relationships and that antigay bias should be outlawed because gay and lesbians are subject to unique types of discrimination.[26] The court specifically rejected the privacy argument. In the United States, the right-to-privacy argument has never been successful in any case dealing with homosexual concerns.

Likewise, most courts have been unwilling to classify homosexuality as a "suspect category" requiring a more strict constitutional scrutiny. The *Baehr* court did not address the issue of homosexual bias and even went so far as to state that homosexual marriage was not synonymous with same-sex marriage, and that parties to a same-sex marriage could theoretically be either homosexual or heterosexual.[27] The court seemed to intentionally avoid the issue of homosexuality. Arthur Leonard, a New York Law School professor, said the courts focus on gender-based discrimination and refusal to equate same-sex marriage with gay and lesbian marriage led to a "disingenuous" decision.[28]

Legal Culture of Hawaii

The multicultural, predominately liberal political and social views of Hawaii may have contributed to an environment that supported the state's supreme court judges in rejecting past legal doctrine and applying a gender equality analysis. Hawaii has played a pivotal role in progressive national politics over the past twenty-five years.[29] Hawaii has a history of successful union organizing since the days of the vast sugar cane and pineapple plantations. It was the first state to legalize abortion in 1970 and the first to ratify the Equal Rights Amendment in 1972. Hawaii has had a reputation since the early 1970s as a progressive state on issues of sexuality and has one of the most liberal criminal codes on homosexuality in the nation.[30] The state was one of the first in the country to enact laws which include sexual orientation among those classes protected from discrimination in employment. In 1978, the state constitutional convention discussed discrimination based on sexual orientation, and a privacy measure was passed protecting gay people. The law requires all employers to provide universal health care.[31] Attorney Dan Foley commented that "Hawaii has had a tradition of protecting civil liberties more broadly than they are protected by the U.S. Constitution and the U.S. Supreme Court."[32]

The religious right is not active in the state. Even the local Catholic bishop defied Vatican pronouncements and publicly supported gay rights legislation. However, opposition to same-sex marriage is being led by the Catholic and Mormon churches.[33] The Republican Party is overwhelmingly the minority party. All statewide elected officials in 1990 were Democrats, and only nine Republicans are members of the seventy-six-seat state legislature. Members of the state's congressional delegation are some of the most liberal on Capitol Hill.[34]

In Hawaii, there is no cultural majority. Instead, there are many minorities of Asian, Polynesian, European, and African heritage. As Michelangelo Signorile observed, "[P]eople more freely take on each other's customs, collapsing cultures to form one rather than tensely coexisting.... [U]nlike everywhere else in America and the Western world, in Hawaii people of different races, colors, ethnicities, and religions readily intermarry with little or no social stigma."[35]

Even some supporters of gay civil rights, however, do not endorse expanding marriage rights to same-sex couples. Polls in Hawaii show 58 percent of those surveyed are against same-sex marriages, while 32 percent are supportive and 10 percent are undecided.[36] A *Honolulu Star-Bulletin* poll in July 1993 revealed that 61 percent of those surveyed were opposed to same-sex marriage. A 1996 poll indicated that views on same-sex marriage had not changed much, with 70 percent of Hawaiian residents opposed to it.[37] Gay activists responded that the poll was biased and that the opinion of a large number of people, mostly nonwhite, living in rural areas was not included.

There is evidence that same-sex relationships existed in precolonial Hawaii. Robert Morris published an article in the *Journal of Homosexuality* in 1990 entitled, "Aikane: Accounts of Hawaiian Same-Sex Relationships in the Journal of Captain Cook's Third Voyage (1776-80)."[38] Morris defines Aikane as men who had sex with men and contends that such relationships were common and that several of the kings had their own coteries of Aikane. When the Christian missionaries arrived in the 1800s, Hawaiians were indoctrinated with the prevailing puritan views of sexuality.

Despite the Hawaiian culture and the progressive legal environment, concepts of equality and due process can conflict with the intensity of traditional, and often religious, views defining marriage. For example, Democratic Governor John Waihee III, who signed the gay antidiscrimination bill, said, "Marriage is a form of historical and cultural relationship that exists between a man and woman. There may be other types of personal relationships that exist, but they are not universal nor culturally or historically accepted as being a marriage."[39] The governor's comments and the response of many legislators show the psychological and emotional ties many people feel to the traditional institution of marriage.

Proponents of same-sex marriage, however, feel very strongly that the issue is one of fairness and equality. Daniel R. Foley, attorney for the plaintiffs, commented, "If Martin Luther King had gone to the Alabama state legislature for help, the schools would still be segregated today." Hawaii State Senator Matthew Matsunaga remarked, "This is not about publicly approving or disapproving of a form of relationship. It is about safeguarding the rights of citizens regardless of attitudes."[40] Jane Gross explains, "Whether by sanctioning gay marriage, which no other nation has done, or by passing Americas first state-wide domestic partnership act, Hawaii would lead the way in this fundamental redefinition of family, which some see as a sweeping expansion of civil rights and others see as an erosion of traditional values."[41]

Public Opinion in the Twenty Years of Legal Challenges
Another factor to be considered is the extent to which public opinion on homosexual relationships has changed in the twenty years that same-sex marriage has been before the courts. If public opinion has grown more favorable toward gay and lesbian relationships, this may have made it easier for the Hawaii Supreme Court to rule that the denial of a marriage license to two people of the same sex requires a compelling state interest.

The public opinion data on gay rights do not provide any definite answer to questions about attitudes toward gay rights. A poll conducted by the National Opinion Research Center (NORC) at the University of Chicago in 1972 found that 73 percent of the respondents characterized homosexuality as "always wrong" compared to 75 percent in 1991.[42] In a Gallup Poll conducted in June 1992, 48 percent of those questioned said gay sex should be legal, while 44 percent said it should not. The same question was asked in 1977 with similar results.[43] However, a Gallup Poll in 1977 asked whether gays and lesbians should have job opportunities equal to those enjoyed by heterosexuals, and 56 percent responded positively. In 1992, 74 percent were in favor of equal job opportunities. In 1977, 27 percent of the respondents felt that gays should be allowed to be elementary school teachers, but by 1992 that number had risen to 41 percent.[44]

A Gallup Poll asking whether homosexual relationships should or should not be considered legal found that in 1977, 43 percent favored legality and 43 percent did not, with 14 percent undecided. In 1982, 45 percent favored legality, 39 percent did not, and 16 percent had no opinion. In 1987, 34 percent favored legality; 54 percent did not, and 12 percent had no opinion. In 1992, 48 percent favored legality; 43 percent did not, and 9 percent had no opinion. A 1989 *Time* magazine poll indicated that 69 percent of Americans disapproved of the legal recognition of homosexual marriage.[45] *Newsweek*, in 1992, found that 35 percent of those surveyed approved of legally sanctioned gay marriage, and 58 percent disapproved.[46] These findings suggest that the AIDS epidemic created a backlash against homosexual relations from 1982 to 1987, with a more positive trend of opinion on homosexual relations emerging in 1987 and continuing to the present. They also indicate that an increasing number of people are developing an opinion on the issue.

While the public opinion polls do not reflect a consistent trend in the perception of homosexuality and homosexual lifestyles, other sociological indicators point toward a greater acceptance of gay and lesbian people. Dr. June Reinisch, head of the Kinsey Institute, which studies sexual behavior, comments, "I think there has been a major positive change in the public's perception about homosexuality.... I don't think [societal change] is easy or going to happen quickly, but it's going in the right direction. People are coming out of an incredible well of ignorance."[47] She explains that in the past twenty-five years the public has gone from not knowing much about homosexuality to seeing it become a central issue on the political agenda.

The legal and political climate has also changed. Four states and about seventy-five municipalities had laws in place prohibiting discrimination based on sexual orientation at the time of the first Hawaii trial.[48] The city council of Washington, D.C. passed an antidiscrimination ordinance, but Congress struck it down. In November 1992, voters in Colorado revoked the ability of cities to enact statutes protecting against discrimination based on sexual orientation. The state's authority to limit cities in this way was struck down by a federal court, and the United States Supreme Court upheld this decision in Romer v. Evans.[49] The electorate in cities such as Tampa, Florida, however, overturned by initiative petition the protection for homosexuals in the workplace granted by city councils and county commissions.

The sentiments of leading jurists have also evolved. Retired Justice Lewis Powell has publicly said that he thinks he was wrong in making the majority in *Bowers v. Hardwick*, which upheld the Georgia sodomy law.[50] President Reagan's last solicitor general, Charles Fried, also indicated that he now disapproves of the decision.[51]

Openly gay and lesbian political candidates have successfully run for office. The first openly gay or lesbian public official was elected in 1974. Twenty years later there were seventy-one openly gay or lesbian public officials out of the 497,155 elected officials in the United States.[52] National gay and lesbian civil rights marches in Washington, D.C., in 1987, 1993, and 1998 exemplify the political activism and prominence of the gay rights movement.

In addition, the legal status of "family" is changing, affecting the notion of same-sex relationships. A number of court cases have found same-sex relationships to be families for a variety of legal purposes.[53] These rulings help establish a legal precedent for recognizing same-sex marriage.

The media have increased their coverage of homosexual issues and have portrayed gay men and lesbians in more positive, less stereotypical ways. The 1997 "coming-out" of Ellen DeGeneris as a lesbian in person and in character on her prime-time television show, "Ellen," received much publicity and put homosexuality in the forefront of popular culture. Newspapers such as the Minneapolis *Star Tribune* have changed their wedding and engagement section to a "Celebrations" page that includes announcements of the formation of domestic partnerships.[54] Many same-sex couples are formalizing their relationships in religious or secular services. Businesses are now courting the gay and lesbian consumer,[55] and many employers are offering benefits to same-sex couples.[56]

Cultural and social factors have evolved in such a way that acceptance of homosexuality is much greater than it was even five years ago in the United States. It can be argued that the law in this case is following the evolution of social norms. The courts are not leading the way in the protection of civil rights. As Hannah Schwarzschild has commented, "What differences the courts count as "fundamental" vary substantially over time, as normative values change." She goes on to describe the relationship between morality and marriage:

> [M]arriage is an instrument of the state by which the state regulates "morality." What is meant by "morality" will, to be sure, vary significantly over time and between cultures, according to the values that the dominant group holds and seeks to promote.[57]

The *Baehr* court, commenting on the *Loving* case, stated that "constitutional law may mandate, like it or not, that customs change with an evolving social order."[58]

New York Litigation Not Supported by Gay and Lesbian Legal Establishment

Phillip Storrs in 1995 attempted to secure same-sex marriage rights in Ithaca, New York. The City of Ithaca, in fact, entertained the idea of issuing a marriage license to the gay male couple, thus joining the lawsuit when the state objected. The city has been at the forefront in granting gay and lesbian civil rights in the state, having passed nondiscrimination and domestic partnership statutes. However, national and state-based gay and lesbian rights groups thought such efforts were untimely and undeveloped.

There was a fear that the New York courts would ban same-sex marriage, thus creating a bad precedent just before the Hawaii courts decision. Opponents argued that the legal and political climates in New York did not support same-sex marriage and much more educational work was needed. Paula Ettlebrick, legislative counsel for the Empire State Pride Agenda, a gay rights organization, stated in a letter to Ithaca's mayor and city attorney, that "New York is *not* a state that any of us in the lesbian and gay legal community believes is ready for litigation on this issue" (emphasis in original).[59] Evan Wolfson, co-counsel in the *Baehr* case and head of the Lambda Legal Defense and Education Fund's Marriage Project, remarked, "The wrong litigation at the wrong time can have a serious consequence on every aspect of this work, from potential impact on the case in Hawaii to impact on the law of the state where the given couple resides to national ramifications."[60] Wolfson urges that lawsuits seeking marriage rights should be initiated only after significant political groundwork and public education have been completed to support the legal challenge.

Storrs went ahead with his lawsuit without the support of the City of Ithaca.[61] His case was initially dismissed due to a procedural flaw: the required state defendant was not named. The procedural corrections were made, but the case was eventually dropped by Storrs. Storrs' effort remained a mostly solitary endeavor with officials of the gay and lesbian movement discouraging it.

Alaska Trial Court Finds "Fundamental Right" to Marry

On 27 February 1998, the Alaska trial court was the first court in the United States to hold that the right to choose one's marriage partner is a fundamental right. Most other courts had framed the issue as whether same-sex marriage is a fundamental right. The Alaska court stated, "The relevant question is not whether same-sex marriage is so rooted in our traditions that it is a fundamental right, but whether the freedom to choose one's life partner is so rooted in our tradition.... It is the decision itself that is fundamental, whether the decision results in a traditional choice or the nontraditional choice.... The same constitution protects both." Since a fundamental right is at stake, the state must show a compelling reason for its policy. The case, *Brause v. Bureau of Vital Statistics*,[62] was brought by a gay male couple who had been together for eighteen years.

The Alaska case is unique in that it dealt with a state law enacted in response to the Hawaii case, a statute that specifically defines marriage "as a civil contract entered into by one man and one woman" and explicitly bans recognition of same-sex marriages. The trial court stated, however, that it was "not enough to say that marriage is marriage and accept without any scrutiny the law before the court." The court commented that "in some parts of our nation mere acceptance of the familiar would have left [racial] segregation in place."[63] The decision is even more significant as the judge in this case, Peter Michalski, is considered by many observers to be generally conservative. Conservative judges do not usually favor the expansion of the definition of rights considered to be fundamental under the constitution.

The same-sex marriage ban was held to violate Article 1, Section 22 of the Alaska Constitution, which was added in 1972 and guarantees the right to privacy. The section states, "The right of the people to privacy is recognized and shall not be infringed." The court evaluated the interests implicated in marriage and Alaska precedent. Citing a case from the 1970s successfully challenging a public schools restriction on student hairstyles, the court concluded that "the right to choose one's life partner is quintessentially the kind of decision which our culture recognizes as personal and important."[64]

Conclusion

The Hawaii court declined to expand the existing jurisprudence on the right to privacy. It deferred to the decisions of the United States Supreme Court and chose to adopt the more restricted federal interpretation of privacy. The court also refused to support the expansion of the fundamental right to marry to include same-sex couples, stating that "the precise question facing this court is whether we will extend the *present* boundaries of the fundamental right of marriage to include same-sex couples"(emphasis in original).[65] The Hawaii Supreme Court found that the right of gays and lesbians to marry is not essential to liberty and justice.

The power of the court to expand legal definitions is clearly expressed by the emphasis given to the *present* boundaries of the terms at issue. The importance of the language used to define the dispute is also evident. The Hawaii decision reflects the changing social context regarding homosexuality, improves the status of gays and lesbians, and expands the traditional notion of family. While rejecting the right to same-sex marriage, the court embraced the right to choose a marriage partner free from the sex-based restrictions imposed by the state.

Unlike the Hawaii Supreme Court, the Alaska trial court did recognize a "fundamental right" to marry the person of choice. The court did draw on the precedent that prevented the state from regulating marriage for the criminally incarcerated or for those who failed to honor their child support agreements. This court was willing to expand the substantive due process right of privacy to include the intimate associations of marriage. The state supreme court, however, has not ruled on whether this interpretation is consistent with the state constitution, especially in light of the constitutional amendment restricting marriage to opposite-sex couples.

In Hawaii and Alaska, the courts required the state to show a "compelling" reason to discriminate against gays and lesbians in the issuing of civil marriage licenses. This is the most difficult constitutional standard to meet. The Hawaii court, after a lengthy evidentiary hearing, ruled that the government had failed to meet its burden of proof. The Hawaii court even declared that the state had failed to meet the lower standard of demonstrating a rational reason to ban same-sex marriage.

The voters of Hawaii and Alaska removed the issue from the judiciary and did not have to justify their exclusion of same-sex couples from the institution of marriage. The Hawaii case sparked a political response unequaled by any other state court decision.

Notes

1. Paul M. Barrett, "I Do/No, You Don't," *Wall Street Journal*, 17 June 1996, 1.
2. Daniel Foley, plaintiff's attorney, interview by author, 27 November 1996.
3. Barrett, "I Do/No, You Don't."
4. Fern Shen, "A Same-Sex Couple Married to the Cause," *Washington Post*, 10 September 1996, A1.
5. Shen, "A Same-Sex Couple Married to the Cause," A1.
6. Shen, "A Same-Sex Couple Married to the Cause," A4.
7. Baehr v. Lewin, 852 P.2d 44. The case was restyled Baehr v. Miike when Lawrence Miike became state health director.
8. Baehr v. Lewin, 55.
9. Hawaii Constitution, Article I, Section 6.
10. Committee of the Whole Report No. 15, in 1 Proceedings of the Constitutional Convention of Hawaii of 1978, 1024 (1980).
11. Griswold v. Connecticut, 381 U.S. 479 (1965), 486.
12. Maynard v. Hill, 125 U.S. 190 (1888), holding that marriage is a social relationship subject to state regulation; Zablocki v. Redhail, 434 U.S. 374, 98 S.Ct. 673, 54 L.Ed.2d 618 (1978), holding that the right to marry is part of the fundamental right of privacy implicit in the Fourteenth Amendment due process clause.
13. Hawaii Constitution, Article I, Section 5.
14. Loving v. Virginia, 388 U.S. 1 (1967)(87 S. Ct. 1817, 18 L. Ed.2d 1010).
15. Baehr v. Lewin, 63.
16. Baehr v. Lewin, 74.
17. Linda Hosek, "Judge in Same-Sex Court Case Considers Community Opinion," *Hawaii Star-Bulletin*, 12 October 1996, 3.
18. Susan Essoyan and Bettina Boxall, "Gay Marriages on Hold While Ruling Is Appealed," *Los Angeles Times*, 5 December 1996, A3.
19. Baehr v. Miike, No. 91-1394.
20. Susan Essoyan and Bettina Boxall, "Hawaii Ruling Lifts Ban on Marriage of Same-Sex Couples," *Los Angeles Times*, 4 December 1996, A1.
21. Baehr v. Miike, No. 91-1394.

22. Ibid.
23. Honolulu Star Bulletin, 24 December 1998.
24. Barrett, "I Do/No, You Don't," A4.
25. Foley interview.
26. John Gallagher, "Till Death Do Us Part," *The Advocate*, 15 June 1993, 25.
27. Baehr v. Lewin, 52. Plaintiff's complaint did not allege that the plaintiffs were homosexual, and the health department's attorney raised the question in his pleadings.
28. Arthur Leonard quoted in Gallagher, "Till Death Do Us Part," 25.
29. Mary A. Wilkowski, "Rutherford Institute Challenges Fledgling Law And Loses," *Island Lifestyle*, August 1992, 28-29.
30. "End Victimless Crime, Hawaii Citizens Urge," *The Advocate*, 20 December 1972, 6.
31. Michelangelo Signorile, "Bridal Wave," *Out*, December/January 1994, 70.
32. Essoyan and Boxall, "Hawaii Ruling Lifts Ban," A1.
33. Susan Essoyan, "Hawaii Tries to Take a Stand against Same-Sex Marriages," *Los Angeles Times*, 26 April 1994, A5.
34. Michael Barone and Grant Ujifusa, "Hawaii," *The Almanac of American Politics 1990* (Washington, D.C.: National Journal, 1989), 319-330.
35. Signorile, "Bridal Wave," 71.
36. Polls cited in Essoyan, "Hawaii Tries to Take a Stand."
37. Essoyan and Boxall, "Hawaii Ruling Lifts Ban," A1.
38. Robert J. Morris, "Aikane: Accounts of Hawaiian Same-Sex Relationships in the Journal of Captain Cook's Third Voyage (1776 - 80)," *Journal of Homosexuality* 29 (1990): 124-135.
39. Linda Hosek, "Hawaii Considers Same-Sex Marriage," *Honolulu Star-Bulletin*, 11 May 1993, 3.
40. Ibid.
41. Jane Gross, "After a Ruling, Hawaii Weighs Gay Marriages," *New York Times*, 25 April 1994, A1.
42. John Gallagher, "What America Thinks of You," *The Advocate*, 6 October 1992, 91.

43. Ibid., 94.

44. Ibid., 93.

45. Walter Isaacson, "Should Gays Have Marriage Rights?" *Time*, 20 November 1989, 101.

46. James D. Wilson, "Gays under Fire," *Newsweek*, 14 September 1992, 37.

47. Gallagher, "What America Thinks of You," 92.

48. "Developments in the Law–Sexual Orientation and the Law," *Harvard Law Review* 102 (1989): 1668.

49. Romer v. Evans, 116 S. Ct. 1620, 134 L.Ed. 2d 855 (1996).

50. Linda Greenhouse, "Washington Talk; When Second Thoughts in Case Come Too Late," *New York Times*, 5 November 1990, A14; Anand Agneshwar, "Ex-Justice Says He May Have Been Wrong: Powell on Sodomy," *National Law Journal*, 5 November 1990, 3.

51. Charles Fried, *Arguing the Reagan Revolution: A First-Hand Account* (New York: Simon & Schuster, 1991).

52. Rick Elsaser, Gay and Lesbian Victory Fund, interview by author, Washington, D.C., 19 October 1994.

53. After a lengthy legal battle, the court in In re Guardianship of Kowalski, 382 N.W. 2d 861 (Minn. App.), cert. denied sub. nom., Kowalski v. Kowalski et al., 475 U.S. 1085 (1986), considered a woman the spouse of another woman who was incapacitated due to an automobile accident. Braschi v. Stahl Associates Co, 74 N.Y. 2d 201, 543 N.E. 2d 49 (1989), held a long-term homosexual relationship to constitute a family under rent control regulations. State v. Hadinger, 573 N.E.2d 1191 (Ohio Ct. App. 1991), ruled that a member of a same-sex couple was protected under the state's Domestic Violence Act, which applied to persons living together in a spousal relationship. Other cases have declined to recognize gay or lesbian partners and children as family or ruled gay and lesbian parents unfit.

54. "Paper Includes Gay Couples on What Was Wedding Page," *New York Times*, 22 March 1991, A20.

55. Consumer United Insurance Company of Washington, licensed to do business in forty-five states, provides a plan in which domestic partners may be named on policies. The Fireman's Insurance Company of Washington has a plan that extends home ownership and renters' coverage to domestic partners of policyholders. Kay Longcope, "Gay Couples Fight for Spousal Rights," *Boston Globe*, 4 March 1991, 38.

56. Since *Baehr* has been before the court, many Fortune 500 companies, such as IBM, Disney, Coors, and Bank of America, have instituted domestic partner benefits.

57. Hannah Schwarzschild, "Same-Sex Marriage and Constitutional Privacy: Moral Threat and Legal Anomaly," *Berkeley Women's Law Journal* 4 (1988): 110.

58. Baehr v. Lewin, 63

59. Ettlelbrick letter of 22 May 1995 to Chuck Guttman, Ithaca City Attorney on file with author.

60. Lisa Keen, "Marriage Battle Erupts in Vermont," *Washington Blade*, 25 July 1997, 1.

61. Storrs v. Holcomb, 245 A.D. 2d 943 (N.Y. 1997).

62. Brause v. Bureau of Vital Statistics, slip op., No. 3AN-95-6562 Cl (Alaska Super. Ct., 27 February 1998).

63. Ibid.

64. Ibid.

65. Baehr v. Lewin, 56.

Chapter Four
The Political Response to the Courts

When Ninia Baehr and Genora Dancel, Joseph Melillo and Patrick Logan, and Tammy Rodrigues and Antoinette Pregil filed for marriage licenses, they did not think they were about to start one of the most contentious political debates of the decade. These individuals felt their liberty was being unfairly restricted by the state and sought redress from the judiciary. The Hawaii court's unexpected decision propelled the issue of gay and lesbian relationships to the forefront of the policy agenda, alarming the religious right and astonishing the leadership of gay and lesbian organizations. Beginning in 1995 with Utah, every state in the nation has considered the issue of same-sex marriage. The *Baehr* decision even motivated Congress to intercede in regulating marriage, an area of law that is primarily defined by state statute. Vermont's *Baker* decision inspired a second wave of legislation against gay and lesbian couples that denies recognition of civil unions or domestic partnerships.

Hawaii Responds to Its Courts

The Hawaii state legislature did not expect the courts to expand the definition of marriage as they did. Many legislators felt that the decision was a blatant example of judicial activism and usurpation of the legislative function by the courts. The Hawaii legislature was quick to respond to its Supreme Court's ruling which required the state to show a compelling reason for prohibiting same-sex marriage. In 1994, a broad domestic partnership act was considered in an attempt to undermine claims of discrimination against gays and lesbians but was rejected as legislators did not want to embrace this issue during an election year.[1]

A bill defining marriage as the union of a man and a woman and creating a commission to propose remedies for the inequities same-sex couples experience was passed.[2] Some legislators felt that this bill would aid the state attorney general in demonstrating a compelling state interest for rejecting same-sex marriage. They reasoned that the bill clarifies the language of the marriage statute and may persuade the court that the restriction on marriage is only a benign form of discrimination while the establishment of the commission demonstrates that the state is committed to civil rights for gay and lesbian couples. The bill notes the state's intent to "foster and protect the propagation of the human race" and directs the court to desist from making social policy. It also states that the court's ruling encroaches on the legislature's lawmaking function and infringes on the separation of powers of the respective branches of government.[3]

Proponents of same-sex marriage argued that such legislation will have little effect on the Hawaii court case since the case deals with a constitutional issue. A law passed by the legislature addressing the issue will be invalid if it does not meet the constitutional standards required by the state supreme court as outlined in the case. In 1996, Republicans in the legislature called for a constitutional amendment prohibiting same-sex marriage. A constitutional amendment is the one sure way of restricting marriage to that of a man and a woman. Attempts to ban same-sex marriage by constitutional amendment failed, however. The Hawaii House of Representatives, controlled by the Republican party, passed the measure, but the Democratic Senate would not consent without the inclusion of a domestic partnership program which was intolerable to the House.

The state supreme court granted the state a continuance to allow the Commission on Sexual Orientation and the Law an opportunity to conduct research and report on the issue. The commission, however, was mired in political controversy from the start. Originally, the commission was to include representatives from the Mormon and Catholic churches. This was successfully challenged under the United States Constitution's First Amendment religious establishment clause, and the commission had to be reconstituted. The governor appointed a new commission of seven members with at least two members coming from lists provided by both the state senate president and the Speaker of the House. The commission recommended legislation to allow same-sex couples to marry as well as the creation of a comprehensive domestic partnership law for all couples.

In 1996, an issue before Hawaii's voters was whether to call for a constitutional convention which would allow marriage to be limited to a man and a woman despite the state supreme court's ruling. The results of this vote led to a protracted legal battle. At issue was whether the convention would be called if a majority of people voting on that specific issue endorsed the convention or whether a majority of all people voting had to endorse it. If the voter did not mark the convention issue on the ballot, should that ballot be counted in the total number of ballots received? The federal trial court ruled that the statute was not clear as to how the ballots should be counted, and a new election would have to be held. Proponents of same-sex marriage hoped that the supreme court would have rejected the state's final appeal by the time another vote was taken because the convention would not be likely to take marriage rights away once they had been granted.

In the meantime, the legislature approved a ballot measure for the November 1998 general election that allowed voters to amend the state constitution and permit the legislature to reserve marriage to opposite-sex couples. The legislature would then still have to pass the amendment. As part of this legislation, a compromise bill was also approved establishing "reciprocal beneficiaries," who are entitled to approximately fifty of the rights enjoyed by married couples, such as health care provisions, the ability to sue for wrongful death, access to insurance and state pensions, joint tenancy, and property inheritance without a will. Reciprocal beneficiaries are defined as two people who have economic responsibility for each other regardless of gender. Reciprocal beneficiary status became available on 1 July 1997.

An organization aimed at defeating the proposed constitutional amendment, Protect Our Constitution, pulled together a coalition that included gay and lesbian groups, civil rights organizations, the League of Women Voters, the Japanese-American Citizens League, unions, and members of the clergy. Opponents of same-sex marriage have organized two groups, Save Traditional Marriage '98 and the Alliance for Traditional Marriage. The debate attracted the interest of many groups from the mainland who feel strongly about the issue. Groups such as the American Family Association, the Christian Coalition, the Family Research Council, the American Civil Liberties Union, and the Human Rights Campaign have contributed money and have organized political events in Hawaii. Many Hawaiians are resentful of this intrusion into their local affairs.

Hawaiian voters approved the constitutional amendment allowing the legislature to restrict marriage to heterosexual couples by a margin of two-to-one in November 1998, and the state assembly acted promptly. The call for a constitutional convention was rejected by the electorate, and the state supreme court dismissed the case. Both the opponents and the proponents of the amendment each spent just over a million dollars to publicize their position. The activities of these organizations have not been limited to Hawaii. The fight for and against same-sex marriage has been waged in every state and in Congress.

Alaska Responds

A ballot proposal to amend Alaska's constitution was placed on the November 1998 ballot by the state legislature. The amendment would define marriage as being limited to "one man and one woman." The Alaska Civil Liberties Union and the ACLU's Gay/Lesbian Rights Project filed a lawsuit to remove the amendment from the ballot, arguing that it amounted to a revision of the constitution, not an amendment. Constitutional revisions have to be proposed at a constitutional convention. Jennifer Rudinger, executive director of the Alaska Civil Liberties Union, explained, "Our whole system of government in Alaska, as set forth in the Alaska Constitution, is based on the fundamental notion that all people are entitled to equal protection under our laws. Measure 2 so radically alters this underlying principle of equality that it amounts to a revision of the Alaska Constitution and not an amendment at all."[4] It was also argued that the amendment upsets the balance of governmental power by curtailing the power of judges to interpret the constitution. The court rejected these claims, however. The Alaska Supreme Court did strike from the proposal the statement that "No provision of this constitution may be interpreted to require the state to recognize or permit marriage between individuals of the same sex." The court agreed with the state that this language was superfluous and thus should not be added to the constitution.

The proposed amendment generated much support from outside the state, primarily from the Mormon Church. The Alaska Family Coalition, supporting the amendment, received $500,000 from the Mormon Church and $50,000 from Gary Bauer's American Renewal, Inc., a conservative political action committee. Less than $40,000 of the proponent's total funding of over $600,000 came from individuals. Alaskans for Civil Rights, the organization fighting the amendment, reported just over $108,000 in contributions with 94 percent of the funds coming from Alaskan residents. Dan Carter, treasurer of Alaskans for Civil Rights, commented, "Today's reports clearly demonstrate what's at stake in this election. Do we really want Alaska's constitution, our most precious document, to be rewritten by outside religious and political groups?"[5] Voters approved the constitutional amendment by a margin of two-to-one. The legislature filed a suit to have the marriage case dismissed.

Political Response of the States

Preemptive legislation takes two forms. The first type prohibits same-sex marriages and civil unions from being performed within the state, and the second kind refuses to recognize these relationships between people from other states. Some state marriage statutes already define marriage as between a man and a woman and would presumably prevent gays and lesbians from marrying in these states. The other issue considers whether gay and lesbian residents of one state could potentially go to Hawaii, get married, and have their relationship acknowledged in their state of residence. The civil union legislation in Vermont made this concern more concrete as out-of-state residents who have been joined in civil unions in Vermont return home.

States Passing Same-Sex Marriage and Civil Union Bans

In the 1995 through 2000 legislative sessions, thirty-six states approved laws denying same-sex marriage.[6] In sixteen of these states this legislation had been considered but failed to be accepted in an earlier session. In Indiana, five bills were stopped before the sixth one was passed in the 1997 legislative session. In Nebraska and West Virginia, such statutes were introduced in four earlier sessions of the legislature without success, and California's assembly rejected them three times before the law was adopted by the voters through an initiative petition. In Spring 2001, ten states were still considering anti-marriage legislation with eight of them adding bans against civil unions.

Religious views, traditional family values, and the devaluation of marriage were most often cited as reasons for the legislation. Sponsors said male-female marriages are the "societal cornerstone,"[7] and marriage rights are given because they are unions that will raise children. Georgia Representative Ron Crews (R) remarked that he wrote the nonrecognition legislation to avoid God's wrath being visited on Georgia if it began accepting homosexual marriages. Georgia law requires marriages to be consummated, which is interpreted as being consummated by a man and a woman.[8] Homosexuality was blamed for the deterioration of the

76   Same-Sex Marriage, Legal Mobilization, and the Politics of Rights

American family in some states. In a slippery-slope argument, proponents claimed that if one accepted same-sex marriage, nothing would prevent the

Table 4.1: Non-recognition Bills Passed

State	Year	Notes
ALABAMA	1998	(first two attempts failed in 1996, 1997)
ALASKA	1996, 1998	(first attempt failed in 1995; constitutional amendment vote in 1998)
ARIZONA	1996	
ARKANSAS	1997	
CALIFORNIA	2000	(legislation defeated in 1996, 1997, 1998; first initiative petition failed to collect enough signatures)
COLORADO	2000	(one attempt failed in 1999; governor vetoed legislation twice)
DELAWARE	1996	
FLORIDA	1997	(first attempt failed in 1996)
GEORGIA	1996	
HAWAII	1998	(first two attempts failed in 1996, 1997)
IDAHO	1996	
ILLINOIS	1996	
IOWA	1998	(first two bills failed in 1996, 1997)
INDIANA	1997	(first five bills failed in 1997)
KANSAS	1996	
KENTUCKY	1998	(first two attempts failed in 1997, 1996)
LOUISIANA	1999	
MAINE	1997	(first attempt failed in 1996)
MICHIGAN	1996	
MINNESOTA	1997	
MISSISSIPPI	1997	(first attempt failed in 1996; executive order issued in 1996)
MONTANA	1997	
NEW JERSEY	2000, 2001	
NEW YORK	2001	
N. CAROLINA	1996	
N. DAKOTA	1997	(not effective until another state recognizes same-sex marriage)
OKLAHOMA	1996	
PENNSYLVANIA	1996	
S. CAROLINA	1996	
S. DAKOTA	1996	(first attempt failed in 1995)
TENNESSEE	1996	
UTAH	1995	
VIRGINIA	1997	(first attempt failed in 1996)
WASHINGTON	1998	(one attempt in 1996 and two bills in 1997 failed; governor vetoed twice, overrode in 1998)
WEST VIRGINIA	2000	(bills failed in 1996, 1997, 1998, 1999)

recognition of other unnatural unions such as those between a parent and a child or between animals and people. Proponents of same-sex marriage bans warned that the drive for recognition of these relationships results from accepting other types of gay rights laws.

Other proponents of the legislation claimed they were not acting against same-sex couples but were merely asserting the state's sovereign right to make its own policies. In Tennessee, the bill's sponsor did not want his actions to be seen as discriminating against any one group so he amended the legislation to extend the ban to polygamous marriages and marriages between siblings. Supporters indicated that this legislation allows the people of the state to consider same-sex marriage rather than having it thrust on them by a court 3,000 miles away.

North Dakota's statute has a unique provision that keeps the law from going into effect until another state legalizes same-sex marriage. Sponsors warned that if same-sex marriage rights were not denied before Hawaii authorized them, the state would have to recognize these unions. Idaho House of Representatives Speaker Michael Simpson urged his chamber to act: "If we do nothing, we will be setting public policy. It will be contrary to what has been public policy for the last one hundred years."[9] The Idaho legislation refuses to recognize marriages performed outside the state that violate state policy. By preventing evasion of Idaho's law, the legislature is attempting to prohibit gay and lesbian citizens from going to Hawaii to marry. The passage of nonrecognition statutes in other states was sometimes cited to justify the legislation. Political columnist M. Charles Bakst responded, "I hate to think that Rhode Island would look to Mississippi for guidance on a civil rights matter."[10]

Instead of taking the high moral ground, some proponents of legislation denying same-sex marriage attempted to appeal to a more moderate audience. Supporters of the legislation in Indiana and Illinois claimed that economic considerations were their motivation, not moralistic concerns. Same-sex unions could require spousal protection such as health insurance. David Curtin, executive director of the Illinois Christian Coalition, suggested, "This would be a considerable burden to businesses, especially small business."[11]

New Jersey proponents developed a novel argument for their anti-gay marriage bill. Without this law, a heterosexual couple might marry, and then, if one spouse underwent a sex-change operation, the state would legally have to recognize a same-sex union. Despite this extreme reasoning, there are, in fact, cases of married relationships continuing after sex-change operations, creating legal same-sex relationships.

A typical strategy for defeating recalcitrant committee chairs and opponents was to attach this bill as a rider to another piece of legislation. A more extreme measure was to substitute the marriage legislation for another entire bill that had moved further along in the process in a "strike everything" amendment. In Minnesota, the same-sex marriage ban was attached to a $5.3 billion dollar, two-year health and human services budget bill which members were reluctant to jeopardize for any reason.[12] Examples of sacrificing another piece of legislation in order to substitute the anti-marriage bill are seen in Arizona and Indiana.

Proponents in the Texas legislature tried these tactics a number of times in an attempt to get their bill heard. First, a House of Representatives bill was stripped down in committee in order to add the text of the ban against same-sex marriage. The House Calendars Committee pushed the bill far down on the agenda, effectively killing it, but attempts were made to suspend House rules to try and get a vote on the bill. Representative Glen Maxey (D-Austin), the state's only gay lawmaker, threatened to offer 500 amendments to the bill if the House were to begin debating it, effectively halting all work in the chamber and killing every bill that was to follow as the chamber adjourned.[13] Finally, there was an attempt to amend an amendment to a bill on the House floor in order to force a roll call vote on the issue, but the amendment with the ban failed when the substantive amendment was withdrawn. Dale Carpenter of the Texas Log Cabin Republicans, the gay and lesbian Republican organization, observed, "The overall lesson of this session is that we need to begin trying to influence the outcome of Republican primaries. Until now the gay civil rights movement has failed to argue its positions in terms that appeal to Republicans. That is a fatal mistake in a majority Republican state like Texas."[14]

The legislation was used as a wedge issue by Republicans against Democrats. For the most part, Republicans sponsored and promoted anti-recognition bills. In 1997, twenty-eight of the thirty-nine anti-gay marriage bills were introduced by Republicans. Nine were introduced by Democrats, one by a bipartisan pair of legislators, and one in the unicameral, nonpartisan legislature in Nebraska.[15]

In Kansas, the gay and lesbian community did not lobby against this type of legislation, hoping it would not be introduced and hoping to avoid mobilizing conservatives, but they suggest in hindsight that this was a bad strategy. The majority of Kansas legislators voting against the bill were not facing reelection. In Missouri, Democrats introduced and supported the bill to protect themselves from election-year Republican attacks.[16]

The governors of Florida and Maine let these bills become law without their signatures. Governor Lawton Chiles allowed Florida to ban recognition of same-sex marriages from other states in this manner. Chiles reaffirmed his commitment to equal rights regardless of sexual orientation but said that today domestic partnerships are not viewed as an acceptable part of life.[17] Several Florida companies and local governments expressed concern that the legislation would affect their domestic partnership policies, but Chiles concluded it would not.[18] The bill's language may be ambiguous as it bars recognition, for any purpose, of same-sex relationships that are "treated as marriages in any jurisdiction, whether within or outside the state of Florida." The legislature and the governor are promoting a pro-business attitude, and opponents of the bill argued that this law undermines that effort. More than 18,000 people wrote letters, signed petitions or called the governor's office to support the legislation while only 2,400 Floridians lobbied against it.[19]

Executive orders attempting to ban same-sex marriages were issued in 1996 in two states, Alabama and Mississippi. The constitutionality of such actions is not clear as they may amount to the governor making law by fiat. Mississippi Governor Kirk Fordice denounced same-sex marriage as "perverse" and stated, "For too long in this freedom-loving land, cultural subversives have engaged in trench warfare on traditional family values." The governor's moralizing was seen as somewhat hypocritical since he was recovering from injuries suffered in a car accident while he was driving with an unidentified woman while his wife was out of town. Lawmakers in Mississippi reinforced the governor's executive order with legislation in 1997. A ban on whites and blacks marrying each other was repealed only in 1987, twenty years after the United States Supreme Court declared such prohibitions unconstitutional.

Table 4.2: Executive Orders Banning Same-Sex Marriage

ALABAMA	1996
MISSISSIPPI	1996

The legislatures in Hawaii and Alaska placed on the ballot constitutional amendments to ban same-sex marriage, and they were approved by the voters. In Nebraska and Nevada, citizens through initiative petitions put the issue to the people. In the November 2000 election, Nebraska voters by a 70 to 30 percent margin approved a constitutional amendment to prevent recognition of same-sex marriages or any civil unions or domestic partnerships. The broad language of the amendment may even prevent the state from recognizing contracts such as relationship agreements and wills between same-sex individuals. Nebraska was one of the first states to face such a comprehensive ban, and the impact of the Vermont case is evident with the inclusion of civil unions and domestic partnerships. The Nebraska amendment was proposed by initiative petition, and supporters spent $739,715 on the campaign. Opponents of the initiative spent only $146,897 and were not able to rebut the advertisements of the anti-marriage committee. The American Civil Liberties Union of Nebraska is challenging the ballot measure in federal court as a violation of the Equal Protection Clause of the U.S. Constitution. The ACLU claims that an entire group of people is placed in second-class status. ACLU spokesman Eric Ferrero said, "This is about whether or not the rights of a population of people depend on majority will. Obviously, we believe that is not the way constitutional rights work."[20]

The Nevada ballot initiative was also approved in November 2000 and could amend the state constitution to ban same-sex marriage. To ratify the amendment, voters need to approve the amendment a second time in 2002. An 1861 law already defines marriage as between a male and female. The anti-marriage campaign material suggested that homosexuality is a health risk with economic consequences and is comparable to smoking and drug use.

Unsuccessful efforts to place constitutional amendments on the ballot have been made in New Mexico, Louisiana, Mississippi, Colorado, and Oregon. These legislative proposals failed to be reported out of committee or to garner the super-majority votes needed for passage, and a number of petition efforts failed to receive the necessary number of valid signatures. Once again, the Mormon and Catholic churches strongly supported these initiatives.

Initiative petitions to prevent recognition of same-sex marriages by statute have been launched in Washington, Maine, and California. A voter referendum was proposed in Washington in order to bypass the governor's veto but died in committee due, in part, to internal disagreement between moderate and conservative Republicans. In the 1996 election, the Republicans recaptured the state senate and retained the House, but the moderate wing of the party joined with the Democrats to frustrate the legislation.

Table 4.3:
Constitutional Amendments to Ban Same-Sex Relationships

ALASKA	1998 (referendum in response to *Brause v. Alaska*)
HAWAII	1998 (referendum in response to *Baehr v. Lewin* ; permits legislature to amend constitution but does not require it)
NEBRASKA	2000 (initiative petition, also bans civil unions or domestic partnerships)
NEVADA	2000 (initiative petition, needs to be approved again in 2002)

This effort was almost undermined by the gay and lesbian community itself. One of the reasons advanced for not allowing the ballot initiative to go forward was that it was too divisive. The gay rights group, Hands Off Washington, however, was mounting its own initiative on sexual orientation nondiscrimination. Proponents of the antigay marriage bill argued that this initiative would polarize the citizenry just as much as the anti-marriage bill. When the nondiscrimination initiative was organized, it appeared that the anti-marriage bill would easily pass the new Republican-controlled legislature. Both proposals were eventually withdrawn.[21]

In Maine, the 1997 legislature chose to enact the nonrecognition law in order to avoid inciting antigay sentiment in a public referendum. Gay rights activists waged only a limited fight against the legislation, indicating the same concern after having defeated a constitutional amendment prohibiting sexual orientation nondiscrimination protection just two years earlier. The sponsor of the initiative, Concerned Maine Families, collected 62,000 signatures to put the measure on the ballot. Governor King allowed the legislation to become law without his signature, stating, "I just couldn't in good conscience put my name on it. It's an unconstitutional solution in search of a nonexistent problem."[22] Maine legislators also passed "An Act to End Discrimination," which adds sexual orientation to the categories protected against discrimination by the Maine Human Rights Act. The volatile nature of the process of securing civil rights through the legislative process is clear in Maine. The nondiscrimination act was rejected by voters after being placed on the ballot by initiative petition.

California State Senator William (Pete) Knight (R) introduced legislation to ban same-sex marriage in 1996, 1997, and 1998 without success. Knight, who has a gay son, attempted an initiative petition in 1998 but failed to collect enough signatures. Finally, the issue was put to the voters in the March 2000 ballot. The initiative was originally named "Definition of Marriage," but a challenge by the Lambda Legal Defense and Education Fund persuaded Attorney General Bill Lockyer to rename the proposition "Limit on Marriage." Proposition 22, declaring that "only marriage between a man and a woman is valid and recognized in California," passed by 63 to 37 percent of the vote.[23] The Proposition 22 campaign was expensive with proponents spending about $8 million. The No-on-Knight organization spent nearly $5.5 million to fight the initiative. Yes-on-22's Robert Glazier said of his group's victory, "As Californians, we are proud of our diversity and tolerance, but there are societal boundaries which should be preserved. Tonight we have preserved traditional marriages." The No-on-Knight organizers said that despite the loss at the polls, the gay, lesbian, bisexual, and transgendered community in California is more politically motivated than when the campaign began and will continue to fight for full equality.

Exit polls indicated that a majority of men and women of all races and income levels supported the proposition. However, 58 percent of young voters under thirty rejected the ban on same-sex marriage, suggesting that people who grew up with the gay rights movement are more supportive. A number of prominent Republicans, including the mayors of San Diego and Los Angeles, came out against the proposition.

States Rejecting Legislation Banning Same-Sex Marriage

At the beginning of the 2001 legislative session, fifteen states rejected legislation banning recognition of same-sex marriage.[24] In a number of these states, multiple bills were introduced and thwarted. Bills have been introduced in New Mexico every year from 1996 to 2001, and Maryland, New Jersey, and New York have considered, and rejected, these bills five times.

The arguments against the anti-marriage bills emphasized fairness and equality. This legislation was considered unnecessary by many lawmakers, especially if the state marriage statute was already worded in terms of a union between one man and one woman. The motivation behind these bills was seen by many as fear and bigotry. The law was considered divisive for the community. Some officials did not want to have their state recognized for intolerance. This reputation could hurt tourism and discourage potential employers and employees from relocating in the state.

Elected officials feared the bills might encourage violence toward gays and lesbians as was the case when states addressed other gay rights issues. In Oregon in 1991, there were 968 antigay attacks after the introduction of Ballot Measure 9, which would have prohibited antidiscrimination protection based on sexual orientation if it had passed. Oregon recorded more violent attacks on gays and lesbians than any other state that year. In Colorado in 1992, hate crimes towards gays increased 129 percent as Amendment Two, an antigay ballot measure, was considered. When Maine voters considered a similar measure in 1995, hate crimes more than doubled.[25] Republicans in the State of Washington attempted to avoid criticism of the anti-marriage referendum by adding an amendment to the bill denouncing violence against gays and lesbians.

Legislators who were undecided on the issue stated that they opposed such bills after proponents took extreme religious positions or equated homosexuality with child abuse. The debate was often heated, and Indiana Republican Floor Leader Brian Bosma said it included the most offensive discussion he had ever heard in the chamber. Representative Vernon Smith (D-Gary) chastised supporters of the bill: "I say to you that you are hypocrites who hide behind religious issues and walk around looking pious."[26] Maine Senator Susan Longley (D-Liberty) said that the acerbic remarks of proponents of these bills "made the decision real easy for me. I know I want to stand with those who are targeted for discrimination."[27] Opponents stressed the need to strengthen committed, if diverse, families.

The religious arguments for the legislation were countered by biblical references that outlaw divorce and premarital sex. Divorced legislators favoring the law were called hypocritical. Nebraska Senator Ernie Chambers remarked, "With their unclean hands, they are going to tell others that their (same-sex) relationship is unfit."[28] The religious right was accused of trying to cut off debate on gay and lesbian relationships before the people had time to thoughtfully consider the issue, since no state had yet even granted same-sex marriage rights.

Opponents of these measures contend that the state should not discriminate or follow one set of religious beliefs. Pat Robertson's Christian Coalition and a number of other religious right organizations have led a coordinated effort to initiate and support antigay marriage legislation in all fifty states. The religious right continues to use the issue as a fund-raising point and often distorts the issue for dramatic effect, claiming that gay marriage is just the first step in an effort to legalize multiple-partner homosexual relationships. The Roman Catholic and Mormon churches have also been deeply involved in the issue, and the Mormon Church donated half a million dollars to support the Alaskan constitutional amendment banning same-sex marriage.

Many legislators who questioned the constitutionality of these bills were worried that the legislation would make the state vulnerable to years of expensive, time-consuming court challenges. A constitutional argument suggests that these nonrecognition statutes violate the Equal Protection Clause of the United States Constitution. The American Civil Liberties Union argues that a distinction between the recognition of foreign same-sex marriages and foreign opposite-sex marriages lacks a rational relationship to legitimate state interests. Advocates of this position cite the 1995 United States Supreme Court case, *Romer v. Evans*,[29] which struck down Colorado's constitutional amendment prohibiting the passage of any laws protecting the rights of gays and lesbians. Concerns were raised that these laws are so broad that they might block recognition of opposite-sex couples whose marriages from another state do not meet specific marital requirements. For example, employers in a state with an age of consent of eighteen might be permitted to drop benefits for employees who were married in a state that allowed consent at age sixteen. Proponents of same-sex marriage countered the arguments that such unions were too costly by suggesting that the state could save money by allowing them. In Maryland, a woman testifying before a House committee argued that she could be taken off the welfare rolls if she were allowed to marry her lesbian partner. Since 1992, the woman has collected $42,380 dollars in health and other federal benefits for herself and her children. The woman claimed to know fourteen other lesbians in similar situations costing the state approximately $593,000 dollars.[30]

The antirecognition laws proposed in two states included penalties against anyone legally entitled to officiate who performs a same-sex marriage ceremony. In Alabama, the fine would have been $1,000 dollars, and in New Mexico, it would have been $50 dollars. The Reverend Troy Perry, founder and moderator of the Universal Fellowship of Metropolitan Community Churches (UFMCC), the largest religious organization with a primary ministry to the gay and lesbian community, called for the largest-ever mass wedding for the gay community on the steps of the Alabama Capitol if the law had passed. Reverend Perry had officiated at a mass gay and lesbian wedding in Washington, D.C., during the March on Washington in 1992 where 3,000 couples participated. He called the legislation "unconstitutional religious bigotry" and said, "Holy Union and Holy Marriage are rites and sacraments of all UFMCC congregations. I will serve time in jail before I will allow the government to dictate our religious practices."[31] The UFMCC has 42,000 members in 300 congregations in nineteen countries.

The legislative battles mobilized the gay and lesbian communities in most states. After Montana passed nonrecognition legislation, the gay and lesbian group Pride! announced plans for a mass same-sex marriage ceremony. The Montana *Bozeman Chronicle* stated, "At a time when many gays and lesbians in Montana are still afraid to admit they are gay, such a public ceremony would be unprecedented in the state."[32] Coalitions of people supportive of equal rights claims and those troubled by government entanglement with religion spoke out against efforts to ban same-sex unions. Many editorials in the leading newspapers of cities across the country were against legislation prohibiting same-sex marriage.[33]

The first tactic was an attempt to prevent the introduction of this legislation, but this effort was not successful. A common strategy for defeating these bills was to tie them up in the legislative committee to which they were assigned. Even if one chamber of the legislature passed the bill, a committee chair could prevent the other chamber from hearing it. If a bill fails to meet the legislative deadline for action, it dies when the legislature adjourns. The experience of same-sex marriage legislation reinforces the power that committee chairs wield in the legislative process. In California and New Mexico the Democratic leadership was considered to be more liberal than the legislative membership as a whole and exercised its power to defeat anti-recognition statutes.

Another tactic used was to add amendments to these bills that were unacceptable to the sponsors. These "poison pill" amendments most often created domestic partnership rights in the state. This tactic was used successfully in California. In Arizona, the language banning gay and lesbian marriages was amended in a 31 to 22 vote to read simply that the state "promotes strong family values."[34] In New Jersey, gay and lesbian rights activists successfully lobbied the Assembly's Health Committee to remove the clause stating that same-sex marriage "is against the public policy" of the state.[35] Eliminating that provision is thought to make the legislation more susceptible to a court challenge.

On some occasions, legislators lobbied the bill's sponsor to withdraw the measure, fearing a vote on the issue during an election year. Some legislators were reluctant to alienate their conservative constituency while others responded that they favored the bill but were afraid to offend the members of the gay community and their liberal supporters.[36] Only once did a chamber of one state legislature reject a bill in a full vote of the members; this was a Louisiana bill calling for a constitutional amendment which required a two-thirds majority vote. While more than half of the legislators supported the bill, it failed to pass the super-majority requirement by just two votes.

In Nebraska, opponents of the bill banning same-sex marriage staged a filibuster. At first, amendments making small, inconsequential grammatical modifications were introduced.[37] Time-consuming amendments creating sexual orientation nondiscrimination provisions and domestic partnership rights were subsequently introduced to prevent the legislation from being heard.[38] Supporters of the bill were not organized enough to end the filibuster, lacking just one vote.[39]

The controversial tactic of "outing" was considered in North Dakota. Keith Elston, a Bismarck-based spokesman for the American Civil Liberties Union, threatened to announce the names of gay legislators if they supported the bill. Ira Glasser, the ACLU's national director, later repudiated Elston's suggestions.[40] Oregon Senator Kate Brown (D-Portland), who is bisexual, disclosed the names of past and current state legislators who are gay.[41]

Governors prevented anti-marriage laws from being implemented in two states. Washington's Governor Locke vetoed a bill in 1997, although a state-wide poll indicated public opposition to banning same-sex marriages. Fifty-six percent of those polled opposed changing state law to "withhold legal status to same-gender marriages performed in other states."[42] In 1998, however, the legislature had the votes to override Locke's veto.

Table 4.4: Bills to Ban Recognition of Same-Sex Marriage Defeated

IOWA	1996, 1997
MARYLAND	1996, 1997, 1998
NEBRASKA	1997
NEW HAMPSHIRE	1997
NEW MEXICO	1996, 1997, 1998
OHIO	1997
OREGON	1997 (three bills would have allowed referendum vote), 1999
RHODE ISLAND	1996, 1997
TEXAS	1997
VERMONT	1997
WISCONSIN	1996, 1997
WYOMING	1996, 1997

Governor Romer of Colorado vetoed the marriage ban in both the 1996 and 1997 legislative sessions. The governor vetoed the bill in 1996 primarily because its language equated homosexuality with bigamy and incest.[43] Colorado law already reserves marriage to the union of one man and one woman. Romer cited two reasons for his 1997 veto. First, the language of the bill could threaten thousands of common-law marriages in the state. Second, "regardless of how benign the wording is, this bill is fundamentally negative and divisive."[44] The bill targeted gay and lesbian people to exclude and stigmatize them. The governor said that not only was the legislature taking the wrong approach, but it should focus on the real-life problems of same-sex relationships in the civil law. He also appointed a commission to investigate discrimination against gay and lesbian couples when the legislature failed to do so. This is an interesting twist from the governor who defended Colorado's constitutional amendment prohibiting sexual orientation antidiscrimination provisions. The United States Supreme Court found the amendment unconstitutional in *Romer v. Evans*.[45] In 2000, however, the Colorado legislature and governor approved the anti-marriage bill.

Gays and lesbians offered passionate testimony about the basis of their relationships and the discrimination they faced. Hearings in Rhode Island touched on whether homosexuality is an inherited trait or a chosen behavior. Massive grassroots organizing and educating is being undertaken by groups affiliated with the Freedom to Marry coalition, a project of the Lambda Legal Defense and Education Fund which became co-counsel in the *Baehr* case. Karen Geraghty, president of the Maine Lesbian/Gay Political Alliance, stated that "The focus of the gay community and our supporters over the next year will be to talk to our co-workers and neighbors about the discrimination we face every day."[46] Evan Wolfson, co-counsel in the Hawaii case and director of Lambda's Freedom to Marry Project, remarks that the legislative success at the state level is considerable. Gay rights are prevailing half the time. Wolfson states:

> We are in a struggle for the map of the country.... All of America is now talking about our equality and families, and our freedom to marry. It is our task at this time to engage, fully and with determination, knowing that history is with us as we move forward in Hawaii, throughout the country, and, indeed, across the globe, to full equality and inclusion for lesbians, gay men, and those we love. It is a struggle not just for marriage, not just for gay people, but for what kind of country we want this to be.[47]

Legislation Attempting to Recognize Same-Sex Marriages

Since the *Baehr* case, bills have been introduced to recognize same-sex marriage or civil unions in thirteen states.[48] In Washington Governor Mike Lowry became the first chief executive to call for legislation removing barriers to same-sex marriage. All the bills to recognize same-sex marriage were introduced by Democrats and were defeated without advancing very far in the legislative process. Texas was the first state to consider such legislation in 1993. Initially, the value of these bills was primarily symbolic, but with Vermont as a role model, other states may recognize the merit of extending the legal definition of marriage. Governor Dean predicted that half a dozen states will accept civil unions or domestic partnerships in the next five or six years. Proponents of these bills argued that the state's commitment to family, long-term relationships, and healthy stable environments which foster the development of children would be strengthened. By introducing these bills, sponsors hoped to counter the antirecognition legislation and ensure a fairer debate on the issue.

Table 4.5: Bills Introduced to Recognize Same-Sex Marriage

CALIFORNIA	2001
HAWAII	2001
MARYLAND	1997, 1998, 2000
MASSACHUSETTS	1999
NEBRASKA	1996, 1997
NEW YORK	2001
NEVADA	2001
OREGON	1997
RHODE ISLAND	1998, 1999, 2000, 2001
TEXAS	1993
VERMONT	2000
WASHINGTON	1997, 2001
WISCONSIN	1997

None reported out of committee.

Table 4.6: State-wide Domestic Partnership Laws

VERMONT	Civil Union Law: Grants all the state rights and responsibilities associated with marriage.
HAWAII	Reciprocal Beneficiaries Law: Grants any two single adults approximately 50-60 spousal rights, such as health care decisions, joint tenancy, property inheritance, wrongful death suits, insurance, and state pensions.
NEVADA	Proposed 2001

Congress Responds: The Defense of Marriage Act

The Defense of Marriage Act (DOMA)[49] denies federal benefits to married people of the same sex and permits states to ignore such marriages occurring in other states. After hours of passionate and often bitter debate, the bill easily passed both chambers of Congress.[50] The House voted 342 to 67 in support of DOMA, which was authored by Representative Jack Barr (R-Ga.). Twenty-two of the sixty-seven members opposing the legislation were from California. On the floor of the House, Barr charged that opponents of the legislation wanted to "throw open the doors of the

U.S. Treasury . . . to be raided by the homosexual movement."[51] Republicans touted the bill as part of their "family values" legislation, which also included a parental rights act and a bill relaxing restrictions on state aid to religious institutions.

The House also rejected a proposal to have the General Accounting Office, an investigative arm of Congress, determine the potential cost of extending federal marriage benefits to same-sex couples. In an emotional speech on the House floor, Representative Steve Gunderson (R-Wis.), then the only openly gay Republican member of Congress, urged the Republican leadership to create a commission to study the cost of extending rights to gays and lesbians. Their refusal to support this commission, Gunderson said, "exposes this legislative initiative for the mean political game that it is."[52] Gunderson was the only Republican to vote against DOMA.

The Defense of Marriage Act passed in the Senate in a vote of 85 to 14. No Republican voted against the bill, but votes on the legislation did not translate into political repercussions. All the senators that opposed DOMA were reelected. Senator Carol Moseley-Braun, an opponent of the measure, stated, "This bill expands government intrusiveness into our everyday lives and represents just the opposite of smaller government."[53]

President Clinton signed the legislation without fanfare in the middle of the night. Clinton was strongly supported by the gay and lesbian communities in his 1992 presidential campaign, and the president said his record on gay rights was second to none. While Clinton does not favor same-sex marriage, he accused Republicans of using the issue as a divisive election-year ploy. He decried the debate as "gay baiting, pure and simple" and chastised Republicans for rushing the politically sensitive issue onto the legislative agenda during an election year. Clinton was determined "to stop this election from degenerating into an attempt to pit one group of Americans against another." White House Press Secretary Mike McCurry said, "It's a classic use of wedge politics designed to provoke anxieties and fears. That being the case, though, the president has very strong views, personal views, and he has to act consistent with those views."[54]

Democratic strategists warned that a presidential veto would be politically disastrous. For instance, Brian Lunde, former executive director of the Democratic National Committee, stated, "Clinton is trying to neutralize any issue that might give Senator Dole an advantage. It's a no-brainer in a presidential election year. This is an uncontrollable issue, and very frankly, most voters are opposed to the idea of gay marriage." The president's support of the legislation was seen as an attempt to appease conservative voters. Gary Bauer, Family Research Council spokesman, stated that Clinton had merely removed "another issue in an effort to get re-elected."[55]

Opponents of the bill argued that the legislation is unconstitutional and violates the Full Faith and Credit Clause, which requires states to recognize the "public acts, records and judicial proceedings" of other states. Attorney General Janet Reno, however, responding to queries by the White House, said she believed the bill would withstand a constitutional challenge. Many other constitutional scholars disagree, however.[56]

Refusing to recognize one state's marriage license could lead to policies invalidating other types of contracts. A state could decide it does not like another state's incorporation requirements, if, for example, the corporation gave benefits to domestic partners. Interstate commerce depends on mutual recognition of all contracts, and a marriage license is one form of contract. If anti-marriage laws are enforced, gay and lesbian couples will face uncertainty in their relationships as their legal status will vary throughout the country. The fundamental right to interstate travel is compromised under nonrecognition laws because a couple's legal status will change as they cross state lines. This discourages good, productive citizens from seeking employment in certain states and limits these couples' ability to move or to remain in a state. If a partner in a same-sex couple is transferred for business to a state that does not recognize the union, he or she will have to choose between the employment and the relationship, which is unnecessarily burdensome and places an unfairly high restriction on the constitutional right to interstate travel.

The United States Supreme Court's decision in *Romer v. Evans*,[57] declaring unconstitutional Colorado's Amendment 2, prohibiting the state from recognizing claims of discrimination based on sexual orientation, may support the claim that DOMA is also unconstitutional. The *Romer* decision stated that "Laws singling out a certain class of citizens for disfavored legal status or general hardships" violate even minimal equal protection standards. The Defense of Marriage Act creates two classes of matrimony with the federal government withholding benefits sanctioned by a state if the marriage is between same-sex couples. Evan Wolfson, Lambda senior staff attorney and director of Lambda's Marriage Project, explained, "This anti-gay effort to create two classes of lawful marriage is precisely a classification of persons undertaken for its own sake. We hope *Romer* will help in our efforts to demonstrate this."[58]

The Employment Nondiscrimination bill was taken up in the Senate at the same time as the Defense of Marriage Act but was defeated 50 to 49. This legislation would prohibit discriminatory employment practices aimed at gays and lesbians. President Clinton supported this legislation, and Vice-President Gore was standing by to cast the tie-breaking vote if it was needed. Public opinion polls suggest that 58 percent of Americans oppose same-sex marriage but that 84 percent support rights for gays and lesbians in employment.[59] The bill was introduced in the following Congress, but with the Republicans in the majority it never passed out of committee. Support for the legislation is growing, and passage is predicted in the next few years.

Conclusion

Fighting these battles has taken time and energy away from other efforts to secure gay and lesbian rights. However, the protracted legislative debates on gay and lesbian marriage have altered the nature of the dispute so that now non-discrimination and domestic partnership provisions are considered much less radical and much more acceptable. Since 1991, many states have considered sexual orientation nondiscrimination provisions, and twelve states have enacted such provisions.[60] In Maine, a nondiscrimination bill was enacted by the legislature but was repealed later by the voters.

A resolution to the same-sex marriage issue is years away and is most likely to be decided by the United States Supreme Court. Same-sex marriage bans will be challenged under the Equal Protection Clause and the Full Faith and Credit Clause of the United States Constitution. If these arguments succeed, it will not matter what individual state constitutions or statutes proclaim. The Hawaii marriage case demonstrates the power of rights claims presented in courts to initiate social change. To ensure lasting social transformation, however, the grassroots political work of organization, education, and persuasion must follow judicial decrees.

Notes

1. Susan Essoyan, "Hawaii Tries to Take a Stand Against Same-Sex Marriage," *Los Angeles Times*, 26 April 1994, A5.

2. Hawaii Act 217 (1994); 1994 Haw. Sess. Laws 217; 1994 Hi. HB 2312.

3. Ibid.

4. Alaskans for Civil Rights, press release, 5 October 1998.

5. Ibid.

6. These states and the years of passage are as follows: Alabama (1998), Alaska (1998), Arizona (1996), Arkansas (1997), California (2000), Colorado (2000), Delaware (1996), Florida (1997), Georgia (1996), Hawaii (1998), Idaho (1996), Illinois (1996), Indiana (1997), Kansas (1996), Louisiana (1999), Maine (1997). Michigan (1996), Minnesota (1997), Mississippi (1997), Missouri (1996 but struck down by court on a technicality), Montana (1997), Nebraska (2000), New Jersey (2001), New York (2001), North Carolina (1996), North Dakota (1997), Oklahoma (1996), Pennsylvania (1996), South Carolina (1996), South Dakota (1996), Tennessee (1996), Utah (1995), Virginia (1997), Washington (1998), and West Virginia (2000).

7. California Assemblyperson Pete Knight, quoted in Greg Lucas, "Anti-Marriage Bill Killed in CA Senate," *San Francisco Chronicle*, 23 April 1997, 3.

8. "Georgia Senate OKs Ban on Same-Sex Marriage," Associated Press, 27 February 1996.

9. "Same-Sex Marriage Bill Easily Passes in the House," Associated Press, 21 February 1996.

10. M. Charles Bakst, "Same-Sex Marriage," *Providence Journal-Bulletin*, 13 March 1997, 22.

11. Michael Dizon, "House Forwards to Edgar Bill on Same-Sex Unions," *Chicago Tribune*, 26 April 1996, 3.

12. Lynda McDonnell, "Senate Rise to Occasion with Eloquent Debate," *St. Paul Pioneer Press*, 17 May 1997, 13.

13. "Tradition Snags Gay Marriage Ban," *Austin American Statesman*, 14 May 1997, 8.

14. Steve Labinski, "Session Ends in Standoff on Gay Issues," *Houston Voice*, 9 June 1997, 4.

15. Lisa Keen, "Virginia House, Senate Approve Anti-Marriage Bill," *Washington Blade*, 7 February 1997, 5.

16. Editorial, "GOP Plays the Gay Card," *St. Louis Post-Dispatch*, 16 April 1996, 28.

17. Tyler Bridges, "Same-Sex Marriage Ban Broadened," *Miami Herald*, 30 May 1997, 3.

18. Editorial, "Let Employers Handle Benefits," *St. Petersburg Times*, 28 May 1997, 33.

19. Peter Wallsten, "Same-Sex Marriage Ban Raises Legal, Business Issues," *St. Petersburg Times*, 27 May 1997, 23.

20. Lisa Neff, "ACLU Sues Nebraska over Gay Marriage Ban," *Chicago Free Press*, 29 November 2000, 5.

21. Peter Callaghan, "Allies Impair Bid to Defuse Gay Marriage as State Issue," *Tacoma News Tribune*, 20 April 1997, 3.

22. Bill Nemitz, "King's Stand Spoils Cosby's Celebration," *Portland Press-Herald*, 2 April 1997, 5.

23. Lisa Neff, "Knight Has Its Day," *Chicago Free Press*, 15 March 2000, 1.

24. The states and the years the legislation was considered are as follows: Connecticut (1997, 1999), Hawaii (1999, strengthening current restrictions), Maryland (1996, 1997, 1998, 1999, 2001), Massachusetts (1999, 2000, 2001), Missouri (1996 law overturned by court, 1999, 2000), New Hampshire (1997, 2000, 2001), New Jersey (1996, 1997, 1998, 1999, 2000), New Mexico (1996, 1997, 1998, 1999, 2000, 2001), New York (1996, 1997, 1998, 1999, 2000), Ohio (1997, 1998, 2000) Oregon (1997, 1999), Rhode Island (1996, 1997, 2000), Texas (1997, 1999), Vermont (1997, 1998, 1999, 2000), Wisconsin (1996, 1997, 1998, 2000), and Wyoming (1996, 1997, 2001).

25. "Anti-Gay Marriage Bill Passes House, Stalls in Senate," *Seattle Gay News*, 21 March 1997, 1.

26. Stuart Hirsch, "Ban on Gay Marriages Will Go to Governor," *Indianapolis Star*, 25 April 1997, 3.

27. Denise Goodman, "Maine Legislators Avoid Referendum," *Boston Globe*, 27 March 1997, 17.

28. Erin Schulte, "Debate Heard on Gay Unions," *Daily Nebraskan*, 19 March 1997, 14.

29. Romer v. Evans, 116 S. Ct. 1620, 134 L. Ed. 2d 855 (1996).

30. "Montgomery County Woman Challenges House to Weigh Same-Sex Unions," *Annapolis Daily Capital*, 13 March 1997, 13.

31. "Gay Cleric Denounces Proposed Law on Marriages," UFMCC Press Release, 2 June 1997, on file with author.

32. "Governor Signs Bill, Gays Plan Mass Wedding," *Bozeman Chronicle* (Montana), 1 May 1997, 7.

33. For example, the *Denver Post*, the *Rocky Mountain News*, the *Arizona Daily Star*, the *Portland Press Herald*, the *Detroit Free Press*, the *Daily Nebraskan*, the *Los Angeles Times*, and the *New York Times* were against same-sex marriage bans.

34. "Lawmaker's 'Family Values' Vote Kills Gay-Marriage Ban," *Arizona Daily Star*, 2 April 1996, 33.

35. James M. O'Neill, "NJ Bill Opposing Same-Sex Marriages Passes First Hurdle," *Philadelphia Enquirer*, 24 January 1996.

36. Liz Chapman, "Gay Rights Bill Being Withdrawn," *Sun Journal* (Maine), 17 January 1996, 7.

37. Erin Schulte, "Same-Sex Marriage Bill Held up by Filibuster," *Daily Nebraskan*, 4 April 1997, 5.

38. Erin Schulte, "Senators Try Amendments to Resolve Gay-Union Bill," *Daily Nebraskan*, 9 April 1997.

39. Editorial, " Same-Sex Marriage Bill Teetering," *Omaha World-Herald*, 11 April 1997, 21.

40. Dale Wetzel, "House Votes to Not Recognize Gay Marriage," Associated Press, 15 March 1997.

41. Jeff Wright, " Anti-Gay Bill Passes Oregon Senate," *Eugene Register-Guard*, 24 May 1997, 12.

42. Keen, "Virginia House, Senate Approve Anti-Marriage Bill," 6.

43. "A Solid Legislative Session," *Boulder Camera*, 13 May 1997, 23.

44. Text of Governor Romer's veto message, quoted in Michelle Dally Johnston, "Romer Kills Gay-Wedding Bill," *Denver Post*, 6 June 1997, 3.

45. Romer v. Evans.

46. Chapman, "Gay Rights Bill Withdrawn."

47. Evan Wolfson, "The Freedom to Marry: Eyes on the Prize," *The Lambda Update*, Fall 1996, 1.

48. California (2001), Hawaii (2001), Maryland (1997, 1998, 2000), Massachusetts (1999), Nebraska (1996, 1997), New York (2001), Nevada (2001), Oregon (1997), Rhode Island (1998, 1999, 2000, 2001), Texas (1993), Vermont (2000), Washington (1997, 2001), and Wisconsin (1997).

49. Defense of Marriage Act, Public Law No. 104-1909, sec. 3(a), 110 Stat. 2419 (1996).

50. Eric Schmitt, "Senators Reject Both Job-Bias and Gay Marriage," *New York Times*, 11 September 1996, A1; Andrew Sullivan, *Same-Sex Marriage: Pro and Con* (New York: Vintage Books, 1997), 200-238.

51. Schmitt, "Senators Reject Both Job-Bias and Gay Marriage."

52. Melissa Healy, "House Backs Curbs on Gay Marriages," *Los Angeles Times*, 13 July 1996, A13.

53. Eric Schmitt, "Senators Reject Both Job-Bias and Gay Marriage."

54. Melissa Healy, " House Backs Curbs on Gay Marriages."

55. Melissa Healy, "Clinton Signals He'd Sign Anti-Gay Marriage Bill," *Los Angeles Times*, 23 May 1996, A15.

56. Laurence Tribe, "Toward a Less Perfect Union," *New York Times*, 26 May 1996, 32.

57. Romer v. Evans.

58. Lambda Legal Defense and Education Fund, press release, 24 May 1996, on file with author.

59. James D. Wilson, "Gays under Fire," *Newsweek*, 14 September 1992, 37.

60. The twelve states prohibiting such discrimination are California, Connecticut, Hawaii, Maryland, Massachusetts, Minnesota, New Hampshire, New Jersey, Rhode Island, Vermont, and Wisconsin. The District of Columbia also has a nondiscrimination provision, and Maine's law was repealed by initiative petition. Similar bills have been introduced in New Mexico, Nevada, Oregon, and Texas but have not yet been approved.

Chapter Five

Vermont's Supreme Court Grants Benefits of Marriage

Three same-sex couples joined the litigation battle to secure marriage rights in Vermont in the summer of 1997. After being denied marriage licenses, they brought suit in the case *Baker v. State*.[1] The plaintiffs were two lesbian couples and one gay couple: Lois Farnham and Holly Puterbaugh who had been together for more than 26 years, Nina Beck and Stacy Jolles, and Stan Baker and Peter Harrigan.

Nina Beck and Stacey Jolles experienced the discrimination gay and lesbian couples face as parents. When Beck was rushed to the hospital due to complications during childbirth, having been impregnated by a sperm donor, Jolles would not have been allowed in the labor ward if she had not remembered to bring her power of attorney with her. Jolles had no legal relationship with her son, so when Vermont became the first state to allow second-parent adoptions, Beck and Jolles moved there. Jolles notes, "Now the state says I'm fit enough to be a parent, but not fit enough to be a spouse. It makes no sense." Stacy Jolles says her children motivated her to seek marital rights despite the depositions, publicity, and public attacks that would come with the litigation. Jolles remarks, "This is about protecting Seth, who shouldn't be a second-class citizen because his parents are lesbians."[2]

The plaintiffs argued that Vermont law allows same-sex marriage, and if not, the statute violates the state's constitution. Their case is based on the Common Benefits Clause which states:

> That government is, or ought to be, instituted for the common benefit, protection, and security of the people, nation, or community, and not for the particular emolument or advantage of any single person, family, or set of persons, who are a part only of that community.[3]

This clause is usually interpreted like the Equal Protection Clause of the U.S. Constitution.

There are three levels of analysis under the equal protection doctrine. The most demanding review applies when fundamental rights are infringed upon or when the group of people affected has historically been discriminated against or is politically powerless. These "suspect" groups have been defined by race, religion, alienage, and national origin. In these cases, the courts strictly scrutinize the law, and the government must have a compelling reason to justify the discrimination. The burden is on the government to demonstrate why it needs the policy.

The lowest level of review requires the state only to show a rational basis for a legitimate policy. The government wins most of these cases because the court usually defers to the judgment of the elected members of the legislature. An intermediate level of review, "heightened scrutiny," asks whether the policy is related to an important government objective. This analysis has often been used in claims of gender discrimination. The level of review used by the court is often a cue as to which party will prevail.

One of the first determinations that the Vermont trial court made was what test to use. Judge Linda Levitt ruled that sexual orientation is not a suspect class necessitating strict scrutiny because being gay "is not a characteristic that is as readily determinable by third parties as race, gender or alienage" and because gays and lesbians are not politically powerless. No federal court to date has considered gays and lesbians a suspect class.

Judge Levitt held that there is no gender discrimination claim because men and women are treated the same; both are prevented by the definition of marriage from marrying the same sex. Such circular reasoning had been used earlier to justify antimiscegenation statutes. Interestingly, the Hawaii Supreme Court did find the ban on same-sex marriage to be a violation of its equal rights amendment prohibiting gender discrimination.

Courts have also been reluctant to expand the definition of fundamental rights. While the state must have a compelling reason to restrict heterosexual marriage, the "right" to choose one's partner has not been extrapolated from the state or federal constitutions. Heterosexual marriages, Judge Levitt wrote, receive constitutional protection because they are connected with procreation, childbirth, abortion, and child rearing. Judge Levitt relies heavily on the precedent denying same-sex marriage and cites *Baehr* only to support her argument that same-sex marriage is not a fundamental right. Conspicuously absent from her analysis is any discussion of the Hawaii court's determination of gender discrimination and the failure of the state to show a compelling interest in prohibiting same-sex marriage.

When neither a fundamental right nor a suspect class is at issue, the court evaluates whether the state law reasonably relates to a legitimate public purpose. The State of Vermont gave seven reasons to support its policy of prohibiting gays and lesbians from marrying. Uniting men and women allows them to "bridge their differences" and promotes a setting which provides both male and female role models. The "time honored" institution of marriage should be preserved, and Vermont marriages need to be recognized in other states. The legislature's authority to channel behavior and make normative statements should be preserved. The use of modern fertility treatments should be minimized in order to avoid increased child custody and visitation disputes. Finally, the state has an interest in furthering the link between procreation and child rearing.

Judge Levitt rejected the first six justifications, but the marriage statute was deemed constitutional based on the state's desire to encourage procreation and support children. This is an explanation that the Hawaii court rejected. Plaintiffs Nina Beck and Stacy Jolles remarked, "The Judge's reasoning is ironic. Gay and lesbian individuals and couples like us have children. We share the State's concern for promoting stable homes for children. That's why we wanted to marry."[4] The court also failed to explain why heterosexual families enjoy greater protection than gay and lesbian families under the Common Benefits Clause, which specifically requires that families be treated equally.

The gay and lesbian couples appealed the case to the state supreme court. In Vermont, the supreme court is the appellate court of last resort and has mandatory jurisdiction. At oral argument, the supreme court challenged a number of the state's assertions. Chief Justice Amestoy asked if marriage should not be replaced with domestic partnership given the "wreck" heterosexuals have made of the institution of marriage. Justices also questioned the notion that procreation is the basis of marriage. When the attorney general noted that no state or country permits same-sex marriage, a justice asked, "Doesn't someone have to be first?"

The Vermont Supreme Court issued its opinion on 20 December 1999 and concluded that "none of the interests asserted by the state provides a reasonable and just basis for the continued exclusion of same-sex couples from the benefits incident to a civil marriage license under Vermont law."[5] This landmark decision was considered by many to be one of the most significant legal victories ever for the gay rights movement.[6] It certainly is the most important decision regarding gay and lesbian couples. The Vermont court is the first state supreme court in this country to rule that prohibiting gay and lesbian couples from marrying is a constitutional violation. The reasoning of the court, however, took three different positions.

Chief Justice Jeffrey Amestoy wrote the opinion for the court and based his decision on the Common Benefits Clause of the Vermont Constitution. Interestingly, he rejected the three-tiered analysis used under the Equal Protection Clause of the Fourteenth Amendment of the U.S. Constitution. While the Vermont court has often referred to the Equal Protection Clause when evaluating claims under the Vermont Constitution, the state can adopt more stringent standards for government action. Amestoy also pointed out that the U.S. Supreme Court itself has deviated from its rational-basis/strict-scrutiny test.

The Vermont Constitution should be interpreted in such a way as to be faithful to the core values of its framers rather than being rigidly attached to labels. The values underlying the Common Benefits Clause are those of inclusion and a "vision of government that afforded every Vermonter its benefit and protection and provided no Vermonter particular advantage."[7] Chief Justice Amestoy continued, "Out of the shifting and complicated kaleidoscope of events, social forces, and ideas that culminated in the Vermont Constitution of 1777, our task is to distill the essence, the motivating ideal of the framers. The challenge is to remain faithful to that historical ideal, while addressing contemporary issues that the framers undoubtedly could never have imagined."[8] The proper analysis under the Common Benefits Clause is first to define the group disadvantaged by the law and then to determine whether such classification is reasonably necessary to achieve the state's objectives. Amestoy explained:

> Consistent with the core presumption of inclusion, factors to be considered in this determination may include: (1) the significance of the benefits and protections of the challenged law; (2) whether the omission of members of the community from the benefits and protections of the challenged law promotes the government's stated goals; and (3) whether the classification is significantly underinclusive or overinclusive.[9]

When weighing the relative importance of the competing interests, the court will look to the "traditions from which [the state] developed" as well as those "from which it broke." This assessment of the state's traditions will prevent judges from deciding cases according to their personal views.

The test he outlined was then applied. The marriage laws apply to opposite-sex couples, thereby excluding anyone who wants to marry someone of the same sex. The government's purpose for the statutory classification is "furthering the link between procreation and child rearing." Since gay and lesbian couples cannot conceive a child on their own, the legislature is justified in limiting marriage benefits to opposite-sex couples. Chief Justice Amestoy recognized that the state has a "legitimate and long-standing interest in promoting a permanent commitment between couples for the security of their children."[10]

The statutory exclusion of same-sex couples, however, is significantly under-inclusive as many people marry for reasons unrelated to procreation and never intend to have children. In addition, many children today are being raised by same-sex parents. Therefore, Justice Amestoy concluded that the "law extends the benefits and protections of marriage to many persons with no logical connection to the stated governmental goal." In fact, the Vermont legislature in 1996 removed all legal barriers to adoption for same-sex couples and provided for parental rights for unmarried persons in domestic partnerships. Excluding same-sex couples from the legal protections of marriage exposes their children to the "precise risks that the State argues the marriage laws are designed to secure against." Commenting on the state's case, Amestoy remarked that "it is not a failure of proof that is fatal to the State's arguments, it is a failure of logic."[11]

The chief justice then turned to the significance of denying marriage benefits to same-sex couples. The United States Supreme Court in *Loving v. Virginia*, which struck down that state's antimiscegenation law, noted that the "freedom to marry has long been recognized as one of the vital personal rights."[12] One hundred thirty-seven years before *Loving*, the Vermont Supreme Court stated that marriage is part of the "natural rights of human nature." The opinion then lists a dozen benefits or protections that Vermont bestows upon married couples. Considering the significance of these marriage rights, the court concluded that "[t]he laudable governmental goal of promoting a commitment between two married couples to promote the security of their children and the community as a whole provides no reasonable basis for denying the legal benefits and protections of marriage to same-sex couples, who are no differently situated with respect to this goal than their opposite-sex counterparts." Chief Justice Amestoy concluded concluded that "The extension of the Common Benefits Clause to acknowledge plaintiffs as Vermonters who seek nothing more, nor less, than legal protection and security for their avowed commitment to an intimate and lasting human relationship is simply, when all is said and done, a recognition of our common humanity."[13]

The State of Vermont, however, was not required to issue marriage licenses to same-sex couples, and the court held only that the benefits and protections of marriage could not be denied. Some future case may attempt to establish that the denial of a marriage license *per se* is a constitutional violation, but that was not the issue before this court. The court did not want to "infringe upon the prerogatives of the Legislature to craft an appropriate means of addressing this constitutional mandate."[14] The legislature could simply add same-sex couples to the marriage statute or could create some other alternative, parallel licensing scheme. The legislature was given a reasonable period of time to implement such legislation so as to avoid any unforeseen, disruptive consequences of a sudden change in the marriage laws.

Justice John A. Dooley wrote a concurring opinion. Justice Dooley considers gay men and lesbians a suspect classification for equal protection analysis under Vermont's Article 7. No federal court has included gays and lesbians as a suspect class, but the Oregon Court of Appeals did so in 1998. Justice Dooley found the Oregon analysis instructive for defining a suspect class. The United States Supreme Court has defined suspect classes in terms of historical discrimination, political powerlessness, and immutable characteristics. The Oregon appellate court noted, however, that religious affiliation and alienage may be changed, and yet these characteristics might elevate a claimant to a suspect class depending upon the nature of the discriminatory government action. Justice Dooley concludes that Vermont would be wise to follow Oregon's lead and define suspect class by "(1) whether the characteristic has historically been regarded as defining a distinct socially-recognized group, and if so (2) whether that group has been the subject of adverse social or political stereotyping."[15] Under this definition, gays and lesbians are members of a suspect class. The courts will evaluate any law that applies to this suspect class with strict scrutiny, and the state must show that the statute promotes a compelling governmental interest through the least restrictive means. This is a difficult standard for the state government to meet.

Justice Dooley found the well-established three-tier system of analysis for discrimination claims under the Equal Protection Clause of the U.S. Constitution suitable for Vermont's Common Benefits Clause cases. The evaluation under the Equal Protection Clause distinguishes between claims of civil rights discrimination and economic discrimination with great deference to the legislature regarding economic regulations. Justice Dooley accused the majority opinion of blurring this distinction and failing to provide any guidelines for such claims in future cases.

Justice Denise Johnson concurred in part and dissented in part. Justice Johnson objected to the court's remedy and would have required the state to issue marriage licenses to same-sex couples. Under the majority opinion, the plaintiff same-sex couples are subjected "an uncertain fate in the political caldron."[16] While the state may establish age and consanguinity restrictions for public health and safety concerns, the state in granting a marriage license is "not espousing certain morals, lifestyles, or relationships, but only identifying those persons entitled to the benefits of the marital status." In this case, the state has not raised any legitimate public health or safety arguments for denying same-sex couples the benefits of marriage. Justice Johnson argued that the court has a great deal of responsibility to fashion remedies for civil rights violations.

Justice Johnson also asserted that this is a straightforward case of sex discrimination, as the marriage statutes establish a classification based on sex. Citing the Hawaii Supreme Court and the Alaska Superior Court, Justice Johnson concluded, "A woman is denied the right to marry another woman because her would-be partner is a woman, not because one or both are lesbians."[17] The state argued that it is the definition of marriage that restricts the institution to a man and a woman, that such an argument is circular, and that it is the very definition of marriage that is being challenged. While men and women are both prevented from marrying someone of the same sex, the fact that a woman cannot marry a person of her choice based on the sex of that person is a type of sex discrimination. Most courts have held that the state's sex-based classifications are subject to heightened scrutiny; the level of review in this case is not an issue because the exclusion of same-sex couples from the benefits of marriage does not even pass the rational-basis test.

Justice Johnson framed the question "as whether the sex-based classification in the marriage law is simply a vestige of the common-law unequal marriage relationship or whether there is some valid governmental purpose for the classification today."[18] Vermont precedent has established that the state's rationale cannot rest on outdated prejudices or presumptions that are not reasonable today given the vast cultural and social changes that have occurred. The state, according to Johnson, offered three types of public purposes served by excluding same-sex couples from marriage.

First, current marriage laws provide male and female role models for children and celebrate the "rich physical and psychological differences between the sexes." Interestingly, the state relied upon feminist literature and affirmative action cases to show that there are differences between men and women. Requiring couples in a marriage to be "different" and "complementary" to each other involves the state too much in such a personal decision. Justice Johnson concluded, "In short, the 'diversity' argument is based on illogical conclusions from stereotypical imaginings that would be condemned by the very case cited for its support."[19]

Second, the state claims an interest in preserving the existing marital structure. The state's desire to retain the *status quo*, however, does not address the issues of why the state should maintain these classifications. This is mere tautological, circular reasoning.

The third category of arguments offered by the state assume, a highly questionable public purpose and is only remotely related to the sex-based classifications. These arguments deal with technologically assisted reproduction issues and potential custody and visitation disputes arising from such issues. The state argues that it wants to make sure that couples accept responsibility for any children they bring into the world, but denying marriage benefits is completely at odds with this purpose. Deterring marriages of convenience is another ground given for denying same-sex marriage, but once again this exclusion is under-inclusive as it does not address such marriages for opposite-sex couples. Justice Johnson concludes that none of the state's justifications meets the rational-basis test under the Common Benefits Clause.

Case Analysis

The Vermont Supreme Court's ruling in *Baker* is a landmark decision for gay and lesbian rights. This court goes further than any other U.S. court in granting legal recognition to same-sex couples. Interestingly, the majority and concurring opinions reflect the divergent constitutional grounds used to support these claims. The majority opinion in *Baker* rests upon a type of equal protection argument with gays and lesbians as the group of people to be protected, but this group does not constitute a "suspect class" that would mandate a strict scrutiny of the law. Chief Justice Amestoy departed from the usual equal protection analysis, which distinguishes the standard of review of the government action according to the nature of the group of people targeted. Instead, he evaluated the significance of the issues at stake, asking whether the group distinction promotes the government's goals and whether the classification is overly broad or too narrow. This shift in doctrinal analysis seems unnecessary and encourages critics of the decision to argue that the court is overstepping its bounds and forcing citizens to accept lifestyles of which they disapprove.

Justice Johnson applied the established equal protection analysis and found sex discrimination that could not be justified under the rationale given by the state, the lowest standard of review. Chief Justice Amestoy's opinion is a stronger precedent for the gay and lesbian social movement because it uses sexual orientation as its basis rather than gender, but Amestoy does not define sexual orientation as a suspect class as Justice Dooley did. However, Amestoy could have reached the same result without modifying Vermont's Common Benefits Clause jurisprudence.

The remedy provided by the court is also controversial. By requiring the legislature to act, Chief Justice Amestoy forced the issue onto the political agenda of elected officials. The court did not surrender its authority to order that marriage licenses be issued to same-sex couples if the legislature did not act, however. James E. Tierney, a former Maine attorney general and a friend of Amestoy, noted:

> I'm sure he was the one who crafted the decision in a way that would bring people together. He sent it to the Legislature but he put them in a box. He knew the process; he's a great believer in the process, and he knew the same process he led the court through would then be gone through in the Legislature: You start with the hatred and the reaction and the extremes, and you work on it and work on it and you find your way. His bottom line is to do this with dignity and respect. What would possibly be the sense of doing this if you end up with a state that's divided and filled with hate and anger?[20]

Brian Burgess, Amestoy's deputy attorney general from 1985 to 1992 and now a district court judge, remarked that the court's decision to bring the legislature into the process "reflects a recognition that the court does not have the monopoly on right answers, which is his approach to things."[21] In his acceptance speech as chief justice, Amestoy commented, "I believe in 'civility in public discourse and constancy in private affection.' And I believe, with Learned Hand, that 'the spirit of liberty is the spirit that is not too sure it is right.'"[22] In his opinion, he reiterates his view of judicial power and quotes Cass Sunstein:

> [I]t cannot be doubted that judicial authority is ultimate authority. It is certainly not the only repository of wisdom. When a democracy is in moral flux, courts may not have the best or final answers. Judicial answers may be wrong. They may be counterproductive even if they are right. Courts do best by proceeding in a way that is catalytic rather than preclusive and that is closely attuned to the fact that courts are participants in the system of democratic deliberation.[23]

Chief Justice Amestoy found the Hawaii decision and political response "instructive." He noted with what seems a bit of sarcasm that a judicial edict would avoid a political reaction, "even allowing for the welcome lack of political sophistication of the judiciary," is "significantly isolated from reality."[24]

Justice Johnson, however, dissented from Amestoy's remedy. She would have required the issuance of marriage licenses to same-sex couples. For her, it is not a matter of which branch of government is wiser, but rather that "one of the fundamental principles of our tripartite system of government is that the judiciary interprets and gives effect to the constitution in cases and controversies concerning individual rights." Forbidding the state to deny same-sex couples marriage licenses would "provide prompt and complete relief to plaintiffs and create reliable expectations that would stabilize the legal rights and duties of all couples."[25] Justice Johnson is aware that granting outright marriage privileges to same-sex couples may precipitate a political backlash like that in Hawaii and Alaska, but this should not be grounds for denying the plaintiffs the remedy to which they are entitled. She explains: "However much history, sociology, religious belief, personal experience or other considerations may inform our individual or collective deliberations, we must decide this case, and all cases, on the basis of our understanding of the law, and the law alone." Justice

Johnson notes that the court has a responsibility to hear controversial cases even when the "outcome may be deeply offensive to the strongly held beliefs of many of our citizens."[26]

The court itself wrestles with defining the appropriate degree of judicial activism, and the opinion justifies the tribunal's exercise of power. First, there is no intermediate appellate court in Vermont, so the state supreme court had to hear the case. The United States Supreme Court has mostly discretionary jurisdiction, and the decision when to hear a case is an element of how judicial authority is exercised. While legal traditions and procedural rules provide some constraint on the granting of writs of *certiorari*, the justices still have a great deal of prerogative. The opinion also notes that courts have defined a greater role for themselves when addressing civil rights and liberties. Courts give much more deference to the legislature when considering economic regulations. Justices Dooley and Johnson in their opinions express concern that the court's role will be expanded because it does not have a clear standard by which to judge future cases.

Chief Justice Amestoy argued that his test provides clear guidelines for future cases, but the other authors contended that it opens the decision-making process to the judge's personal values. Amestoy noted the need for "reasoned judgment" and argued that the approach necessarily "calls for a court to assess the relative 'weights' or dignities of the contending interests."[27] The traditions of the state ground this analysis and prevent a judge's personal notions from determining the case. Amestoy noted that what constitutes a suspect class under the Vermont Constitution has not been well defined and the "adverse stereotyping" standard recommended by Justice Dooley and the Oregon Court of Appeals gives a court even more freedom. Same-sex couples, said Amestoy, "are afforded the common benefits and protections of Article 7, not because they are part of a 'suspect class,' but because they are part of the Vermont community."[28]

Justice Dooley responded:

> It is difficult to conceive that any persons sitting on this Court, whatever their philosophical persuasions, would be insensitive to the history and traditions from which Vermont developed, and those from which it broke, but how this standard will be applied to Article 7 challenges is not at all predictable. In the end, the approach the majority has developed relies too much on the identities and personal philosophies of the men and women who fill the chairs at the Supreme Court, too little on ascertainable standards that judges of different backgrounds

and philosophies can apply equally, and very little, if any, on deference to the legislative branch. The final irony in this decision for me is that the balancing and weighing process that set forth in the Court's opinion describes exactly the process we would expect legislators to go through if they were facing the question before us. We are judges, not legislators.[29]

Justice Johnson thinks it is important to distinguish whether the group being discriminated against has been historically disadvantaged, thus requiring a heightened scrutiny of the law. While the balancing approach of the majority is "superficially attractive" in its attempt to provide fairness for all Vermonters, the most important purpose of Article 7 is to protect those "whose exclusion from full participation in all facets of society has resulted from hatred and prejudice."[30] The tiered approach makes courts more skeptical of cases where there is a greater chance that illegitimate motives are at work. It also disciplines judicial discretion and provides predictability for future cases as the court articulates its rationale for defining a suspect class. While the court's analysis should be disciplined, once a constitutional violation is found, the court has an obligation to correct the injustice. Justice Johnson would grant the most sweeping remedy, requiring the state to issue marriage licenses to same-sex couples.

Comparing *Baker, Baehr,* and *Brause*

Unlike the cases in Hawaii and Alaska, the Vermont case does not raise the substantive due process issue of privacy. The Hawaii Constitution explicitly recognizes a right to privacy, unlike the U.S. Constitution. If the right to privacy exists in the U.S. Constitution, it is found in the "penumbras" of rights in the first ten amendments. Many of the conservative justices currently on the U.S. Supreme Court reject this doctrine and interpret the document more literally and according to the original intent of the framers. For this reason, many civil liberties such as abortion and assisted suicide do not have strong constitutional underpinnings. Despite a specific privacy provision in the Hawaii Constitution, the Hawaii Supreme Court defined this right according to the parameters of the federal courts. Since same-sex marriage is neither rooted in the "traditions and conscience" of our people nor a fundamental principle of liberty and justice, the right to privacy does not cover it. The Alaska Trial Court, applying its own constitution's privacy amendment, included same-sex marriage within the right.

The Hawaii court also failed to consider the right of same-sex couples to marry as a fundamental principle that would be protected by more stringent constitutional standards, at least at the time of writing. This court seemed to recognize that the definition and legal needs of a family evolve over time. The Alaska court finds a fundamental right to marry. Rather than defining the issue as whether there is a fundamental right to same-sex marriage, the Alaska Trial Court framed the question as whether there is a fundamental right to choose one's life partner. The Vermont Supreme Court suggests that the marriage right is fundamental because the benefits and protections flowing from it cannot be denied without sufficient, unquestionable justification.

Table 5.1:
Constitutional Theories for Recognizing Same-Sex Marriage

	Hawaii	Alaska	Vermont
Fundamental Right to Marry	not at present; boundaries expanding	yes	yes (dicta)
Marriage Protected by Privacy Rights	no	yes	not addressed
Equal Protection: Sex Discrimination	yes	yes	minority option
Equal Protection: Gays and Lesbians	no	not addressed	yes
Gays and Lesbians: Suspect Class	no	not addressed	minority opinion

The Hawaii court and the majority in the Vermont court did not define gays and lesbians as a suspect class requiring a strict scrutiny of the government's action. A concurring opinion in *Baker* would grant this additional protective status, but it does not seem likely that most courts will be receptive to expanding the categories of people considered to be a suspect class. One of the criteria often used to define suspect class is political powerlessness, and the success of gay and lesbian candidates and the passage of supportive legislation has been used to counter any such claim. Another criterion is a history of discrimination against the group, but some people justify their animus towards gay and lesbian people as being warranted by religious or moral convictions. The Vermont and Hawaii courts considered two types of equal protection claims. The Hawaii court based its ruling on the sex discrimination claim, and one of the concurring opinions of the Vermont court agreed. If a man cannot marry another person because of gender, it is a form of sex discrimination. The majority opinion in the Vermont court was persuaded by the argument that prohibiting same-sex couples from marrying unfairly discriminated against gays and lesbians. This rationale goes much further in protecting gays and lesbians based on their sexual orientation. The Hawaii court evaded the issue of sexual orientation discrimination and even noted that homosexual marriage and same-sex marriage were not necessarily the same.

Vermont's Political Response

Vermont's same-sex marriage case, *Baker v. State*, is a milestone for gay and lesbian couples. As noted in the opinion, the court did not require the state to issue marriage licenses to same-sex couples. Rather, it mandated that the legislature devise a means for providing them with the state rights and responsibilities that are associated with marriage. This shifted the debate on gay and lesbian relationships to the political arena.

Political Culture

Statistically, Vermont is one of the most rural states in the union. Rural attitudes are often considered conservative or libertarian. Yet, the state is known for its liberal, back-to-the-land contingent as well as its strong traditional heritage. Vermont is represented in Congress by the only socialist, Bernie Sanders, and its two U.S. senators, Patrick Leahy (D) and James Jeffords (R), are from the liberal wings of their respective parties. The Vermont Constitution of 1777 was the first in the United States to prohibit slavery.

Vermont has extensive laws protecting gays and lesbians from discrimination. A state law protects lesbians and gays from discrimination in employment, housing, and public accommodation. A hate crime law punishes violence against gays and lesbians. The state has been at the forefront of recognizing "second-parent adoptions," which allow a gay partner to become the second parent of a child that is not biologically related to that partner.

It is difficult to characterize the Vermont Supreme Court as liberal or conservative. Chief Justice Jeffrey L. Amestoy was a seven-term, Republican state attorney general before being appointed to the supreme court in 1997 by Democratic Governor Howard Dean. On the day the governor signed the civil union bill into law, he said of Amestoy, "I think Jeff has a lot of wisdom. I appointed him as a moderate, and I think this ruling was a moderate ruling."[31]

It does not appear that Vermonters see the ruling as moderate. A 1998 poll sponsored by a group opposed to same-sex marriage, Take It to the People, showed 53 percent of respondents opposed to gay marriage and 38 percent in favor. A January 1999 poll for Vermont Public Radio showed 43 percent in favor of same-sex marriage, 48 percent opposed, and 7 percent undecided, with a five point margin of error.

Circumventing the Court

Opponents of same-sex marriage learned in Hawaii and Alaska not to rely on, or wait for, the courts to resolve the claim of discrimination. With public opinion polls showing opposition to same-sex marriage and a history of success in amending state constitutions, opponents were once again ready to take the issue to the people. An Ohio-based group, Citizens for Community Values, spent $40,000 on a statewide mailing opposing same-sex marriage. The mailing contained a letter from Mike Gabbard, chairman of the Hawaiian Alliance for Traditional Marriage, who warned that "The decisions made in Vermont will impact the entire nation and the world. If Vermont allows 'same-sex marriage,' the 18 other states without DOMA [anti-gay marriage] bills may be forced to accept those marriages as legal."[32] The letter provides information on the Vermont organization formed to oppose same-sex marriage, Take It to the People (TIP). This group was not consulted about the mailing, however.

Susan Murray, a member of the Vermont Freedom to Marry Task Force, responded that "the Alliance for Traditional Marriage has a return address from an organization in Cincinnati, Ohio but still purports to be an open letter from the citizens of Hawaii. Hawaiians are entitled to do what they did with their votes, but I don't think that it is appropriate for them to be purporting to tell Vermonters how to think about this issue."[33] Two Democratic politicians, Lt. Governor Doug Racine and Speaker of the House Michael Obuchowski, voiced their support for same-sex marriage to counter the letter. Many Vermonters resented outside political groups coming into the state and trying to divide the population.

To the People's Branch

Once the court had ruled, the political focus shifted to the state legislature. While drafting their bill, both the House and the Senate judiciary committees held hearings in which gays and lesbians were called perverts and child molesters. Randall Terry, founder of the antiabortion group Operation Rescue, set up camp just outside the capital. Republican presidential candidate Alan Keyes and Traditional Values Coalition director Rev. Lou Sheldon visited the state to campaign against the legislation. Opponents took out full-page ads in newspapers listing the home phone numbers of legislators supportive of the bill. Barbara Dozetos, editor of the state's gay, lesbian, bisexual, and transgendered newpaper, observed that "It brought to the surface a lot of homophobia that previously lived silently in this state. The excitement has been mixed with equal parts pain."[34] Several legislators reported damage to their cars, and some requested that their special license plates be replaced.

On 16 March 2000, the Vermont House passed 76 to 69 the most expansive gay rights legislation in the country with the civil union bill. Approximately 300 state benefits and privileges available to married couples would be granted to same-sex relationships in the areas of inheritance, property transfers, medical decisions, workers' compensation, insurance, and taxes. Couples must fill out the form provided by their town clerk, who provides a certificate or license. As with marriage, the union must then be certified by a justice of the peace, clergy member, or judge. Partners who want to separate have to go through Family Court proceedings and have the same rights and responsibilities associated with divorce. Legislators adopted an amendment which made clear that the term "marriage" was reserved for the union of a man and a woman, but they rejected an amendment that would have prohibited the recognition of gay marriages performed in other states.

The debate on the bill was "unusually ugly," "bitterly contentious," and opponents vehemently spoke against the legislation and its moral implications. Some said that homosexuality was against God's will, was unnatural and unhealthy, and that civil unions would undermine traditional marriage. The bill was called "social rape" and a sign of "moral rot." Opponents argued that civil unions were marriage in all but name. They waged a newspaper and radio campaign arguing that if something looks, talks, and swims like a duck, then it is a duck, and small, yellow plastic ducks were distributed to legislators. Concern about the state's business climate and potential boycotts against the state for recognizing same-sex relationships were also raised. Representatives were accused of ignoring the views of their constituents. Proponents responded that their marriages were not at all threatened by civil unions and that the issue is about equality and fairness. Representative Donny Osman (D) explained, "This bill is not about perversion in any way. It is about love. It is not about sex, it is about relationship."[35]

The state senate approved the law on April 19th 19 to 11. Prior to the vote, the Senate rejected constitutional amendments overturning *Baker v. Vermont* and defining marriage as the union between a man and a woman. Existing Vermont statutes already define marriage as between one man and one woman. Only three senators spoke against the bill. Mary Bonauto, an attorney with the Gay and Lesbian Advocates and Defenders and one of the counsels in the *Baker* case, remarked, "Many [senators] talked about new insights they gained into discrimination faced by gay people because of the hate mail they received from opponents of the bill."[36]

The House accepted the Senate's changes in the bill on April 25th in a 79 to 68 vote. A review commission was established to follow the results of the civil union law and "note its strengths and shortcomings" and to analyze how other states will address the dissolution of civil unions. Another amendment emphasized that the Free Exercise of Religion protections of the Vermont and U.S. Constitutions apply to the civil union law.

Governor Dean boasted that many officials were supporting the bill at the risk of being defeated in the November elections. He noted, "This is not politics as usual. My guess is that there are just twenty people out of one hundred-eighty lawmakers who have voted on this so far who are thinking about political considerations. Most of them are just looking into their heart and trying to figure out what the right thing to do is."[37] Lawmakers often had to choose between voting their conscience rather than with the views of a majority of their constituents. Dean signed the bill into law at the end of April 2000 saying the legislation "speaks to the heart of this state and certainly to my heart."[38] He observed that Vermont needed time to heal after addressing this contentious issue that almost evenly divided the state.

The civil unions law went into effect July 1, 2001. It is unclear whether other states will recognize Vermont's civil unions. State laws preventing the recognition of same-sex marriage might not apply to civil unions. Thirty-five states and the U.S. Congress have passed "defense of marriage" laws.

Gay and lesbian Vermonters had mixed feelings about the law. Many were pleased by this monumental first step to marriage and were proud that their state was leading the way. Paula Ettelbrick, family policy director for the National Gay and Lesbian Task Force, suggested that politically it might be wiser for other states to press for civil unions rather than marriage. She points out that civil unions provide "a really wonderful, clean slate for defining family relationships" without being "tethered to religion or a history of sexism."[39] As well as the material gains, gay and lesbian couples win "public recognition that our relationships are valid and worth officially recognizing. So in addition to the tangible benefits are the social benefits," said Stan Baker, the lead plaintiff in the Vermont case.[40]

Others, however, considered this a compromise that enshrined same-sex relationships as second-class. The federal government and other states do not have to recognize this status creating "separate but equal" treatment for gay and lesbian couples. Some people also expressed concern about registering with the government as a gay or lesbian person.

"Take Back Vermont" in the November Election

The religious right and many Republicans vowed to defeat candidates in favor of the law, including Democratic Governor Howard Dean, and to make overturning the law central to the campaign. The issue divided the Republican Party, and five incumbent House members were defeated by more conservative members in the primary. The House considered delaying the vote until after the election but the move was defeated. The Catholic bishops of Maine, Massachusetts and New Hampshire attacked the statute. The only gay member of the Vermont legislature at the time, Democrat Bill Lippert, acknowledged the issue was very volatile. Both proponents and opponents of civil unions established political action committees to support candidates favoring their position.

Vermonters remain divided over the civil union law. A May 2, 2001, poll found 51 percent of the respondents want to repeal the law while 46% oppose repeal. Asked whether they approve of the one-year old law, 53% said no and 45 % said yes. These findings are basically unchanged from a poll a year earlier.[41] The April 2000 poll brought relief to lawmakers, though, because more than 50% of the respondents said that passage of the civil union bill would not affect their vote in the November election compared to 25% who said it would be an important factor.[42]

While Governor Dean retained his seat, a voter backlash in the November 2000 elections gave the Republicans a majority in the state house for the first time in fourteen years. Bills were introduced to repeal the civil unions act, to outlaw same-sex marriage, and to ban the discussion of homosexuality in public schools. Only the Marriage Restoration Act repealing the civil union bill was approved by this chamber of the legislature, and the Democratically controlled state senate did not endorse the measure.[43] These bills helped fuel the anti-civil unions crusade, however.

A lawsuit aimed at preventing the law from taking effect was rejected by the supreme court. The suit argued that a betting pool among some state representatives on how the legislature would vote created a conflict of interest. If these members' votes were disqualified, the House would not have approved the legislation. A number of town clerks also claimed that homosexuality is immoral and that sanctioning gay relationships violates their religious beliefs.

The Vermont Attorney General's office testified that it would be a mistake to repeal or replace the civil unions act and could open the state up to another costly lawsuit. Chief Assistant Attorney General William Griffin warned, "Leave well enough alone. Your lawyer, as the attorney general, says we'll defend (civil unions). We think we'll win."[44]

The civil union bill went into effect on July 1, 2000, and in the first six months nearly 1,500 civil unions were performed. About three-fourths of these have been couples from out of state. Numerous legal issues will be tested as these couples return home and test their state's recognition of the Vermont law. Dick McCormack, vice chair of the senate judiciary committee and majority leader, commented, "When all the screaming, gnashing of teeth, and breast-beating is done, people across the country will come to see that only one thing has changed in Vermont: Life will be a little better for gay and lesbian citizens."[45] The Freedom to Marry Task Force and the Committee for Vermont Families released a publication in late November 2000 to encourage individual dialogue about the civil unions law. "Common Ground: Respect and Dignity for All" focused on creating harmony in communities, providing respect for all people, and obeying the laws of the state.

In May 2001, the Republican majority in the Vermont House once again considered legislation to undermine civil unions. The Marriage Restoration Act would have repealed civil unions and all benefits to same-sex couples. Nancy Sheltra (R), the sponsor of the bill, remarked, "Civil Unions, homosexual marriage has given rights to individuals because of what they do, not because [of] who they are." This legislation was defeated in the House.

A bill that was passed would replace civil unions with a reciprocal partnership program. Civil union licenses and the requirement of a ceremony would be eliminated and instead, same-sex couples and blood relatives would file applications with the state for tax breaks and other benefits. The legislation passed by only a few votes after more than five hours of debate. The sponsor of the bill, Peg Flory (R), said, "We should be giving benefits on the worth of people to the community rather than based on their sexual orientation."[46] The legislation is not supported by the governor, a majority in the Democratically controlled senate, or the state attorney general. The security of the civil union legislation may once again depend on the outcome of the next election.

Notes

1. Baker v. Vermont, 744 A2d. 864 (1999).
2. David Goodman, "A More Civil Union," *Mother Jones*, July/August 2000, 49.
3. Vermont Constitution, Ch. 1, Art. 7.
4. Vermont Freedom to Marry Task Force, "Explanation of Trial Court Opinion," 1998.
5. Baker v. Vermont, 886.
6. Editorial, "Vermont's Momentous Ruling," *New York Times*, 22 December 1999, A26.
7. Baker v. Vermont, 875.
8. Ibid., 874.
9. Ibid., 879.
10. Ibid., 881.
11. Ibid., 885, footnote 14.
12. Ibid., 883.
13. Ibid., 889.
14. Ibid., 886.
15. Ibid., 893.
16. Ibid., 898.
17. Ibid., 905.
18. Ibid., 909.
19. Ibid., 910.
20. Carey Goldberg, "How Vermont's Top Judge Shaped Law on Civil Unions," *New York Times*, 28 April 2000, A12.
21. Ibid.
22. Ibid.
23. Cass Sunstein, "Foreword: Leaving Things Undecided," *Harvard Law Review* 110 (1996), 101.
24. Baker v. Vermont, 888.
25. Baker v. Vermont, 900.

26. Baker v. Vermont, 888.
27. Souter concurring in *Washington v. Glucksberg*, 521 U.S. 702, 767 (1997).
28. Baker v. Vermont, 878, footnote 10.
29. Baker v. Vermont, 897.
30. Baker v. Vermont, 907, footnote 13.
31. Goldberg, "How Vermont's Top Judge Shaped Law on Civil Unions."
32. Paul Olsen, "Vermont Officials Back Marriage for Gays," In Newseekly, 28 April 1999, 1.
33. Olsen, "Vermont Officials Back Marriage for Gays."
34. Mubarak Dahir, "A Battle of the Unions," *The Advocate*, 23 May 2000, 58.
35. Quoted in Carey Goldberg, "Vermont Supreme Court Takes up Gay Marriage," *New York Times*, 19 November 1998, A18.
36. Lisa Neff, "Senate Passes Vermont Civil Unions Bill," *Chicago Free Press*, 26 April 2000, 1.
37. Ibid.
38. Lisa Neff, "No Backlash for Vermont Lawmakers," *Chicago Free Press*, May 10, 2000, p. 4.
39. Ibid.
40. Dahir, "A Battle of the Unions."
41. "Vermonters Divided on Civil Unions," *Chicago Free Press*, 9 May 2001, 5.
42. Neff, "No Backlash."
43. Lisa Neff, "Vermont House Votes to Ban Gay Marriage," *Chicago Free Press*, 21 March 2001, 6.
44. Lisa Neff, "Vermont Lawmakers Warned against Repealing Civil Union Act," *Chicago Free Press,* 11 April 2001.
45. Dahir, "A Battle of the Unions."
46. Lisa Neff, "Vermont House Votes to Repeal Unions," *Chicago Free Press*, 30 May 2001, 6.

Chapter Six
Comparative Perspectives on the Recognition of Same-Sex Relationships

Gays and lesbians throughout the world have transformed their discrimination disputes into important public policy debates in legislatures, courts, and international tribunals. Litigation and legislative strategies for homosexual rights have considered laws dealing with sodomy, the age of sexual consent, military service, and discrimination in employment and housing. Gays and lesbians have also resorted to international tribunals to force domestic compliance with regional interpretations of human rights under international law. As basic protections have been afforded gays and lesbians in some countries, demands have been made for legal recognition of same-sex relationships. Denmark is at the forefront of this movement as the first country to pass broad domestic partnership legislation in 1989. Nearly a decade later, the Netherlands earned the distinction of being the first nation in the world to offer gay and lesbian couples access to the institution of marriage.

This chapter traces current global efforts to recognize same-sex relationships.[1] Political, legal, and educational tactics promoting the recognition of same-sex relationships may be engaged in simultaneously within a country; this analysis highlights these strategies by looking at representative examples from around the globe. Obviously, the activities of every country cannot be covered. The effort to validate gay and lesbian families is, however, clearly a worldwide movement.

The first section surveys legislative efforts to recognize same-sex relationships. Since Denmark was the first country to allow domestic partnerships, the Danish treatment of gay and lesbian couples is explored in depth. The other Scandinavian countries have followed Denmark's lead and enacted similar laws, and the Netherlands has removed any gender requirement for marriage. For many of these countries, the most pressing issue regarding same-sex relationships is whether to allow the adoption of children, which, for the most part, is currently prohibited. Many Western European countries have considered domestic partnership legislation and have such provisions at the national, provincial, or municipal level.

The second section depicts a number of attempts through litigation to have gay and lesbian couples recognized under the law. In Canada, Israel, and New Zealand, the courts have been utilized with varying degrees of success. Attempts have also been made to extrapolate protection for same-sex couples from other nondiscrimination and privacy clauses in statutes and human rights treaties. International tribunals have not as yet been willing to extend the definition of family to same-sex couples. As of 1997, the Republic of South Africa is the only nation to include protection against discrimination based on sexual orientation in its constitution. It will be interesting to observe how same-sex relationships are treated here. Finally, examples of symbolic and educational activities from Asia and South America are described. A comparative analysis of the political treatment of gay and lesbian relationships reveals interesting insights into the efficacy of judicial and legislative strategies for securing gay and lesbian rights and the impact that the social context has on these dispute resolution processes.

Legislation
Denmark's Domestic Partnership Registration Act

Because Denmark was the first nation to enact significant protections for same-sex couples,[2] it serves as a valuable case study with which to compare other activities. In Denmark, the national legislature passed a same-sex domestic partnership bill in 1989.[3] While these laws extend many of the benefits, protections, and duties afforded by the status of marriage, there are a number of areas where equal rights have not been granted. Nonetheless, these laws are significant for their recognition of the legal status of same-sex relationships.[4]

A commission appointed by Parliament in 1984 studied the social situation for homosexuals and issued a report to the Folketing, the legislative body, in January 1988. In that report, only a minority in the commission proposed the registered partnership provisions, yet the partnership bill was introduced in Parliament that month. Parties aligned with social, liberal, center, and left wing politics in close cooperation with the National Danish Organization for Gays and Lesbians introduced the bill. Legislation on homosexual partnership had been discussed and proposed since the late 1960s. A majority of the Folketing passed the bill with the support of some members of right-wing parties and the ultra-liberal, *Fremskridtsparti*. Seventy-one legislators supported the bill, forty-seven opposed it, and five abstained from voting.[5] The bill became law 1 October 1989.

The domestic partnership registration act provides some of the rights and benefits of marriage. As in marriage, the registered partnership creates mutual obligations of maintenance, rights regarding compensation, and insurance benefits. Registered partners have inheritance rights, rights of survivorship, and responsibility for funeral arrangements on the same scale as spouses.

The conditions for entering into a registered partnership are similar to those for entering into a marriage. A person cannot be a party to an existing marriage or registered partnership when registering. It is not a requirement for registered partnership or marriage that the parties intend to live together or have sexual relations. The state issues a "partnership certificate" to the couple and records the relationship. While two foreigners visiting Denmark for a short time can get married there, a registered partnership requires that at least one party to be a Danish citizen domiciled in Denmark. The rationale given for this requirement was the probability that the relationship would not be recognized abroad. Provisions in certain international treaties require the other country's approval of a registered partnership for the foreign granting of spousal rights. Registered partners do not have a right to a Danish church wedding. Blessings by a vicar are performed on a private basis in homes and are tolerated by some bishops.

Parties to a registered partnership cannot adopt a child and cannot have joint custody of a child. As Marianne Hojgaard Pedersen of the Ministry of Justice commented, "These rules are based on the assumption that registered partners can have children separately but not together."[6] While heterosexual couples and single women have free access to artificial insemination, registered lesbians are not allowed such access. This reasoning is troublesome and ignores the existence of registered partners who want to raise children together. The domestic partnership registration act limits same-sex couples' ability to form a family. Cohabitants of different sexes are also prohibited from jointly adopting children, in order to give more value to marriage.

A registered partnership can be dissolved under the same conditions and according to the same rules and procedures as those used for the dissolution of marriage. The rules regarding maintenance and the distribution of assets and the home apply to registered partnerships. In Denmark, marriage and registered partnerships have "become simply a contract that may be freely dissolved by either of the parties."[7] A separation of at least six months is required before the relationship can be terminated. Registered partners, however, do not have a right to mediation performed by clergy. This last-mentioned law was passed unanimously a month after the passing of the Partnership Act after complaints from Christian groups. The reasons cited were concerns for the position of vicars who may oppose same-sex relationships.

Same-sex couples who do not register have the same legal status as unmarried cohabitants of different gender. Unmarried cohabitants have pension rights, some rights of survivorship, and the joint right to the home. There are no plans in Denmark to introduce legislation affecting the legal status of unmarried cohabitants, due to the desire to protect the institution of marriage. Changes to the social welfare law have been contemplated to eliminate any economic advantages for individuals who cohabit rather than marry.

From 1989, when the law first came into effect, through 1996, 3,011 partnerships were registered, 2,050 by men and 961 by women. Out of these, 210 male and 147 female partnerships have been terminated. In contrast, nearly 1,063,000 men and women were married in Denmark with approximately 161,000 divorces.[8] The separation rate for gay men and lesbians is lower than that for their heterosexual counterparts. From 1996 to 1998, another 1,327 same-sex couples registered their relationships. In those last two years, more women registered than men. Hanne Moeller, spokeswomen for the National Association of Gays and Lesbians, explained that "Women in the beginning were a bit skeptical of registered partnerships. They did not want to be too much like heterosexuals. They did not like to be 'normalized.' But now we have a new generation of lesbians who find it natural to have a family and to raise kids."[9]

The debate over the legislation contained many of the familiar arguments over homosexuality. Henning Bech noted, "There were, however, some significant shifts of emphasis, and some of the old assertions, though industriously repeated, turned out to have lost their power."[10] The major argument against the act reported in the press was that homosexuality was in conflict with the Bible or with nature. Opponents argued that as homosexuality was sinful and perverse, it should not be officially recognized by society.

Another opposition theme that carried a lot of weight was the decline of marriage and the demise of the traditional family. These arguments were common to various groups. In addition to church organizations, influential conservatives not tied with religious fundamentalism, such as newspaper editors and members of Parliament, articulated this view.

A third type of argument focused on juridical-administrative concerns. Opponents argued that there was no need for the legislation or that no one would use it, yet hundreds of related laws would have to be changed. Another variation on this theme predicted that a new influx of immigrants could be created by expanding access to Danish citizenship. Finally, it was argued that if domestic partnerships were established, Denmark could become the object of ridicule and would lose standing in the world community. Because of their more abstract nature, these issues were usually combined with other arguments.

Opponents' arguments not only constituted the larger part of the printed debate but were also the most widely circulated. Christian groups were largely responsible for this, arranging meetings, writing petitions to Parliament, and contacting the press. The small Christian Party made the legislation a primary theme of their campaign in spring 1988 and put the issue on television. They made the withdrawal of the legislation a condition of their participation in government after the election, threatening to organize a referendum if it was passed. The Christian Party, however, lost popularity in the election, declining from 2.4 percent of the vote to 2 percent, and was not able to gather support in Parliament to call a referendum after the bill was passed. Opinion polls in 1988 and 1989 reported that the majority of Danes supported the legal recognition of same-sex relationships.[11]

The arguments described above are based on the notion that homosexual relationships are of lesser value than heterosexual relationships. Others critics of the bill opposed it because they felt the legislation did not do enough and in fact perpetuated discrimination. The law institutionalized homosexual relationships as second-class by omitting the rights to adoption and church weddings.

A "radical" criticism of the legislation was expressed by a minority in the gay and lesbian community. This minority argued that marriage denied individuality, repressed conflict, and created economic dependence, social isolation, emotional stagnation, and physical violence. Bent Hanson, a gay activist and AIDS hotline manager who worked on the partnership law, stated that "Especially women objected because of the negative influence from marriage, of being oppressed and dependent on men."[12] By suggesting a common model of marriage, the bill discouraged an acceptance of alternative lifestyles and traditions, and the progressive nature of the legislation was questioned.[13] Since only a small number of people expressed radical criticism, this view did not receive much attention in the public debate. Inge-Lise Paulsen, a travel books editor and lesbian activist who supported the partnership law as an avenue to equal rights, remarked, "Is this selling out to middle-class values or is this radical? It was both."[14]

Proponents' arguments centered around the principles of equality, freedom, and justice. It was suggested that the realization of these principles had value in their own right. Legal equality implied an official, societal acknowledgment of the equal value of homosexual and heterosexual relationships. In Danish, "equal value" (*ligevaerd*) is a matter of human worth and dignity, and "equality" (*lighed*) refers to social and legal rights and opportunities. Legal recognition of homosexual relationships would increase the positive image of the homosexual community within itself and would positively influence the attitudes of others. Inge-Lise Paulsen, who is registered with another woman, said, "It's about identity. It's about pride in who you are."[15] These arguments were espoused by politicians from left and center parties, the national organization of gays and lesbians, and some newspaper editors.

Proponents of the bill also used Denmark's status in the world as an argument. They claimed that Denmark has a reputation for tolerance and equal rights that puts the country in the forefront of civilization. Danes think of Denmark as the country of *frisind* ("free mind or free spirit"), broadmindedness, tolerance, and social responsibility in securing real equality for everyone. As Henning Bech explains, "In its idealized form, [*frisind*] does not simply denote permissiveness, but enlightened tolerance in matters of personal belief and moral conduct, combined with a social commitment to establish the conditions for individuals to think and live as they prefer."[16] Proponents argued that Denmark has an obligation to set an example and lead the way for other countries in these areas.

The possible benefits of living in registered partnerships were not a main theme. Yet, some pointed out that the legislation provided opportunities for greater emotional and financial security and for seriousness and responsibility in relationships. A more moralistic version of this argument suggested that the bill would strengthen long-term monogamous relationships among homosexuals, which would help prevent the spread of AIDS. Some of these arguments were mentioned in the notes to the bill, but usually they were cited as supplementary reasons for supporting the legislation. Dorte Bennedsen, a nonpracticing ordained minister and health spokeswoman for the Social Democratic Party, actively supported the legislation and thought the gay and lesbian response to the AIDS crisis influenced the vote. She commented that "Society respected how they [gays and lesbians] took up the problem. It made a change in the ordinary population."[17]

The majority of Danes did not base their opinion of the domestic partnership registration act on the "against God/against Nature" or the "dissolution of marriage and society" arguments. "All that can be safely concluded," Henning Bech suggests, "is that they thought homosexuals should be given more of the same rights that heterosexuals had."[18] This was the central argument of the proponents, and it was what the majority actually endorsed in answers to opinion polls, where questions were asked in terms of equal rights. The acceptance of the legislation and the results of public opinion polls do not necessarily suggest that homosexuals were thought to be of equal value to heterosexuals or that homosexuality was not considered "unnatural." Many opponents of the law expressed some sympathy or pity for homosexuals and said their opposition to the law should not be misinterpreted as hostility to them.

Cultural and Sociological Factors in Denmark

To understand the environment in which the partnership legislation was passed, it is helpful to look at social and cultural factors in Danish society. Denmark has a history of progressive legal views regarding sexuality. For example, in 1968, Denmark passed legislation eliminating the censorship of pornography. The bill passed with only 13 objections out of 172 legislators.

Moreover, homosexual relations between consenting adults over eighteen were decriminalized in 1933. A national organization for gays and lesbians was founded in 1948 and has close contacts with influential politicians from various parties. Homosexuality and homosexuals have become increasingly visible in the media in less stereotyped and negative ways since the 1970s. Large-scale public campaigns directed by the health authorities at the prevention of HIV and AIDS did not provoke hostility toward homosexual activity.

Since June 1987, an anti-discrimination law has prohibited public defamation of any group of people based on their sexual orientation. The Danish media's attention shifted from the partnership registration act to a case brought under this law. A woman was prosecuted at the request of the National Organization for Gays and Lesbians for writing a letter describing homosexuality as the most loathsome form of adultery and the homosexual as a sort of thief who steals his neighbor's honor and perhaps his life by inflicting AIDS upon him. When the woman was acquitted, the reasoning for the decision was not outlined.

The position of the Danish Lutheran church was a factor, also. Evidently, the church was not actively opposed to the partnership legislation. Else Slange, chairwoman of the Danish National Organization for Gays and Lesbians, stated that the reason Denmark was the first country to enact such legislation had "something to do with our religious traditions. I think the Lutheran Church has more and more opened itself up to different kinds of things. I think that does something to the community, that thoughts get more free."[19] Reflecting on the legislation, Bert Hansen, who worked on the partnership law, thinks that the state church supports democracy and diversity, and outside religious critics do not play an important role.[20]

Most government officials declare the law a success as it gives committed same-sex couples an official status and enhances the country's reputation. Linda Hosek commented, "Some conservative groups predicted decay for Denmark's society, but seven years of registered partnerships show they offer stability for gays and status for the country." Kim Engelbrechtsen, information manager for Denmark's Tourism Department, commented, "It's had only a positive effect. It's showing we're an open-minded society." Dorte Bennedsen, a Social Democratic Party member and party health spokesperson, who steered the bill through Parliament, stated, "It is completely accepted in the Danish population." While this is too sweeping, even opponents of the initial legislation have changed their views. Per Stig Moller, a Christian Democrat who abstained from voting, was concerned that foreign homosexuals would transform the solemn Danish marriage ceremony into a "circus" in a rush to register. He feels that this fear was misplaced; "Now they [gays and lesbians] live officially. It works."[21]

The Lutheran Church and the Danish Parliament have considered expanding the rights of same-sex couples, and the Church of Denmark appointed a commission in 1995 to study the issue. While the committee recommended allowing same-sex marriages, the bishops voted unanimously in 1997 in order to preserve church unity not to perform such services. Some bishops had previously spoken in favor of same-sex weddings.[22]

In June 1998, the Danish Parliament voted 70-57 against lifting the ban on artificial insemination of single women. It was argued that lesbian motherhood is unnatural and that children should know their fathers.[23] However, Parliament approved a bill in a 61-48 vote in May 1999 to allow a registered partner the right to adopt the other partner's child, unless the child was originally adopted from a foreign country. The legislation did not allow the couple to adopt children from outside the relationship. Under the bill, Denmark will recognize gay and lesbian couples from Norway, Sweden, and Iceland who have registered in their home country. People who are not Danish will be able to register their partnership if they have lived in Denmark for two years.

While Denmark continues to expand the definition of family to include same-sex couples, gays and lesbians still do not have full equality. Bent Hansen, head of the National Association for Gays and Lesbians, commented that "The politicians have realized that we have children, now we must convince them that we should also be allowed to get children."[24] The Danish example illustrates the evolving social acceptance and political recognition of gay and lesbian relationships.

The Netherlands

Holland formed a commission to study the legal implications of opening marriage to same-sex couples in order for them to achieve full social equality. The Dutch Parliament's lower house voted 80-61 in 1996 to study the consequences of same-sex marriage on children and on couples who traveled outside the Netherlands. In October 1997, the Netherlands' special parliamentary committee on gay equality recommended by a 5 to 3 vote to allow gay and lesbian couples to marry. Parliament was expected to pass this legislation, but bills take three to four years to be approved. The committee stated that "Same-sex couples can only be afforded equal treatment if they are allowed to enter into civil marriage."[25] Christian Democrats were the leading opponents of same-sex marriage but were not part of the ruling coalition. Only about 5 percent of Parliament's seats are held by conservative Christian parties, which are vocal but carry little influence.[26]

In January 1998, a Dutch partnership law went into effect giving same-sex couples all the rights of matrimony except access to adoption and artificial insemination. Just a month later, however, the government removed these two restrictions, making registered partnerships legally equivalent to marriage. The cabinet, in a prepared statement, said, "There must be better legal protection of children brought up by two people of the same sex. That means adoption must be possible for two people of the same sex."[27] Nonbiological parents were also guaranteed input into the raising of children born or adopted into a registered partnership.

However, few gay and lesbian couples took advantage of the registered partnership laws. Advocates were still lobbying for the right to actually marry, and they hoped it would be approved in a few years.[28] Some gays and lesbians in the Netherlands opposed marriage as a relationship model. Liberal Party member Annelize Van der Stoel remarked that "The government shouldn't be involved with love," and that officials only need to know the status of a couple for taxation, subsidies, and inheritance purposes. Longtime gay activist Hein Verkerk, stated that individual contracts were supported by the social movement until about five years ago when partnership and marriage became politically correct strategies to end discrimination. He argued that "It's an imitation of a system that refused to recognize gays and lesbians until recently."

Two years after the partnership law went into effect, the Netherlands eliminated nearly every distinction between domestic partnership and marriage. The only difference between opposite-sex and same-sex marriage is that gay and lesbian couples cannot adopt children from overseas because of potential objections from other countries. The legislation was supported by the liberal and labor parties of the governing coalition and by the left-wing opposition parties, and the bill was approved in late 2000. The Christian Democrat party and the small religious parties did not support the law. It became effective on 1 April 2000.

Henk Krol, the driving force behind the domestic partnership and marriage efforts, said that it was a difficult campaign. In the beginning, the gay and lesbian community needed to be convinced that marriage should be a priority and was possible. Krol advised marriage advocates in other countries to discuss the issue thoroughly, give people time to think, and make people understand that there was no reason not to allow it. Opinion polls showed that a large majority of the population was supportive. Dutch society is also one of the most secular in the Western world.[29]

Marriage is available only to citizens and legal residents of the Netherlands, but residency can be established by using a Dutch address for at least four months. Couples from the other fourteen European Union nations do not have to be Dutch residents, however. Pro-marriage activists in the Netherlands are assisting foreigners with obtaining legal addresses so that they can marry. Domestic partnerships can be converted to full, legal marriage status. As of July 2000, approximately 9,500 people were registered as partners.

Nordic Countries

Four other countries besides Denmark and the Netherlands have adopted gay and lesbian registered partnerships: Norway in 1993,[30] Greenland (which is part of the Kingdom of Denmark but enacts its own statutes) in 1994, Sweden in 1994, and Iceland in 1996. Sweden's Parliament legalized gay and lesbian relationships on 7 June 1994 by a vote of 171 to 141 with 5 abstentions and 32 absences.[31] The law became effective on 1 January 1995. Prime Minister Carl Bildt remarked about the legislation, "We accept homosexual love as equivalent to heterosexual. Love is an important force to personal as well as social development, and should therefore not be denied."[32] The Swedish law grants gay spouses many of the benefits of marriage except access to adoption, artificial insemination, in-vitro fertilization, and church weddings.

The Icelandic parliament, the Althingi, created a commission to research gay issues in 1994. The commission recommended domestic partnership recognition, criminalization of discriminatory acts against gays and lesbians, and increased education about homosexuality in schools. In 1996, the government amended the antidiscrimination clause of the penal code to criminalize actions that degrade an individual or group and that deny service or merchandise based on sexual orientation.[33] Parliament voted 44-1 to establish these provisions, and the partnership law took effect on June 27, 1996. Seventeen same-sex couples registered in the second half of that year.[34]

Iceland is unique in that it allows both partners to have joint guardianship and custody of children if the children are related biologically to one of the partners. Adoption of children unrelated to one of the partners is not permitted nor are there any rights to artificial insemination. Klara Bjartmarz, spokeswoman for Samtoekin, a gay and lesbian rights group, stated in January 1997 the organization's future goal: "Our next priority is a bill regarding full rights for step-parent adoption, and we hope that Althingi will come forward with that bill in the next few months."[35] The Swedish government began an eighteen-month study in fall 1999 to determine the ramifications of same-sex partners adopting each other's children or children from outside the partnership. One again, co-parent adoption is seen as one of the most pressing issues for gay and lesbian couples.

Registered partnerships are generally not transportable across national boundaries. However, many Nordic countries have signed interstate compacts agreeing to recognize each other's registered partnerships. Most Nordic countries also distinguish registered partnership from marriage by requiring one partner to be a citizen of the state in which registration takes place, whereas most countries will allow foreign nationals to marry.

Belgium may become the second country to legalize same-sex marriage. Belgium is traditionally more conservative than the Netherlands, its northern neighbor from which it gained independence in the 1830s. Legislation was to be proposed in Spring 2001. Belgium's minister for consumer interests, health, and environment, Magda Aelvoet, explained that "The government considers the right to marry a constitutional right and the chance to marry the sole opportunity to see that homosexual and heterosexual couples are treated in the same way."[36]

The United Kingdom

The United Kingdom does not recognize committed same-sex relationships. Gay and lesbian couples do not have any legal rights with regard to pensions, inheritance, tenancy, compassionate leave, or next-of-kin visiting rights in hospitals and prisons. While there are no legal impediments to gay and lesbian parents having access to or custody of their children, in practice judges often rule that a "normal family life" is essential for the well-being of a child and that a parent's sexual orientation renders him or her unsuitable. In 1989, a judge took away a lesbian mother's

Table 6.1: Countries Recognizing Same-Sex Relationships

DENMARK	Domestic Partnership 1989
NORWAY	Domestic Partnership 1993
GREENLAND	Domestic Partnership 1994
SWEDEN	Domestic Partnership 1994
ICELAND	Domestic Partnership 1996
NETHERLANDS	Domestic Partnership 1998; Marriage 2000

custody of her nine-year-old son, who had lived with her for the eight years since she had divorced her husband. The appellate court upheld the decision because the boy would face "unusual difficulties" growing up, due to the embarrassment and distress of having a lesbian mother.[37] Lesbian and gay couples are prohibited from adopting children in England.

The election of the Labour Party into power in 1997 seems to have signaled a shift in the treatment of gay and lesbian issues in the country. The foreign partners in same-sex and unmarried heterosexual couples are allowed to immigrate as of October 1997. A couple must prove they have lived together for four years, intend to stay together, and can support themselves. Immigration Minister Mike O'Brien stated, "I think it's unfair to destroy their [gay and lesbian couples'] relationships. The position we inherited [from the previous government] for common-law and same-sex couples was unsustainable and may have breached human rights laws."[38] The criteria, however, are much more strict than for couples who can marry.

France

The Parti Socialiste in France endorsed a gay and lesbian partnership bill, the Contrat d'Union Civile, that gives all unmarried couples spousal rights regarding inheritance, housing, taxation, workplace benefits, social security, and welfare. The introduction of the bill was a major goal of the French gay and lesbian political group, Homosexualitié et Socialisme, which had authored a text, Contrat d'Union Sociale, forming the basis of the bill. In 1996, lesbian and gay pride events in cities across the country attracted nearly 300,000 people and were used to promote the bill.[39]

Homosexualitié et Socialisme applauded the Parti Socialiste for the bill and for its commitment to having the legislation enacted if the party regained power. Adeline Hazan, national secretary of the party, and Laurent Fabius, former prime minister under Francois Mitterrand and president of the Socialist MP's Group when the bill was considered, took decisive action in promoting domestic partnership provisions.

France's National Assembly in a 316-249 vote passed the partnership registration bill on 9 December 1998. The controversial bill was debated for over seventy hours, more than any other under the current constitution (of 1958), and nearly 1,000 hostile amendments were introduced. The proposal sparked furious protests and demonstrations across France. President Jacques Chirac spoke out against same-sex marriage, stating:

> The French Republic has a duty not only to recognize and defend the role of the family in our society but also to protect its legal basis in the heart of our Civil Code, I am referring to marriage law, against anything that might damage it. We should not take the risk of distorting this law or making it banal by extending it to cover other contemporary arrangements for social life, which would take it far away from the values on which the family is based.[40]

The legislation was supported by Prime Minister Lionel Jospin's Socialist Party, which had 320 of the 577 Assembly seats, as well as by the Communists and Greens.[41] The French Senate, however, rejected the measure, 216 to 99, in March 1999. They did approve an alternative measure that gave benefits only to heterosexual cohabitating couples by a vote of 192 to 117.

In November 1999, the assembly and the senate reached an agreement on civil solidarity pacts, or Pactes civils de solidarité, known as "PACS." The law allows all couples to share in employment benefits. Both people are responsible for jointly supporting each other. After three years, they can file a joint income tax return and receive the same tax benefits as married couples. Unlike marriage, PACS do not require any type of ceremonial proceedings, and terminating a PACS does not require a lawyer. In France, divorce is a lengthy process involving numerous court appearances, and women have complained that the process favors men. To dissolve a PACS, one partner can give the other notice, and the union is ended in three months. Many areas are not clearly defined by the law, including alimony, disputes over property and joint possessions, and real estate transfers.

In the first four months that PACS were permitted, close to 14,000 couples joined together in civil unions. Experts had predicted that only approximately 10,000 couples would be interested in PACS in the first year, so they were surprised by the popularity of this option. While the government is not permitted to keep statistics on who is "PACS-ed," one estimate suggests that 40 percent are heterosexual couples who seek an alternative or first step to traditional marriage, often with little fanfare. Same-sex couples tend to celebrate the process.[42]

Spain

Spain's government considered creating registered partnerships for gay and straight couples in spring 1995. Legislation written by gay groups received support in the media, regional parliaments, and the federal Parliament, which voted to write its own proposal. Most if not all rights of marriage except adoption by same-sex couples are expected to be included in the final plan. Individuals, however, may adopt in Spain regardless of their sexuality. Approximately thirty Spanish cities register "civil unions," including Barcelona, Cordoba, Granada, Ibiza, and Toledo, and Valencia, has a regional law.

On January 1, 1995, a national law took effect to protect the domestic partner who has not signed a lease when an unmarried couple lives together. If the renter moves or dies, a right of first refusal now goes to "the person who has been cohabiting with the lessee in a similar affective relationship to that of a spouse, regardless of sexual orientation, for at least the two previous years."[43] This legislation provides some security for gay and lesbian partners and is another example of economic rights being recognized as a first step to the implementation of broader civil rights protection. By requiring two years of cohabitation, the law imposes a burden on all unmarried couples that does not exist for married, heterosexual couples.

In July 1998, the Parliament of the Catalonia region of Spain, which includes Barcelona, adopted legislation giving unmarried couples, both homosexual and heterosexual, many of the rights of marriage by a margin of 100-12. Inheritance, alimony, next of kin, apartment leases, and work leave are included, but gay and lesbian couples cannot adopt. Other rights, such as social security, taxation, and immigration, are not included because they are covered under national law. Jordi Petit, secretary general of the International Lesbian and Gay Association, remarked, "The law ... shows that Spain is evolving, modernizing, shunning machismo."[44] The Socialists, an opposition party, introduced a bill to legalize gay marriage in April 2001.

The Czech Republic

A domestic partnership statute was considered in the Czech Republic in 1995. SOHO, the nation's leading gay-rights group, proposed this legislation when parliament updated the family law provisions of the Czech Civil Code. Gay and lesbian couples who registered their partnership would have every right of marriage except the ability to adopt children.[45]

In March 1999, the cabinet of the Czech Republic drafted a same-sex partnership bill that met the approval of all the parties represented in the Chamber of Deputies except the Christian Democrats. The proposed legislation would grant most of the social and property rights of marriage and required the couple to execute a contract before a notary.[46] The bill was approved by the full Chamber of Deputies at its second reading, by 88 to 80 with 13 abstentions. The legislation was ultimately rejected, but the campaign continues.

Brazil

Surveys in 1995 in the Brazilian state capitals of Salvador, Curitiba, and Aracaju found that 60 to 80 percent of Brazilians believe gays must have the same rights as heterosexuals, and 50 to 65 percent think gay couples should be able to marry.[47] Seventy-three Brazilian cities and towns, including Sao Paulo, Rio de Janeiro, and Brasilia, ban discrimination based on sexual orientation. National legislation to create civil-union contracts for same-sex couples was introduced by Worker's Party Deputy Marta Suplicy.

In May 2001, in the lower house of Congress, legislation was considered which would allow partners to transfer property and extend social security benefits and health plans to their companions. The bill has been left pending for six years in an attempt to garner more support, and in an attempt to ease resistance, the definition of "partner" was modified to include family members who were dependent on each other. The prospects for passage are not great as the law is opposed by the Roman Catholic

Church, a growing evangelical Christian population, and conservative lawmakers. Brazil is the world's most populous Catholic country.[48]

Litigation
Canada

Private homosexual acts were decriminalized in Canada in 1969, and legislation at the federal level and in most of the provinces prohibits discrimination based on sexual orientation. In 1998, the Supreme Court of Canada ruled that the guarantees of equality in the Charter of Rights and Freedoms incorporate sexual orientation as a prohibited ground of discrimination, requiring Alberta, Prince Edward Island, and the Northwest Territories to amend their statutes.[49] With sexual orientation legislation covering most Canadians, the gay and lesbian community focused its attention on gaining legal recognition of same-sex couples and securing the benefits of heterosexual marriage. Many statutes, such as the Health Care Consent Act, recognize same-sex couples.

The existing legislation recognizing nonmarital, common-law heterosexual relationships in several provinces formed the basis for claims to gay and lesbian domestic partner rights. Canada has already granted many of the rights and obligations of marriage to same-sex couples. Many people in the Canadian gay and lesbian communities support efforts to achieve full marriage rights. Some have argued, however, that since opposite-sex, common-law couples are treated differently under the law, it would be more realistic and practical to achieve a status equal to common law relationships. This argument ignores the fact that gay and lesbian couples cannot legally marry under the law, while opposite-sex couples do have that option. All rights claims based on provincial law can be appealed to the Canadian Supreme Court. In addition, the national Charter of Rights and Freedoms can be the basis for equality claims. Consequently, litigation in Canada has taken place on both the provincial and the national level. The Supreme Court of Canada has gone the farthest of any judicial tribunal in the world in recognizing the legal rights of same-sex couples. The case, *M. v. H.*,[50] was initiated by a woman who had lived with another woman for twelve years and, upon separating, sued for support. The court ruled that the heterosexual definition of "spouse" in Ontario's Family Law Act violated the Canadian Charter of Rights and Freedoms. In an 8 to 1 decision, the Ontario Family Law Act was held to unconstitutionally prohibit same-sex couples from claiming spousal support when separating.

Supreme Court Justice Peter Cory, writing for the majority, stated, "The exclusion of same-sex partners from the benefits of" the act "promotes the view that M., and individuals in same-sex relationships generally, are less worthy of recognition and protection." The court stressed that it was not changing "traditional conceptions of marriage" since Ontario law already allows heterosexual common-law spouses the right to claim support. Martha McCarthy, the attorney for M., stated that the court's ruling was "the first time that gays and lesbians can say that the charter's promise of equality for them and for their relationships has been fulfilled."[51]

The ruling has broad implications, and the court indicated that its decision "may well affect many other statutes that rely on a similar definition of the word 'spouse.'" Federal and provincial laws contain hundreds of references to "spouse," in statutes addressing adoption, marriage, pensions, and taxes. In January 1999, a gay-rights lobbying organization initiated challenges to fifty-eight federal laws. The federal government has quietly introduced changes eliminating the legal differences between heterosexual and same-sex common-law relationships. Even though M. had already reached an out-of-court settlement with H., Ontario had continued the case out of principle.

Ontario's Family Law Act creates rights and obligations between both married couples and common-law couples. While the benefits and responsibilities accruing to common-law couples are less than those in a marriage, they have been greatly expanded by the judiciary over the years. In fact, the Canadian Supreme Court ruled that legal distinctions between married and common law couples would not survive Charter scrutiny.[52]

The Canadian Supreme Court affirmed the decision of the Ontario Court of Appeal. The lower court also struck the act and stated that requiring same-sex couples to provide support after separation was necessary "for the equitable resolution of economic disputes that arise when intimate relationships ... break down" and eased "the burden on the public purse by shifting the obligation to provide support for needy persons to those parents and spouses who have the capacity."[53]

Interestingly, federal and provincial governments are permitted to ignore the court's decision under a rarely used clause of the Charter. A campaign to encourage the provinces to do this is underway. However, Ontario's prime minister, Mike Harris, said he would not fight the ruling and thought that other governments would also comply with it.[54]

In 1998, the Ontario Court of Appeal also found in *Rosenberg v. Canada*[55] that denying same-sex couples pension rights was unjustified discrimination. Two employees with same-sex spouses and the Union of Public Employees challenged the Income Tax Act which allows tax registration of private pension plans only if benefits are limited to survivors of the opposite sex. The court required that same-sex couples be included in the definition of spouse under the act.

In 1995, the Canadian Supreme Court heard its first case dealing specifically with the legitimacy of same-sex relationships. Jim Egan, a pioneer of the gay rights movement, tried to claim spousal benefits under the Canadian pension plan for his partner of thirty-nine years.[56] The government argued that national pension legislation does not specifically include spousal benefits for same-sex couples and the long-term costs of expanding these benefits may be prohibitive. Conservative religious groups asked the court to deny the claim on moral grounds.

Five of nine justices on the Canadian Supreme Court recognized that differential treatment of same-sex couples was a *prima facie* violation of the equal treatment guarantees of Section 15 of the Charter of Rights and Freedoms. The majority of the Court ruled, however, that state discriminatory practices could be justified pursuant to Section 1 of the Charter, which allows "reasonable limits prescribed by law as can be demonstrably justified in a free and democratic society."[57] The government's unequal treatment of same-sex couples was permissible in this case. Justice Sopinka's was the swing vote, and he said this deferential treatment might not be justified in the future when same-sex couples are no longer "a novel concept."

The history of same-sex litigation in the provincial and lower federal courts shows the judiciary's trend of initially denying benefits to same-sex couples but over time granting these rights. Karen Andrews, a Toronto library worker, unsuccessfully sued for provincial health insurance coverage for her lover and her lover's child in 1988.[58] A federal court ruled in 1989 that a gay man, Les Beau, must be allowed to visit his lover in prison under the Private Family Visiting Program and the "conjugal visit" provisions in a program called Corrections Canada. The law already allowed visitors other than a spouse.

In 1989, the Canadian Human Rights Commission overruled the

federal government's refusal to allow Brian Mossop a day off work to attend the funeral of his lover's father.[59] The Federal Court of Appeal, however, struck down the ruling in 1990. Joining the federal government's case against Mossop was the antifeminist women's organization, R.E.A.L. Women, and evangelical and Pentecostal churches, together with the Salvation Army. In the *Mossop* case the appellate judge writing for a unanimous bench stated that since Parliament had not amended the Canadian Human Rights Act to prohibit discrimination on the basis of sexual orientation, it was not "appropriate for tribunals or courts to preempt the legislative process."[60] The Ontario Divisional Court stated in *Layland v. Ontario*[61] that marriage was constitutionally reserved by definition to opposite-sex couples.

In *Re K.*, the provincial court ruled that same-sex couples could not be legally barred from adoption when one of the partners was a biological parent. While the provincial court is the lowest Canadian court, the case has been widely followed, and the ruling was adopted by the Unified Family Court which has superior jurisdiction. The adoption issue was a controversial point used by the opponents of gay and lesbian rights legislation. Over time, Canadian courts have treated same-sex couples like unmarried opposite-sex couples in some circumstances and have expanded the definition of family.

Israel

Israel's courts have historically been viewed as liberal, while Parliament vacillates between progressive and conservative. On 8 January 1996, the District Court in Tel-Aviv overturned the Israel Defense Force's decision to deny Adir Steiner, the partner of the late Colonel Doron Meisel, benefits under the Regular Service (Pensions) Law.[62] Colonel Meisel, a high-ranking officer in the Medical Corps, died of cancer in 1991. In addition to the fiscal benefits of the pension, Steiner states that the real victory has to do with non-monetary benefits; "One of them is the right to be invited to memorial ceremonies. Another is to be allowed to write an entry in memory of Doran in *Sefer Yizkor*," the IDF's series of memorial volumes.

Judge S. Aloni ruled in a two-page decision that the army's position constituted sex discrimination:

> I believe that at this time ... the principle of sex equality found a permanent place

in our constitutional law and in our world view. The principle of equality and the prohibition on sex discrimination found an appropriate place in our constitution from the Declaration of Independence, through many High Court decisions, and in Basic Law: Human Dignity and Freedom.[63]

Aloni states that if Steiner had been a woman, he would have received the pension, and he was being denied only because he was a man.

Steiner thinks that three elements of his twelve-year relationship with Meisel were relevant to the court's recognition of his status as a common-law spouse: shared finances, a shared home, and public recognition of their relationship. While Steiner and Meisel had a monogamous relationship, the sexual element was not considered to be an issue. Steiner states, "The courts no longer get into a person's underpants. Even a man and woman don't have to prove they had sexual relations to establish their status as common-law spouses."[64]

Steiner was shattered by Meisel's death at the age of forty-six and was not moved to take action until a year and a half later. The Israeli Supreme Court ruling in *El-Al Israel Airline v. Danilowitz*, holding that companies must give gay and lesbian couples the same spousal benefits given to opposite-sex couples also provided motivation to pursue his claim.[65] Steiner's life has changed radically since he initiated his dispute. He stated, "I've gone from being a person with no awareness of civil rights and uninvolved in anything to being involved in my own struggle, the struggle of homosexuals and lesbians in Israel, and the struggle of gay people around the world."[66]

Judge Aloni also referenced the *El-Al v. Danilowitz* decision in his opinion. Aloni's decision expands the reasoning in *El-Al*, which is based on the equal employment law that explicitly prohibits discrimination on the grounds of sexual orientation but does not apply to military service. By invoking sex discrimination, the *Steiner* decision extends protection for gays and lesbians beyond the workplace, where remedies are already available based on sexual orientation discrimination. Prohibitions against sex discrimination are applied more broadly than sexual orientation discrimination. The potential of the case to expand protections under claims of sex discrimination will be tested as Steiner is also appealing a decision under a different statute denying him other rights that family members of deceased army personnel enjoy.

New Zealand

In *Quilter v. Attorney-General*,[67] the New Zealand Court of Appeal, the nation's highest court, upheld the Registrar of Births, Deaths, and Marriage's denial of a marriage license to three lesbian couples. The law does not specifically state that a marriage is between a man and a woman, but the registrar interpreted the statute using the traditional definition. The women argued that the marriage law unjustifiably discriminated against same-sex couples and also constituted sex discrimination. The New Zealand Bill of Rights Act 1990, in section 19, guarantees the right to freedom from discrimination, and the Human Rights Act 1993 includes sexual orientation as a ground to claim unequal treatment. The Bill of Rights also requires that statutes should be interpreted as complying with it whenever possible.

The court by a 3-2 majority found that there was no discrimination and ruled unanimously that the Marriage Act was defined by the traditional meaning. To reinterpret marriage any other way would be to judicially invalidate the statute, in violation of the consistency provisions of the Bill of Rights. There was no sex discrimination since the law applied to men and women on the same basis, prohibiting both equally from marrying someone of their own gender. There was also no sexual orientation discrimination, because heterosexual people would also be prohibited from marrying their own sex. The male-female distinction "has long been conventional in the concept of marriage, ... and it should be ruled unjustifiable only by the legislature because of the social policy implications."[68]

The minority view on the discrimination issue emphasized society's commitment to "the recognition of each person's individual worth regardless of individual differences." The impact of restricting marriage to opposite-sex couples was *prima facie* discriminatory. Only one member of the court argued that this discrimination was not justifiable. The main reason given to support the traditional definition of marriage is the biological ability to procreate, but Justice Thomas countered that "The essence of marriage is to be found in the nature of the relationship, not in some biological purpose." He went on to state that marriage is "a basic civil right of all citizens" and to prohibit same-sex couples from marrying excludes gays and lesbians "from full membership of society" and "can only add to the stigmatization of their relationship and have a detrimental effect on their sense of self-worth."[69]

The New Zealand case shows the difficulty of reconciling constitutional human rights standards with statutes that define key social institutions. Once again, the judiciary deferred the rights claim to the legislature. New Zealand law professor Andrew Butler states that traditionalists will be disappointed by the decision because it suggests that there are no legitimate reasons for different treatment of homosexuals and heterosexuals regarding marriage. Gays and lesbians are displeased because while Parliament has outlawed sexual orientation discrimination, the courts can find traditional marriage not to be discriminatory without giving an objective reason.[70]

Hungary

Hungary's Constitutional Court legalized common-law gay marriage 8 March 1995, effectively making Hungary the first East European nation to extend traditional rights to gays and lesbians.[71] Heterosexual common-law and formally married couples all have the same rights in Hungary. Any couple permanently living together in an intimate relationship is considered married under common law. The court said a law limiting common-law marriages to "those formed between adult men and women" was unconstitutional. "It is arbitrary and contrary to human dignity ... that the law (on common-law marriages) withholds recognition from couples living in an economic and emotional union simply because they are same-sex,"[72] the court wrote. The justices ordered Parliament to make the changes necessary to implement common-law gay marriage by 1 March 1996.

The Parliament, in response to the Supreme Court, amended the civil code so that same-sex couples have the inheritance and pension benefits of unmarried, opposite-sex couples. The *East European Legislative Monitor* states that on 21 May 1996, "Parliament passed an amendment to the Hungarian Civil Code (T/2074) that provides a legal framework for same-sex cohabitation."[73] The law provided legal rights to "a man and woman who are not married, share a household and live together in emotional and economic community."

Paradoxically, the court also ruled that formal civil marriages are for heterosexual couples only. "Despite growing acceptance of homosexuality [and] changes in the traditional definition of a family, there is no reason to change the law on (civil) marriages," the justices wrote. Gay leaders welcomed the ruling. Lajos Romsauer, president of Homeros Lambda, said it does not matter that only common-law marriage was legalized for gays, because the same rights were granted. Homeros initiated the legal action that led to the ruling.

International Tribunals

The European Court of Human Rights has interpreted Article 12 of the European Convention for the Protection of Human Rights and Fundamental Freedoms[74] as applying only to marriage between opposite-sex couples. Article 12 guarantees to men and women the right to marry and the right to form a family. This interpretation was first articulated in the European Court of Human Rights' 17 October 1986 judgment in *Rees v. UK*[75] and was reaffirmed in the 1990 *Cossey v. UK* case.[76] In *Cossey*, a transsexual woman (chromosomally male) was prevented from marrying a man as they were not of the opposite biological sex. The dissenting opinion argued that "a more functional approach . . . tak[ing] into consideration the factual conditions of modern life" should be considered. The dissent, however, would not extend marriage rights to same-sex couples, based on a reading of Article 12 which specifically refers to men and women.[77]

In September 1997, the advocate general of the European Court of Justice ruled that Britain's Southwest Trains violated Article 119 of the European Community Treaty by not extending spousal benefits to the partner of a lesbian employee.[78] Southwest Trains does grant spousal benefits to unmarried heterosexual couples. However, on 17 February 1998, the European Court of Justice overturned the decision. The court held that since the benefits would not have been extended to a male couple either, European Union law banning employment discrimination based on gender was not violated. European law does not ban discrimination based on sexual orientation. The court stated, "Stable relationships between two persons of the same sex are not regarded as equivalent to marriages or stable relationships outside marriage between persons of opposite sex." Angela Mason, head of the British gay lobby group, Stonewall, concluded that "The ruling means the end of the road for attempts to establish through the courts that discrimination on grounds of sexual orientation is a form of sex discrimination." The lesbian couple was represented by Cherie Booth, whose husband is British Prime Minister Tony Blair.[79]

On 19 October 1990, the Dutch Supreme Court denied two women the right to marry each other.[80] The women argued that the International Covenant on Civil and Political Rights (ICCPR).[81] required the Netherlands to recognize their relationship. The Dutch court (Hoge Raad), however, ruled that Article 23 of the ICCPR refers to "the traditional marriage between persons of different sex." Article 23 asserts that the family is the "natural and fundamental group unit of society" and specifically protects the right of men and women to marry. The Dutch court reasoned that this interpretation had to be "assumed" because Article 12 of the European Convention for the Protection of Human Rights and Fundamental Freedoms had been interpreted this way by the European Court of Human Rights. The Dutch Supreme Court held that because the distinction made between persons of different sex and persons of the same sex is "characteristic" of the right to marry as guaranteed by Article 12 of the convention and Article 23 of the ICCPR, that distinction cannot be considered discrimination in the sense of Article 14 of the ECHR and Article 2 of the ICCPR. These provisions forbid discriminatory practices and guarantee equal treatment under the law for all people. The women's claim of privacy under Article 8 of the ECHR and under Article 26 of the ICCPR was also rejected. The European Union (EU) Parliament on 17 March 2000 urged its fifteen member nations to grant same-sex couples marriage rights. The vote was 265 to 125 with 33 abstentions. The EU resolution also condemned discrimination against homosexuals in military service and in the age of consent for sexual relations. Eastern European nations wishing to join the union will ultimately have to comply with these international standards.

Symbolic Action

An Agence France-Press report in *The Independent* on 4 April 1995 indicated that two women were married in a traditional ceremony in Khandal Province of Cambodia and that the wedding generated much publicity in the country. In November 1996, Taiwan's first public gay wedding was held in Taipei. Shu Yu-sheng, a well-known author of books on gay issues, pledged himself to Gary Harriman. The ceremony was attended by prominent members of the Taiwanese media and the former head of Taiwan's main opposition party, the DPP.[82] Taiwan does not legally recognize this union, but gay and lesbian issues are being discussed more openly and more frequently now.

Vietnamese law did not in the past specifically prohibit same-sex marriage, and two Vietnamese women held a wedding in the spring of 1998 despite being denied registration with the local people's committee. Over one hundred relatives and guests were reported to have attended the celebration. Government officials did not approve of the relationship, however, and the Justice Ministry ordered the women to meet with twenty officials from Communist Party groups. The women were required to sign a written promise never to live together again. The provincial justice department spokesperson stated, "They would have had no trouble with their relationship if they had not chosen to have a public wedding."[83] Vietnam's national assembly has now banned same-sex weddings.

Mingshui Xiushu, a well-known Chinese writer and actress who starred in China's first TV comedy serial, held an unofficial wedding ceremony with another woman, Wan Ru, in the fall of 1999. The marriage is not recognized under People's Republic of China's law. The two women met on the Internet. Mingshui has written a novel and a short story about lesbian relationships, but neither has been approved by China's censors. She is disappointed that the work she is proudest of cannot be published. Yet, her views on acknowledging her sexuality reflect Chinese culture:

> But in China, if there's no big suppression, why should we have a revolution? In the West, there's a desire to assert your individuality, but in the space between coming out and not coming out, Chinese think a lot more. If you come out, you will change your family, your work, your friends, your environment. We Chinese think about these issues much more.[84]

Still, China's gay community is gaining acceptance and recognition. Sodomy was decriminalized in 1997; it remains outlawed in twenty U.S. states. Homosexuality is considered a perversion by the medical establishment, but the state has stopped institutionalizing homosexuals. Fang Gang, author of a best-selling book on gay life in China, was fined $7,500 in October 1999 for suggesting that an establishment was a gay bar. The court stated that homosexuality was "abnormal and unacceptable to the Chinese public." Zhang Beichuan, a doctor and publisher of a gay magazine, remarks, "I wish for the day when we live like the Chinese proverb says: 'Radishes or cabbage, everybody's got the thing they love.'"

Two Nepalese women "tied the knot" in August 1998 despite being threatened by their parents and arrested by police. They had to be released by the authorities because same-sex marriage is not specifically prohibited in Nepal.[85]

In Colombia, two gay men signed a joint-ownership-of-property contract in December 1998, affirming that they are homosexual, love each other, and desire economic union. A notary judge read the contract in front of the twenty guests assembled in the location where heterosexual marriages take place. Correspondent David Olson remarked, "This is certainly going to be a precedent. There are many other couples who want to do the same thing but nobody wanted to be the first."[86]

These acts are significant for their generation of publicity, educational impact, and ability to empower supporters of same-sex marriage rights. In the new constitution of South Africa, sexual orientation is specifically mentioned as a status protected from direct or indirect state discrimination. To date, South Africa is the only country that protects gays and lesbians in its constitution. Justice Albie Sachs of the Constitutional Court indicated that the issue of same-sex marriage could come before the court, and the constitutional prohibition against discrimination based on sexual orientation would carry much weight. He mentioned that gay rights organizations had been significant supporters of the fight against apartheid.[87] The African National Congress, the country's ruling party, passed a wide range of resolutions for gay and lesbian rights in December 1997, including equal marriage rights.

Conclusion

This brief survey of developments around the legal recognition of gay and lesbian relationships in other nations is not comprehensive as events in this area are unfolding so quickly. Since Denmark passed its same-sex domestic partnership registration in 1988, gays and lesbians across the world have mobilized politically to undertake litigation, advocate legislation, and engage in symbolic acts in order to have their relationships recognized. At times, these efforts have been rebuffed by courts and legislative assemblies, but in other nations same-sex couples are poised to be fully recognized under the law. The vast number of countries engaging in this debate demonstrates the saliency of the issue and the fact that the concept of family is evolving on a global scale.

There is little indication, however, that there is any coordination between activists in different nations. Given the wide range of experiences and strategies used to secure legal recognition of gay and lesbian relationships, many useful insights regarding the implementation of civil rights could be gleaned from more in-depth studies. The concluding chapter offers a number of observations on the treatment of same-sex relationships around the world, analyzing these developments in light of their social, cultural, and political context.

Notes

1. Interesting work has been done on the status of same-sex relationships in other cultures. For example, Walter L. Williams investigates same-sex relationships in traditional Native American society in *The Spirit and the Flesh* (Boston: Beacon Press, 1986). B. A. Rwezaura discusses the tension between customary law in colonial courts in "The Legal Status of Woman-to-Woman Marriages in Tanzania," *East African Law Review* 7 (1974): 319-325. John Boswell argues for the acceptance of same-sex relationships in premodern Europe, *Same-Sex Unions in Premodern Europe* (New York: Villard Books, 1994).

2. A number of sub-governmental units, such as provinces in Spain and France and cities in the United States, have enacted domestic partnership statutes, but they are not covered here because they generally do not grant many legal rights since "spouse" is defined by state or federal law.

3. Act No. 372 of 7 June 1989, established the registered partnership. Act No. 363 of June 7, 1989 amended various laws to incorporate the registered partnership act.

4. In 1987, Sweden amended its marriage law to allow unmarried cohabitants, including same-sex couples, additional property rights. The Swedish law is much more limited in scope than the Danish act.

5. Linda Nielsen, "Family Rights and the 'Registered Partnership' in Denmark," *International Journal of Law and the Family* 4 (1990): 298.

6. Ibid.

7. Marianne Hojgaard Pedersen, "Denmark: Homosexual Marrages and New Rules Regarding Separation and Divorce," *Journal of Family Law* 30 (1991/92), 291.

8. Linda Hosek, "'I Do' In Denmark," *Honolulu Star Bulletin*, 22 January 1997, 6.

9. Quoted in Rex Wockner, "Danish Politician Marries Gay Lover," *Outlines*, 31 March 1999, 10.

10. Henning Bech, "Report from a Rotten State: Marriage and Homosexuality in Denmark," in Ken Plummer, ed., *Modern Homosexualities* (London and New York: Routledge, 1992), 134.

11. Ibid., 138.

12. Hosek, "I Do."

13. This view is articulated in the United States by people such as Barbara J. Cox, "Love Makes a Family, Nothing More, Nothing Less: How the Judicial System Has Refused to Protect Non-Legal Parents in Alternative Families," *Journal of*

Law and Politics 8 (1991): 66; Ruth Colker, "Marriage," *Yale Journal of Law and Feminism* 3 (1991): 321-326; and Paula Ettlebrick and Thomas Stoddard, "Gay Marriage: A Must or a Bust?," *Out/Look*, Fall 1989, 8-19.

14. Hosek, "I Do."

15. Hosek, "Insight."

16. Bech, "Report from a Rotten State," 143.

17. Hosek, "I Do."

18. Bech, "Report from a Rotten State," 141.

19. Sheila Rule, "Rights for Gay Couples in Denmark," *New York Times*, 2 October 1989, 8.

20. Hosek, "I Do."

21. Ibid.

22. Rex Wockner, "Danish Bishops Nix Gay and Lesbian Weddings," *Outlines*, 12 November 1997, 11.

23. Rex Wockner, "Denmark Nixes Lesbian Insemination," *Outlines*, 8 July 1998, 11.

24. Rex Wockner, "Denmark Expands Partner Rights," *Outlines*, 2 June 1999, 10.

25. Rex Wockner, "The Netherlands Prepares to Legalize Gay and Lesbian Marriage," *Outlines*, 12 November 1997, 11.

26. Kees Waaldjick, Gay and lesbian commission member and associate professor of law, Universiteit Utrecht, quoted in Hosek, "Special Report."

27. Rex Wockner, "The Netherlands OKs Gay and Lesbian Adoption," *Outlines*, 18 February 1998, 11.

28. Rex Wockner, "Dutch Partnerships Unpopular," *Outlines*, 22 July 1998, 11.

29. Rex Wockner, "World First: Dutch Gays Legally Marry," *Windy City Times*, 4 April 2001, 14.

30. Domestic partnership legislation was passed in the Odelsting chamber of the Norwegian Parliament by a vote of 58-40 on 29 March 1993 and the Lagting chamber by a vote of 18-16 on 1 April 1993. The law came into effect 1 August 1993.

31. Swedish Law Allows Marriages for Gays," *Boston Globe*, 8 June 1994, 4.

32. "Sweden Joins in Approving Partnership Law for Gay Couples," *Los Angeles Times*, 15 June 1994, E3.

33. "Iceland Approves Domestic Partnerships," *Frontiers*, July 12, 1996, p. 28; Rex Wockner, "International News, #114"*Outline*, 3 July 1996, 23; *IGLA Euroletter*, April 1996, 3.

34. Samtoekin '78 [Icelandic gay and lesbian organization], *SAMTAKA '78*, January 1997.

35. Ibid.

36. Lisa Neff, "Belgium Looks at Gay Marriage," *Chicago Free Press*, 11 April 2001, 1.

37. In the United States, the Virginia Supreme Court reached a similar decision using the same rational in Pamela Kay Bottoms v. Sharon Lynne Bottoms (Rec. No. 941166, decided 25 April 1995).

38. Rex Wockner, "British Same-Sex Immigration Policy Takes Effect," 29 October 1998, 11.

39. "Gays on the Continental March," *The Economist*, 5 July 1997, 52.

40. Rex Wockner, "French President Denounces Gay Marriage," *Outlines*, 17 June 1998, 11.

41. Rex Wockner, "French National Assembly OKs Partner Bill," *Outline*, 23 December 1998, 7.

42. Suzanne Daley, "French Couples Take Plunge That Falls Short of Marriage," *New York Times*, 18 April 2000, A1.

43. Lesbian and Gay Immigration Rights Task Force, "World News in Brief," *Newsletter*, Spring 1997, 2.

44. Rex Wockner, "Catalonia Passes Partners Law," *Outlines*, 15 July 1998, 11.

45. Lesbian and Gay Immigration Rights Task Force, "World News in Brief," *Newsletter*, Spring 1997, 2.

46. Rex Wockner, "Czech Government OKs Partner Bill," *Outlines*, 31 March 1999, 10.

47. Correspondent Luiz Mott reports from Salvador, Bahia, on the Queer Resources Directory home page, http://www.qrd.org.

48. "Brazil, with Clergy Opposed, Plans Vote on Same-Sex Unions," *New York Times*, 11 May 2001, A5.

49. Vriend v. Alberta, S.C.J. No. 29 (Q.L. 1998).

50. M. v. H. (1996) 31 O.R. (3d) 417 (C.A.), appeal to S.C.C. granted 24 April 1997.

51. "Canada Overturns Definition of 'Spouse' as Heterosexual."

52. Miron v. Trudel, 2 S.C.R. (1995).

53. Ibid.

54. "Canada Overturns Definition of 'Spouse' as Heterosexual," *New York Times*, 21 May 1999, A10.

55. Rosenberg v. Canada, O.J. No. 1627 (C.A.)(Q.L. 1998).

56. Egan v. Canada, (1991), [1992] 1 FC 687 (TD), aff'd, [1993] 3 FC 401 (CA), aff'd (25 May 1995), [1995] 2 SCR.

57. Canadian Charter of Rights and Freedoms, Section 1, RSC 1985, Appendix II, Nos. 44-45, proclaimed in force on 17 April 1982.

58. Andrews v. Ontario (Min. of Health) (1988), 49 D.L.R. (4th) 584 (Ont. HC).

59. Mossop v. Dept. of Sec. State (1989), 89 C.L.L.C. 16,041 (C.H.R.T.); rev'd. (1990), 71 D.L.R. (4th) 661 (F.C.A.); aff'd (1993), [1993] 1 S.C.R. 554 (SCC),

60. Quoted in Bruce Ryder, "Equality Rights and Sexual Orientation: Confronting Heterosexual Family Privilege," *Canadian Journal of Family Law* 9 (1990), 92.

61. Layland v. Ontario (Minister of Consumer and Commercial Relations), 14 OR (3d) 658 (1993).

62. Esther Hecht, "Ruling against IDF Sets Gay Rights Precedent," *Jerusalem Post*, 13 January 1996, 1.

63. Steiner v. IDF, January 1997.

64. Ibid.

65. Dan Perry, "Israel Recognizes Gay Couples," *Boston Globe*, 1 December 1994, 2.

66. Ibid.

67. [1998] 1 N.Z.L.R. 523; (1997) 4 H.R.N.Z. 170; (1997) 3 B.H.R.C. 461.

68. Barillas, C., "New Zealand Court Upholds Gay Marriage Ban," 17 December 1997.

69. Ibid.

70. Andrew Butler, "Same-Sex Marriage and the Freedom from Discrimination in New Zealand," *Public Law*, Autumn 1998, 396-406.

71. Blaise Szolgyemy, "Hungary High Court Gives Blessing to Gay Couples," Reuters, 9 March 1995, REU1922 3 OVR 476 (RWS) J0805922.

72. *East European Legislative Monitor*, vol. 1, no. 3, part 2, June 1996; *IGLA Euroletter*, April 1996; *IGLA Euroletter*, June 1996.

73. Ibid.

74. European Convention for the Protection of Human Rights and Fundamental Freedoms, signed Nov. 4, 1950, entered into force 3 September 1953, 213 U.N.T.S. 222.

75. Rees v. UK, Series A, vol. 106, par. 49 (1986).

76. Cossey v. UK, 27 September 1990, Series A, Vol. 184, par. 46 (1990).

77. Robert Wintemute, *Sexual Orientation and Human Rights* (Oxford: Clarendon Press, 1995).

78. Grant v. South West Trains Ltd. European Court of Justice Case C-249/96 - 17/2/98.

79. Rex Wockner, "Lesbian Loses Benefits Case at Euro Court," *Outlines*, 4 March 1998, 11.

80. Nederlandse Jurisprudentie 1992, nr. 129.

81. International Covenant on Civil and Political Rights, adopted 19 December 1966, entered into force 23 March 1976, G.A. Res. 2200 (XXI), 21 U.N. GAOR, Supp. (No. 16) 52, U.N. Doc. a/6316 (1966).

82. Lesbian and Gay Immigration Rights Task Force, "World News in Brief," *Newsletter*, Winter 1997, 2.

83. Rex Wockner, "World Roundup," *Outlines*, 10 June 1998, 11.

84. Quoted in John Pomfret, "China's Low-Key Gay Liberation," *Washington Post Weekly Edition*, 31 January 2000, 18.

85. "Nepali Women in Lesbian Relationship Face Violence and Jail," *International Gay and Lesbian Human Rights Commission*, press release 12 April 2000.

86. Rex Wockner, "Two Men Marry in Colombia," *Outlines*, 30 December 1998, 10.

87. Michael McLoughlin interview with Justice Albie Sachs, Constitutional Court of the Republic of South Africa, San Francisco, Calif., 24 January 1997, reported in http://www.lgirtf.org.

Chapter Seven
Conclusion

Same-sex marriage is a prominent component of the worldwide struggle for gay and lesbian civil rights. Individuals in many countries have raised legal arguments in judicial proceedings based on equal protection, privacy, sexual orientation discrimination, and gender discrimination. In other nations, organized interest groups have utilized the legislative process to advance the cause of same-sex marriage. Gay and lesbian interest groups, however, have not often initiated test-case litigation to achieve the benefits of marriage, although these organizations have provided support for cases once courts have signaled the possibility that such claims may be accepted. The same-sex marriage debate is a case study shedding light on the merits of legislative and judicial strategies for securing civil rights.

The arguments raised in other countries over same-sex relationships are similar to those raised in the United States. The reasoning of opponents centers on religious and moral issues, and concern for children is often voiced. One typical claim is that the sanctity of marriage would be undermined if its definition were expanded to include same-sex couples. This antiquated view of marriage and family is still embraced despite the fact that it no longer reflects reality. The 2000 U.S. census showed that married-couple families dropped from 55 to 52 percent of all households. Families maintained by women with no husband present had increased three times as fast as married-couple families by 21 percent as against 7 percent. Unmarried, partnered homes, regardless of sexual orientation, had increased by 72 percent from 3.2 million in 1990 to 5.5 million in 2000. The 2000 U.S. census also allowed same-sex households to identify themselves for the first time, but the data from the states with the largest gay and lesbian populations are not yet available.

Proponents argue that the issue centers on fairness, equality, and discrimination. Judicial reasoning might rely on statutes prohibiting discrimination based on sexual orientation in those jurisdictions that have such laws, like Canada. Existing prohibitions against sex discrimination have often been expanded to include gays and lesbians and as a basis for allowing same-sex marriage. Examples of this rationale have been seen in the Hawaii case and in cases in Israel. The Scandinavian countries and Vermont's registered partnership law constructed positive rights by stating that the privileges and duties of marriage should be available unless otherwise stated, and the exceptions were specifically outlined. The Hawaii legislature and various nations took the opposite approach and delineated the specific rights and duties available to same-sex couples in domestic partnership.

In the Scandinavian countries, the legislature proactively addressed gay and lesbian relationships. Commissions were often appointed to study the condition of lesbians and gays in society. The issue was part of the national debate, and public policy was implemented as a result of the give-and-take of the legislative process. In the United States by contrast, the focus has been on limiting Hawaii's *potential* judicial acknowledgment of gay and lesbian relationships. In the 1996 and 1997 legislative sessions, nearly every state considered legislation to ban recognition of same-sex marriages. With same-sex marriage, an idea considered too radical for many elected officials, on the legislative agenda, sexual orientation antidiscrimination provisions have been regarded more favorably. Twelve states passed such provisions after the Hawaii case was initiated and nineteen states passed hate crime laws that cover sexual orientation.[1]

Another significant difference between the arguments raised in the Scandinavian countries and those in other countries is the traditional view that Scandinavians have of their nations as progressive. As Henning Bech stated, "the reasons for support of the registered partnership act in Denmark are in part related to the cultural identity of Denmark as a nation of progressive, equality-minded people."[2] This notion does not seem to affect public opinion in the United States. Some of this sentiment may have been felt in the states and municipalities that enacted domestic partnership legislation, but there is no evidence that these attitudes were a compelling reason for the electorate's approval of the legislation. Only the Hawaii court made any reference to the "progressive" or "conservative" nature of its state. In *Baehr*, the state's pleadings claimed that Hawaii had a "history of tolerance for all peoples and their cultures." Here the notion of a progressive culture in the state was used to suggest that lesbians and gays had not experienced discrimination. While Hawaii has a reputation as a liberal state, so do a number of other states, like Minnesota and

Washington, that have rejected same-sex marriage statutes.

Culture and history affect social mores, which, in turn, influence the law and political institutions. David Rayside offers an insightful explanation of how these elements pertain to sexual politics in the United Kingdom:

> [T]he homophobia embedded in the political culture(s) and institutional practices of England exceeds that to be found in most if not all other countries in the industrialized West. Both of Britain's largest political parties have contributed to the maintenance of a repressive climate for gays and lesbians, the Conservatives through their selective adoption of a morally conservative outlook deeply rooted in a middle-class culture of respectability, and the Labourites through a timidity on matters of sexuality born of a concern for the puritanism of an important element of their working-class constituency.[3]

The Conservative government proclaimed itself as the party of the family, and if gay rights were not banned altogether they were strictly limited to relationships between individuals so that which touched the family and society remained "normal" and ordinary. For the Conservatives, the permissiveness of the 1960s and 1970s, especially regarding sexuality, is a particularly dangerous factor in the decline of traditional standards of respectability and the breakdown of authority. The AIDS epidemic has been used by Conservatives and the media to create a moral backlash against the gay community.

While the Canadian federal elections of 1984 also brought a Conservative Party to power with affinities to that of Margaret Thatcher, "its right-wing moral agenda was never fully developed."[4] There were more similarities between these two governments regarding economic policy than regarding social concerns. The permissive attitudes of the 1960s and 1970s did not create as great a conservative backlash in Canada as they did in the United Kingdom. The enactment of the Charter of Rights and Freedoms in Canada in 1982, along with subsequent court "Charter challenges" on a number of issues,[5] actually caused an expansion in rights discourse as opposed to the contraction experienced in Britain under the Thatcher government.

The jurisprudential basis underlying public sentiments in countries adopting broad domestic partnership registrations and that of the Hawaii and Vermont courts is similar. In Denmark, the passing of the partnership bill reflected a shift from "traditionalist" principles based on morality, culture and society to "modernist" principles based on concepts of social and legal rights. The Hawaii and Vermont courts also embraced theories of equality and justice while previous courts had looked to traditional definitions. As Mary Treuthart explained, "Although a number of state interests have been advanced to justify confining marriage to opposite sex couples, it is primarily the morality concerns raised by Judeo-Christian religious teachings, and not the social values served by marriage, which make it problematic for judges and legislators to sanction same-sex relationships."[6] This distinction between traditional and modern values is useful in understanding cultural influences on the legal system. Professor William Eskridge expanded on this point:

> If a goal of liberalism is the inculcation of the values of tolerance and mutual respect, the way in which liberal projects are accomplished must be consistent with these values. For the judiciary... to tell traditionalist citizens that their time-tested family values count for nothing in the same-sex marriage debate is a time-tested path to political alienation or revolt. The genius of Vermont's [decision] is that the state insisted that traditional family values give way to the recognition of lesbian and gay rights, but lesbian and gay rights give way to accommodation of traditionalist anxieties for the time being.[7]

As social values fluctuate between traditional and modern, there will be corresponding shifts in the reasoning of courts and legislatures.

The trend at present seems to involve a willingness on the part of government officials to grant economic rights as they relate to gays and lesbians and same-sex relationships but an unwillingness to grant legal rights that raise issues of morality and challenge religious notions. The Scandinavian domestic partnership acts are evidence of this distinction as same-sex couples were denied the right to a church wedding and the right to adopt children. This distinction also helps explain legislation and court decisions in the United States. If the gay rights issue before voters, legislators, and judges involves economic concerns, there is a much better chance of change being approved than if the issue involves concepts dealing with familial or personal rights. The Canadian suit for economic support upon separation, *M. v. H.*, specifically made this point. In this case, the state had an interest in recognizing the same-sex relationship in order to avoid having to make financial contributions to one partner in the form of welfare assistance.

In many European countries and in Canada, same-sex couples are being awarded the rights that unmarried, cohabitating opposite-sex couples receive. While the status of marriage is not granted to cohabitating couples, unequal legal treatment in relationships is being eliminated. Canadian courts have recently challenged the distinction between common-law marriage and civil law marriage. In the United States, where common law marriages are recognized, such couples have all the rights attached to marriage. However, no state in the United States has expanded the definition of common-law marriage to include gay and lesbian couples.

A common issue raised in many countries is concern for children. Most legislative acts recognizing same-sex couples have denied them the right to adopt or even seek alternative fertilization methods. The Danish argument against adoption parallels the one presented by the states of Hawaii and Vermont during their trials. Courts have been reluctant to allow children to remain with their gay or lesbian biological parent and have refused to recognize the partner of a gay or lesbian person as a co-parent. As people in the Scandinavian countries have grown accustomed to domestic partnerships, they have become more willing to accept the familial aspects of same-sex relationships. It appears that adoption rights and full marriage status for gays and lesbians may not be far off, with Denmark leading the way once again.

Another factor distinguishing the legal environment around same-sex relationships in various nations is the degree to which laws and legal institutions condone homosexuality. In Denmark, gay and lesbian relationships between consenting adults have been decriminalized for almost sixty years. An antidiscrimination law prohibits public defamation based on sexual orientation. Existing laws and legal institutions in Denmark provide a supportive framework for same-sex relationship issues.[8] This is the case in most of the Scandinavian countries, and they have been the most progressive in recognizing same-sex relationships.

In comparison, there is less structural or institutional basis in law for same-sex relationships in the United States and many other nations. Sodomy laws criminalizing sexual relationships between consenting adults exist in many countries.[9] These statutes are used to deny the expansion of civil rights and have been specifically used as grounds for denying same-sex marriage. Sodomy laws stigmatize gays and lesbians as criminals, thereby reinforcing people's negative attitude to same-sex marriage. Since sodomy laws are rarely enforced, they may still exist as simply a reflection of social bias. To secure human rights for gays and lesbians, sodomy laws will have to be repealed.

The legislative process for addressing same-sex relationships seems to closely reflect the perception of the people's values. The number of legislatures that have passed domestic partnership acts continues to grow, and elected officials are becoming more confident that supporting such a bill will not jeopardize their political careers. The legislative process in the Scandinavian countries was expeditious, but political compromise resulted in only limited benefits being granted to same-sex couples. The experiences of these nations suggest some of the weaknesses of domestic partnership registration: immigration restrictions, prohibition of child rearing, lack of religious support, absence of international recognition, imposition of waiting periods before benefits are granted, and imposition of residency requirements for at least one partner. Over the decade that broad domestic partnership provisions have been in place in the Scandinavian countries, people have found that the institution of marriage has not disintegrated. These examples show that as people become more comfortable with gay and lesbian families, more official recognition will be granted to them, culminating in full marriage rights as in Denmark.

Tension is created when the morals of the majority are challenged through the legal process. In Denmark, Norway, Sweden, and Iceland, the opposing values around same-sex relationships were addressed through the political process in the legislatures. In the United States, Israel, and Canada, these conflicting standards are being juxtaposed against constitutional provisions in the courts. A tenet of constitutional law is that "moral norms that interfere with the exercise of constitutional rights are to be given the force of law only if they prevent objective and concrete harm."[10] Some courts have not embraced this principle, merely accepting the argument that by definition and tradition marriage is between a man and a woman. The courts in Hawaii, Alaska, and Vermont required the state to offer explicit reasons for denying same-sex couples the right to marry. In Hawaii and Vermont, the courts rejected the state's main argument that the welfare of children dictates that the institution of marriage be limited to opposite-sex couples.

Insights from the U.S. Courts

In the United States, the gay and lesbian social movement has a long history of turning to the courts for protection. This is due, in part, to legislative hostility to gay and lesbian rights. Judicial acknowledgment of same-sex relationships has the power to transform the institutions of marriage and the family, making the issue highly contentious. The U.S. litigation for same-sex marriage demonstrates both the weaknesses of relying on courts as an instrument of social change and the promise that a rights discourse holds for securing justice and equality.

A distinction needs to be drawn between test cases orchestrated by interest groups using adjudication in an attempt to achieve some public policy, and rights claims initiated by aggrieved citizens. Courts may make public policy in both instances, but there are tactical considerations that influence an organized litigation strategy. From a strategic perspective, the expense of going to court and the prospect for winning must obviously be taken into account. Individual rights claims are often made out of principle or necessity, and the cost-benefit analysis is greatly different. If a person cannot be with her or his loved one in the hospital emergency room, for example, the circumstances might require legal intervention.

The Hawaii same-sex marriage case was initiated by individuals who felt they had been wronged but were not officially aligned with any organization. Gay and lesbian groups decided to support the individuals involved and help coordinate the effort after the Hawaii court found a constitutional violation. Individuals in New York and Alaska also initiated their marriage suits without the support of the social movement's leadership, which feared the creation of a bad precedent while the Hawaii case was pending. In Vermont, the Gay and Lesbian Advocates and Defenders acted as co-counsel for the plaintiffs. The Lambda Legal Defense and Education Fund indicated that the political climate of Vermont and the educational groundwork that had been done made this action timely. Practically speaking, Lambda might also have recognized that the Hawaii case could be derailed by the political response.

Neo-Realist Perspectives

Gerald Rosenberg has argued that the courts are constrained by legal and institutional factors that limit their ability to make "significant social change."[11] The same-sex marriage cases support a number of his contentions. Past case precedent was used by the courts to restrict their interpretation of marriage statutes and constitutional rights. The early same-sex marriage cases demonstrate how judicial reliance on previous legal opinion reinforces the social *status quo*.

The same-sex marriage cases show that the way in which the court defines an issue is determinative of the outcome. With regard to this litigation, Professor Hannah Schwarzschild stated:

> Like all cultural norms, the institution of marriage itself, its sexual aspects as well as its vaunted emotional infrastructure, is a social construction. Common law and constitutional doctrine have both responded to, and themselves been instrumental in shaping, the meaning ascribed to the term as well as its normative status. Over years and centuries, courts and legal scholars have functioned much like social scientists: as they perceive and attempt to analyze cultural reality, they also play a crucial role in constructing that reality.[12]

Marriage statutes themselves often create language barriers to same-sex unions with references to gender-related terms. In the United States, forty-three jurisdictions have marriage statutes with gender-related terms. Even before the legislation resulting from the *Baehr* case, three states specifically prohibited same-sex marriage: Indiana, Utah, and Virginia.[13] While most of the marriage laws were written decades ago, and many do not necessarily imply an intent to prohibit same-sex marriage, the gender-specific language reveals the deep-rooted traditions associated with the institution of marriage.

The states have primary jurisdiction over family law issues, so state courts have heard cases regarding same-sex marriage. It appears that courts are reluctant to promote social change and more often simply endorse current public sentiments. State court judges are not as insulated from politics as their federal counterparts are. State court judges often have to face the electorate in retention votes or even run for reelection. Voter accountability may make these judges reluctant to uphold the rights of gays and lesbians if these judges sense a lack of popular support. William B. Rubenstein summed up this dilemma:

> Often, convincing four of seven jurists is a quicker and simpler mechanism for change than convincing the public generally, much less its elected representatives, of the equities inherent in a particular situation. Yet in the end judges . . . share all the biases and limitations of the public itself. [W]e cannot

expect them to remain far ahead of society in their willingness to accept social change, even if their own holdings suggest they might.[14]

Given the current social and political climate, it does not seem that a majority of state judges or legislators are likely to be receptive to expanding the status of marriage to include same-sex relationships. Public opinion in Vermont is almost equally split over the civil union law, but it does seem that there is momentum to recognize gay and lesbian couples.

Gerald N. Rosenberg suggested that courts may create social change if they can overcome the factors that constrain them.[15] There needs to be support from the legislative or executive branch or a low level of public opposition to the court's decision. To overcome the court's weak enforcement power, compliance must be induced by some incentive or cost or by the marketplace, or other political forces will implement the decision.

In the Hawaii, Vermont, and Alaska same-sex marriage cases, the courts acted boldly without these additional supports. These cases show that courts have the institutional capacity to make social policy. A lawsuit between two parties, especially a citizen against the government, can have an impact that reaches far beyond the litigants. The same-sex marriage litigation had a significant impact on the national debate over gay and lesbian rights and incited a political response never before seen over a state court case.

Constitutive Perspectives

The critical legal studies, neo-Marxist view of rights rocked the legal academy in the 1980s. According to this theory, law is seen as co-opting and limiting people's perspectives. Law is part of the "superstructure" that supports existing institutions. For the most part, the law does reflect the dominant moral views of the larger society. Yet, it does not appear that gays and lesbians themselves accept the notion that privacy rights, equal protection, and sex discrimination do not apply to their relationships.

The indirect impact of the same-sex marriage cases demonstrates that litigation strategies can make a difference for social movements. While the cases have not granted gays and lesbians the right to wed, their impact on social change has been significant. The court decisions gave the demand for same-sex marriage rights a certain degree of legal, political, and moral legitimacy. Vermont legislators could vote for the civil union bill and say that they were forced to do so by the Supreme Court. The Hawaii case mobilized the gay and lesbian communities. Hundreds of Freedom to Marry organizations were created across the country. By involving the legislature, the court made possible a full public discussion of the issue and provided the time for the educational campaign that was needed to win support. The Vermont case motivated activists in some states to pursue civil unions instead of marriage rights. In Hawaii, an organization called "Civil Unions-Civil Rights" was formed in December 2000, with the aim of expanding the state's domestic partnership program to include medical, custody, and adoption rights.

The same-sex marriage cases raised awareness of the existence of gay and lesbian families and of the issues they currently face without the protection of the law. The litigation educated the public in ways that would not otherwise have been possible. A grassroots campaign to have people and organizations sign a marriage resolution provided a means to initiate this dialogue. The Marriage Resolution simply states:

> Because marriage is a basic human right and an individual personal choice, Resolved, the State should not interfere with same-gender couples who choose to marry and share fully and equally in the rights, responsibilities, and commitment of civil marriage.

Comprehensive domestic partnership provisions are now seen as a viable option and reasonable compromise in regard to the institution of marriage. Without the litigation, statewide domestic partnership registration would probably not have been on the public agenda at this time. The number of companies that grant domestic partnership benefits to their gay and lesbian employees increases every year. A federal domestic partnership bill was introduced in Congress in February 2001 by Rep. Barney Frank (D-MA), one of the openly gay members, which would give gay and straight domestic partners of federal employees health insurance, life insurance, and retirement benefits.

Yet, the indirect and symbolic aspects of the litigation have not all been supportive of the movement to recognize gay and lesbian families. When there is a widespread disdain for a group of people, social biases impede much of the symbolic value that law may have. For the gay and lesbian community, numerous legal claims of discrimination are unsuccessful because many people still believe that it is appropriate to draw distinctions based on sexual orientation. The homophobic views of many judges are evident in their opinions. Legal and political leveraging is unlikely because social attitudes deny any affirmative rights claim needed to form the basis of an argument. Rights claims cannot transcend emotional, religious, or moral positions. Other social movements have been able to use rights claims and the threat of litigation to pressure their opponents into making concessions.[16] The gay and lesbian social movement is less able to use legal mobilization for political leveraging.

Civil union law embeds in the law same-sex couples as second-class citizens by defining marriage as between a man and a woman. This itself marks gay and lesbian couples as inferior and withholds the legitimating social status of marriage. The labels the law places on people shape how society views them and how they view themselves. Anti-marriage laws reflect animosity toward gays and lesbians.

In Vermont, the civil union legislation was a political compromise between proposing same-sex marriage, which would have failed, or doing nothing. The latter two options would have put the issue back before the state supreme court, which would have mandated marriage or some type of sweeping domestic partnership law. The court's actions, however, would not have been seen as less legitimate since the people's representatives had just rejected these options.[17]

The "political reality" that motivated the Vermont legislature to enact civil union legislation rather than simply expand marriage laws to apply to same-sex couples reflects the deep-seated homophobia that exists in this country. David Chambers speculated that the Vermont legislature opted for civil unions rather than marriage for three reasons. First, even liberals may unconsciously believe that gay and lesbian relationships are different from those of heterosexuals; that they have merit, but are not equal. Heterosexism also affects gay and lesbian consciousness, and even same-sex couples see themselves as different. This allows civil unions to be acceptable. "Second, marriage is in part about sexual pleasure, and gay men and lesbians have sex in ways that most heterosexuals find quite uncomfortable to think about. And, third, marriage is about gender roles that most liberals consciously reject but unconsciously embrace."[18] Richard Mohr elaborated on the deep-seated impact of sexual identity in the law:

> To put it bluntly: marriage, viewed now as a symbolic event, enacts, institutionalizes, and ritualizes the social meaning of heterosexuality. Marriage is the chief means by which culture maintains heterosexuality as a social identity.... One does not become a heterosexual by having heterosexual sex. Rather, marriage is the social essence of heterosexuality. In consequence, on the plane of symbols and identities, if one did not marry, one would not be fully heterosexual. And here's the kicker: if others were allowed to get married, one wouldn't be fully heterosexual, either. This analysis explains why the courts, the president and Congress can claim that marriage, by definition, is the union of one man and one woman as husband and wife, even though this definition is circular, lacks any content, and explains nothing. Its function is not to clarify or explain; its function is to assure heterosexual supremacy as a central cultural form.[19]

Mohr suggests that "standard civil rights strategies that appeal to fairness and equality will do no good. Since the problem is chiefly cultural rather than political, we must adopt a cultural strategy."[20] If the court had granted marriage rights, the backlash would have been against the court rather than the legislature, but this is one reason why the judiciary is provided with some insulation from the political sentiments of the day. When the courts uphold and protect the constitutional rights of a disliked group, there is always the risk of some backlash, but protecting minority rights is one of the roles of the judiciary.

Critics of the Vermont civil union law argue that an inferior class of relationships is created and draw an analogy between the "separate but equal" doctrine that defined race relations in this country under the U.S. Supreme Court ruling in *Plessey v. Ferguson*. Vermont law professor Gil Kujovich commented that "Our society's experiences with 'separate but equal' have repeatedly shown that separation can never result in equality because the separation is based on a belief of distance necessary to be maintained between those in the privileged position and those placed in the inferior position."[21] The Hawaii Supreme Court in *Baehr* noted that the same-sex marriage ban violated the state's Equal Protection Clause and possibly the Fourteenth Amendment of the U.S. Constitution. The Hawaii court stated that "substitution of 'sex' for 'race' and article I, section 5 [of the state constitution] for the Fourteenth Amendment yields the precise case before us together with the conclusion that we have reached."[22] The Vermont Supreme Court held that preventing same-sex marriage violates a similar provision in Vermont's constitution.

Individuals using the courts have forced this item onto the agenda of the gay and lesbian social movement without the backing of the leaders or the mass of members. Critics of these individual actions argue that the court cases raised these policy issues before the necessary political groundwork had been completed. In addition to the cost of the litigation itself, millions of dollars were spent fighting the state's defense of marriage acts. The Human Rights Campaign Fund, a gay and lesbian political action committee, spent over one million dollars in Hawaii alone and noted that it did not have the resources to assist financially in Alaska. Nearly six million dollars was spent in California in an unsuccessful attempt to stop the passage of the nonrecognition law. During the 1990s, thirty-five states enacted statutes to prevent same-sex marriage, and the gay and lesbian social movement had to respond to each of these campaigns, using a large amount of time and resources that could have been used on other issues.

As mentioned earlier, there seems to be more public support for sexual orientation nondiscrimination provisions dealing with economic issues. Would the gay and lesbian communities have been better off if they could have focused on repealing sodomy statutes or passing employment protections? Were these higher priorities? The temporary success of the Hawaii litigation removed these options from the political agenda and instead made marriage rights the priority.

Same-sex marriage seems radical even to many liberals. Conservatives used the issue to argue that the "gay agenda" was extreme, possibly undermining attempts at securing other means to prevent discrimination against gays and lesbians. The focus on marriage may also have retarded more progressive change by privileging traditional notions of family rather than looking at alternative ways to allocate social benefits, such as "cafeteria"-style insurance options where all employees receive coverage and have the option of purchasing any additional plans they need.

Courts and the Possibilities for Social Change

Have the same-sex marriage cases *caused* much social change? No state has yet granted marriage rights to gays and lesbians. Civil unions codify same-sex relationships as unworthy of the designation "marriage," according to some critics. The political backlash may have stunted the movement for gay rights. On the other hand, the public awareness of gay and lesbian families has increased dramatically.

The question becomes, when will, or should, the courts expand the prevailing notion of a right? On the state level, the highest court may not have the option of refusing to hear the case. Plaintiffs can force the issue onto the court's agenda. The circumstances under which a court will reject past precedent and prevailing social attitudes are difficult to determine. The influence of judicial decrees, however, is mediated by the political response. The legislative actions in the states and in Congress were an attempt to reject what many elected officials saw as judicial activism on the part of Hawaii's courts. Greg Johnson, who assisted with the Alaska case, explained that the lesson of Alaska and Hawaii is that work in the courts is not enough. "The reason we have some hope here in Vermont is not just because the jurisprudence is good but the body politic is markedly different than in Alaska and Hawaii."[23] Johnson explained that the "one thing that distinguishes Vermont is the remarkable amount of planning and coordination which preceded and accompanied the push for equal marriage rights. In Alaska, the lawyers working on the same-sex marriage case held to a naive belief in the power and primacy of constitutional rights."[24]

What is revealing in Vermont is the political climate over the last three decades. In 1977, the sodomy laws were repealed. Discrimination based on HIV-status was prohibited in 1988, and the first statutory prohibition against discrimination based on sexual orientation was passed regarding insurance decisions. A hate crimes law that included sexual orientation was approved in 1990. Discrimination based on sexual orientation in housing, banking, insurance, public accommodations, and employment was outlawed in 1992.

In 1993, a unanimous Vermont Supreme Court recognized a same-sex partner as the equivalent of a spouse for the step-parent exception in the adoption statute. The court also accepted a state agency's decision that adoptions by same-sex couples were in the best interests of the children concerned. The General Assembly in 1995 revised the adoption statutes to recognize same-sex couples as "family-units" and extended family court jurisdiction to unmarried and same-sex couples parenting a child. In Vermont, the legislature has taken the lead in protecting gays and lesbians, and judicial action was even subsequently ratified by the General Assembly. The court in *Baker* notes these statutes and refutes the contention that state law has "historically disfavored same-sex relationships."[25] Gil Kujovich noted, "Thus, the carefully measured step taken by the majority in *Baker* reflects neither political manipulation nor timidity, but a subtle appreciation of the process by which the Vermont constitutional culture continues to evolve."[26]

A great deal of work within the gay and lesbian communities and within the state's political establishment preceded the *Baker* case, enhancing the possibilities for success. The Vermont Coalition for Lesbian and Gay Rights (VCLGR), formed in 1985, held a debate on the merits of same-sex marriage in 1993 and participated in a national meeting to consider strategies for obtaining same-sex marriage rights in 1994. A year later, a thirty-five-page outline of "speaking points" suggesting style and word choices was circulated. Also in 1995, the Vermont Freedom to Marry Task Force was created. Speaker's bureaus were established; a short educational video was made, and meetings were held with the governor and leaders of the assembly. A team was set up to field questions and conduct interviews, and a positive media climate was established. The litigation was filed two years later, in 1997.

The task force continued to build broad-based support. Women's groups proved to be important allies. The Governor's Commission on Women honored the plaintiffs in 1999 for "their courage, commitment, and willingness to open their private lives to public scrutiny for what is simply a civil rights issue."[27] Women legislators favored the civil union bill by 35 to 9, with four of the twelve Republicans and all but one of the thirty-two Democratic women voting for it. Men, on the other hand, voted against the bill by 60 to 41. While Republicans overwhelmingly voted against the civil union bill by 50 to 14, the chair of the House Judiciary Committee and his fellow party members were instrumental in drafting compromise legislation. The committee approved the bill in a 10 to one vote with all five Republicans voting in favor of it.

Occasionally there is a legal victory that is incongruent with prevailing social mores. The Hawaii Supreme Court's ruling in *Baehr*, the Alaska Superior Court's holding in *Brause*, and the Vermont Supreme Court's opinion in *Baker* are such cases. There is not much indication as to when arguments advocating broad expansion of legal concepts will become persuasive. Attitudes toward gays and lesbians are becoming more tolerant, but there is no widespread social support for same-sex marriage. The courts in rare circumstances are willing to recognize a rights claim before it would receive general public support in a legislature, but these are aberrations and should not be the basis of a litigation strategy. Litigation tactics seem more effective when used to incrementally advance legal doctrine and should be used in concert with grassroots education and other lobbying tactics. Kujovich explains that "Incremental elaboration confers legitimacy on constitutional decisions not only by defining the line between the legislative and judicial functions, but also by fostering a restrained pace in the elaboration of principle. That restraint can be an important factor in a democratic society's understanding and accepting of constitutional decisions with which it may, at first, disagree."[28] The unfolding of constitutional principles is an evolutionary process produced by the courts and society.

The history of the gay and lesbian social movement suggests that courts are more likely to enforce the current understanding of existing rights than to expand the concept of a right itself. If a well-established legal doctrine is not inclusive of a minority group, the court may act as a "shield" and protect the group from being excluded from the benefits being sought. For example, the courts have protected gay and lesbian groups' free speech rights. Richard Abel has contended that rights arguments are better at preserving the *status quo* against greater government intrusion and escalating repression than at promoting social change. Courts are less likely to act as the "sword" of justice striking down every perceived inequality or act of discrimination.[29]

The Hawaii court decision came as a surprise to nearly everyone. It seemed much more likely that yet another jurisdiction would reject any legal recognition of same-sex relationships, adding another layer of bad precedent. A decade-long national debate has ensued with thirty-five states passing legislation to prevent the recognition of same-sex marriage. The controversy continues with states now adding civil unions to those relationships that will not receive public acknowledgment.

Despite the public backlash against the Hawaii court's ruling, gay and lesbian couples in Vermont brought their claim of discrimination to the court. Using an equal protection analysis involving gays and lesbians rather than the Hawaii court's sex discrimination rationale, the Vermont Supreme Court also ruled that same-sex couples should enjoy the benefits of marriage. If the Vermont court had ruled against same-sex couples, this entire litigation effort would most likely be seen as a miserable failure for the gay and lesbian social movement. The Vermont judicial victory may justify all the time and resources that went into the litigation and into fighting the state legislation, unless of course, the people of Vermont amend their constitution.

Amending the Vermont Constitution is more complex than in most other states. Amendments can be considered only once every four years. The senate must approve the amendment by a two-thirds vote, and a majority of the House must concur. In the next session of the General Assembly, each chamber must again pass the amendment by a simple majority. Then, it is submitted to the voters for their approval. Consequently, a constitutional amendment overturning *Baker* will not come before the voters until at least 2005, five years after the court decision. Advocates contend that people will have grown to accept civil unions, and perhaps full marriage rights, by then.

The same-sex marriage cases clearly show that a judicial victory, even one proclaiming a constitutional right, may not be the final resolution of an issue. Likewise, the same-sex marriage politics demonstrate that legislative victories can be temporary. The Vermont legislature's creation of civil unions may not be the end of the debate either. William N. Eskridge commented, "There is a broader lesson for the modern state: its constitution may promise liberal rights that its political system cannot immediately deliver and that its judiciary dare not insist upon."[30] Depending on how easy it is for the constitution to be amended, both judicial and legislative policies can be overturned by citizen initiative. With the low voter turnouts that characterize today's elections, an organized, well-funded group can define the constitutional rights of others despite evolving legal norms or legislative compromise.

The judiciary is called upon to weigh societal norms and values against abstract constitutional principles. The definition of these constitutional principles is influenced by cultural, social, and historical elements. How the issues are defined is also a determining factor in the outcome of the case. According to Vermont law professor Michael Millo, "History teaches that people fear those different from themselves, and that people fear change. The inclusion of every group of outsiders into the full benefits of American citizenship has always come at a cost of social dislocation."[31] The actions of Congress and state legislatures also reinforce the observation that economic and "public" rights will be recognized before privileges associated with the family and the "private" sphere. As social views evolve and when a progressive jurisdiction considers the issue, constitutional protection may be established. Constitutional rights have been expanded when opposition to the minority position has diminished by some degree but prior to the majority's acceptance of the alternative values.

The Future of Same-Sex Marriage Rights

Lawsuits, grassroots efforts, and lobbying in other states continue to build on the impact generated by the same-sex marriage cases. Additional litigation was filed in Massachusetts by seven lesbian and gay couples on 11 April 2001 in *Goodridge v. Dept. of Public Health*. The Gay and Lesbian Advocates and Defenders (GLAD) group, which was co-counsel in the Vermont case, is representing the plaintiffs again. A media blitz was held in three cities across the state on the filing day. Joshua Friedes, volunteer political director for Massachusetts' Freedom to Marry Coalition, said the lawsuit will be used "as an opportunity to educate the public and elected officials about the real lives of gays and lesbians.... We are hopeful that the lawsuit will reframe the issue so that people understand that what we are talking about is civil-marriage rights, and these rights are essential for all families, whether they are headed by opposite-sex couples or same-sex couples."[32] GLAD said the lawsuit will show that there are many common threads that unite us all. Civil unions are a good first step, but they do not go far enough. "Gay and lesbian couples want and need what everyone else has, the right to receive the full protections bestowed by the state and federal government that come through marriage," explained GLAD. The Massachusetts judiciary has a long history of being at the forefront of civil rights issues. An editorial in New England's largest gay and lesbian newspaper argued that GLAD and the fourteen plaintiffs should be thanked for initiating the case despite the fact that it will create some of the "most acrimonious and hate-filled debate" seen in years.[33] Supporters of same-sex marriage were urged to become involved in the educational campaign that will be needed to counter the negative attacks of opponents.

The work to secure same-sex marriage rights by legislative enactment has also gained momentum as more bills are introduced each year. Marriage Equality New York launched a two-year campaign in February 2001 to acquire same-sex marriage rights through the legislative process. The objective of "I Do 2002" is to gather the support of hundreds of local and statewide politicians and organizations. A same-sex marriage bill has been introduced in the New York State Senate.

How other states treat Vermont's civil unions remains to be seen. Courts may recognize particular duties imposed by the civil union law rather than the relationship itself, for example, the obligation of a partner to pay child support. The Georgia courts are being asked to consider civil union as equivalent to marriage, in a contempt case regarding child visitation rights. Susan Freer is contesting a court order that prohibits visitation and residence "by the children with either party during any time where such party cohabits with or has overnight stays with any adult to whom party is not married or to whom party is not related." Susan, divorced from the children's father in 1995, took the last name of her lesbian partner, Debra Freer, when they were joined in civil union in Vermont in July 2000. Debra said they told the children, twelve-year-old twin boys and a nine-year-old boy, about the civil union, "and they said they were happy for their mother and were happy for her." Susan argues that she was not violating the visitation agreement because she was effectively married. The superior court judge said that "while the contentions are arguable, they are not persuasive," and that a trial court is not authorized to consider an out-of-state civil union equivalent to marriage. The federal Defense of Marriage Act and Georgia's public policy, which "as declared by the Legislature is against same-sex marriages" were cited as the justification for the holding. The state court of appeals has agreed to review the claim.[34] While most leaders of the gay and lesbian social movement would agree that Georgia is not the ideal state in which to bring a test case, Susan Freer must exercise her rights claim in order to continue to see her children!

Gays and lesbians around the world are seeking legal protection of their relationships through judicial and legislative means. As society becomes more accepting of homosexuality, legal and political systems evolve as well. Same-sex marriage challenges the traditional notions of family and pits religious and moral beliefs against concepts of equality, freedom, and justice. The highly contentious debate around same-sex marriage demonstrates how deeply these values resonate in nearly every society. The history of other human rights issues suggests that tradition will eventually yield to equality and that the religious beliefs of some people will not prevail against more universal concepts of justice.

Notes

1. The states with nondiscrimination statutes are mentioned in chapter 5. The states with hate crime laws that include sexual orientation are Arizona, California, Connecticut, Delaware, Florida, Illinois, Iowa, Maine, Massachusetts, Minnesota, Nebraska, Nevada, New Hampshire, New Jersey, Oregon, Utah, Vermont, Washington, and Wisconsin. The District of Columbia also has such a law.

2. Henning Bech, "Report from a Rotten State: 'Marriage' and 'Homosexuality' in Denmark," in Ken Plummer, ed., *Modern Homosexualities* (London and New York: Routledge, 1992), 144.

3. David Rayside, "Homophobia, Class and Party in England," *Canadian Journal of Political Science* 25 (March 1992): 122.

4. Ibid., 147.

5. Didi Herman, *Rights of Passage: Struggles for Lesbian and Gay Legal Equality* (Toronto: University of Toronto Press, 1994), 37.

6. Mary Patricia Treuthart, "Adopting a More Realistic Definition of Family," *Gonzaga Law Review* 26 (1990/91): 99.

7. William N. Eskridge, Jr., "Equality Practice: Liberal Reflections on the Jurisprudence of Civil Unions," *Albany Law Review* 64 (Spring 2001): 853.

8. The European Court of Human Rights found that since Ireland had refrained from enforcing its law regarding homosexual sodomy and the moral standards of the Irish people were not injured, there were no socially pressing needs to make such acts criminal offenses. Norris v. Ireland, 142 Eur.Ct.H.R. (ser. A)(1988). This decision has precedential authority in all twenty-one Council of Europe states.

9. Twenty-five states decriminalized homosexual sodomy between 1968 and 1983.

10. Alissa Friedman, "The Necessity for State Recognition of Same-Sex Marriage: Constitutional Requirements and Evolving Notions of Family," *Berkeley Women's Law Journal* 3 (1987/88): 167.

11. Gerald N. Rosenberg, *The Hollow Hope: Can Courts Bring about Social Change?* (Chicago: University of Chicago Press, 1991).

12. Hannah Schwarzschild, "Same-Sex Marriage and Constitutional Privacy: Moral Threat and Legal Anomaly," *Berkeley Women's Law Journal* 4 (1988): 110.

13. Michael L. Closen and Carol R. Heise, "HIV-AIDS and the Non-Traditional Family: The Argument for State and Federal Judicial Recognition of Danish Same-Sex Marriages," *Nova Law Review* 16 (1992): 826-829.

14. William B. Rubenstein, "We Are Family: A Reflection on the Search for Legal Recognition of Lesbian and Gay Relationships," *Journal of Law and Politics* 8 (1991): 105.

15. Rosenberg, *The Hollow Hope*.

16. Michael McCann in *Rights at Work: Pay Equity Reform and the Politics of Legal Mobilization* (Chicago: University of Chicago Press, 1994) outlines how this strategy was effective in the comparable worth movement. In this social struggle it may be possible to get an agreement, in principle at least, that comparable work deserves comparable compensation. The legal claim of equality can be used to gather support from the public at large and in court to pressure companies to institute equitable pay schemes.

17. Eskridge, "Equity Practice," 853.

18. David L. Chambers, "An Introduction and a Speculation," *Vermont Law Review* 25 (2000): 12.

19. Richard D. Mohr, "The Stakes in the Gay-Marriage Wars," in Robert M. Baird and Stuart E. Rosenbaum, eds. *Same-Sex Marriage: The Moral and Legal Debate* (Amherst, N.Y.: Prometheus Books, 1996): 106.

20. Mohr, "The Stakes in the Gay-Marriage Wars."

21. Gil Kujovich, "An Essay on the Passive Virtue of *Baker v. State*," *Vermont Law Review* 25 (2000): 134.

22. Baehr v. Lewin, 68.

23. Carey Goldberg, "Vermont Supreme Court Takes up Gay Marriage," *New York Times*, 19 November 1998, A18.

24. Greg Johnson, "Vermont Civil Unions: The New Language of Marriage," *Vermont Law Review* 25 (2000): 26.

25. Baker v. Lewin, 886.

26. Kujovich, "An Essay on the Passive Virtue of *Baker v. State*," 109.

27. Ibid.

28. Kujovich, "An Essay on the Passive Virtue of *Baker v. State*," 106.

29. Austin Sarat and Kearns, *Identities, Politics and Rights* (Ann Arbor, Mich.: University of Michigan Press, 1995): 13.

30. Eskridge, "Equality Practice," 853.

31. Michael Millo, "For Today, I'm Gay: The Unfinished Battle for Same-Sex Marriage in Vermont," *Vermont Law Review* 25 (2000), 266.

32. Beth Berlo, "Marriage Lawsuit Filed on Behalf of Seven Couples," *Bay Windows*, 12-18 April 2001, 1.

33. Jeff Epperly, "The Battle Begins in Massachusetts," *Bay Windows*, 12-18 April 2001, 1.

34. "Question of 'Marriage' in Custody Case," *Gay Chicago Magazine* 10-20 May 2001, 16.

Bibliography

Abt, Clark C., and Kathleen M. Hardy, eds. *AIDS and the Courts* (Cambridge, Mass.: Abt Books, 1990).

Adam, Barry D. "Winning Rights and Freedoms in Canada," in Aart Hendriks, Rob Tielman, and Evert van der Veen, eds., *The Third Pink Book* (Buffalo, N.Y.: Prometheus Books, 1993), 25-37.

_____. *The Rise of a Gay and Lesbian Movement* (New York: Twayne Publishers, 1995).

Adams v. Howerton, 486 F. Supp. 1119 (C.D.Cal.1980); aff'd, 673 F.2d 1036 (9th Cir.1982), cert. denied, 458 U.S. 1111, 102 S.Ct. 3494, 73 L.Ed.2d 1373 (1982).

Agneshwar, Anand. "Ex-Justice Says He May Have Been Wrong: Powell on Sodomy," *National Law Journal*, 5 November 1990, 3.

Andrews, John. "Homosexual Rights in the United Kingdom," *European Law Review* 5 (December 1980): 515-517.

_____. "Homosexuality and the Right to Family Life; Application No. 9369-81, X v. United Kingdom," *European Law Review* 9 (June 1984): 204.

"Anti-Gay Marriage Bill Passes House, Stalls in Senate," *Seattle Gay News*, 21 March 1997, 1.

Apple, R.W. Jr. "Carter Promises No. 2 Spot Will Go to 1 of 7 Queried," *New York Times*, 12 July 1976, 1.

Baehr v. Lewin, 852 P.2d 44 (Ha.Sup.Ct. 1993).

Baehr v. Miike, Hawaii Civil Case No. 91-1394, decided 3 December 1996.

Baker v. Nelson, 191 NW 2d. 185 (Minn. 1971).

Baker v. Nelsen, 409 U.S. 810 (1971), appeal dismissed.

Baker v. State, 744 A.2d 864 (Vt. 1999).

Barone, Michael, and Grant Ujifusa. "Hawaii," in *The Almanac of American Politics 1990* (Washington, D.C.: National Journal, 1989), 319-330.

Bakst, M. Charles. "Same-Sex Marriage," *Providence Journal-Bulletin*, 13 March 1997, 22.

Barrett, Paul M. "I Do/No You Don't," *Wall Street Journal*, 17 June 1996, 1.

Bech, Henning. "Report from a Rotten State: 'Marriage' and 'Homosexuality' in Denmark," in Ken Plummer, ed., *Modern Homosexualities* (London and New York: Routledge, 1992), 134-147.

Ben-Asher, David Ari. "Legal Discrimination against Homosexuals in America, and a Comparison with More Tolerant Societies," *Journal of Human Rights* 7 (1990): 157-178.

Berger, Vada. "Domestic Partnership Initiatives," *DePaul Law Review* 40 (Winter 1991): 417-458.

Blair, William G. "City's Homosexuals Protest High Court Sodomy Ruling," *New York Times*, 3 July 1986, B5.

Blasius, Mark. *Gay and Lesbian Politics* (Philadelphia: Temple University Press, 1994).

Boswell, John. *Same-Sex Unions in Premodern Europe* (New York: Villiard Books, 1994).

Bowers v. Hardwick, 478 U.S. 186 (1986).

Boxall, Bettina. "Hawaii Court Revives Suit on Gay Marriage," *Los Angeles Times*, 7 May 1993, A3.

Bradley, Gerard V. "Remaking the Constitution: A Critical Reexamination of the *Bowers v. Hardwick* Dissent," *Wake Forest Law Review* 25 (1990): 501-546.

Braschi v. Stahl Associates Co, 74 N.Y. 2d 201, 543 N.E. 2d 49 (1989).

Brause v. Bureau of Vital Statistics, slip op., No. 3AN-95-6562 CI (Alaska Super. Ct., 27 February 1998).

Bridges, Tyler. "Same-Sex Marriage Ban Broadened," *Miami Herald*, 30 May 1997, 3.

"Bronx Hospital Gives Gay Couples Spouse Benefits," *New York Times*, 27 March 1991, 1.

Brown, Roger. *Social Psychology*, 2d ed. Section V, "Some Issues of Sexual Liberation" (New York: The Free Press, 1986), 309-377.

Brown, Wendy. "Rights and Identity in Late Modernity: Revisiting the 'Jewish Question,'" in Austin Sarat and Thomas R. Kearns, eds., *Identity, Politics, and Rights* (Ann Arbor, Mich.: University of Michigan Press, 1995), 85-130; and Morris B. Kaplan, *Sexual Justice: Democratic*

Citizenship and the Politics of Desire (New York: Routledge, 1997).

Buchanan, G. Sidney. "Same-Sex Marriage: The Linchpin Issue," *University of Dayton Law Review* 10 (Spring 1985): 541-73.

Burke, Marc. "Homosexuality as Deviance: The Case of the Gay Police Officer," *British Journal of Criminology* 34 (Spring 1994): 192-203.

Cain, Patricia A. "Litigating for Lesbian and Gay Rights: A Legal History," *Virginia Law Review* 79 (1993): 1551-1643.

Callaghan, Peter. "Allies Impair Bid to Defuse Gay Marriage as State Issue," *Tacoma News Tribune*, 20 April 1997, 3.

Campbell, Duncan. "No to Prejudice," *New Statesman*, 15 January 1988, 8.

Caragata, Warren. "Taking a Stand," *MacClean's*, 28 February 1994, 28.

Case, Mary Anne. "Couples and Coupling in the Public Sphere," *Virginia Law Review* 79 (1993): 1643-1689.

Casper, Jonathan D. "The Supreme Court and National Policy Making," *American Political Science Review* 70 (1976): 50-63.

Chambers, David L. "An Introduction and a Speculation," *Vermont Law Review* 25 (2000): 12.

Chapman, Liz. "Gay Rights Bill Being Withdrawn," *Sun Journal* (Maine), 17 January 1996, 7.

Chayes, Abram. "The Role of the Judge in Public Law Litigation," *Harvard Law Review* 89 (1976): 1281.

Clark, Keith. "Legal Battle for Equality in Canada," *Gay and Lesbian Times*, 19 January 1995, 16.

Closen, Michael L., and Carol R. Heise. "HIV-AIDS and the Non-Traditional Family: The Argument for State and Federal Judicial Recognition of Danish Same-Sex Marriages," *Nova Law Review* 16 (1992): 809-845.

Closen, Michael L., et al., eds. *AIDS: Cases and Materials* (Houston, Tex.: John Marshall, 1989).

Colker, Ruth. "Marriage," *Yale Journal of Law and Feminism* 3 (1991): 321-326.

Cooper, Davina, and Didi Herman. "Getting "The Family Right": Legislating Heterosexuality in Britain, 1986-1991," *Canadian Journal of Family Law* 10 (1991): 41-78.

Cox, Barbara J. "Love Makes a Family – Nothing More, Nothing Less: How the Judicial System Has Refused to Protect Non-Legal Parents in Alternative Families," *Journal of Law and Politics* 8 (1991): 5-67.

Crenshaw, Kimberle Williams. "Race, Reform and Retrenchment: Transformation and Legitimation in Antidiscrimination Law," *Harvard Law Review* 101 (1988): 1331-1402.

Cruikshank, Margaret. *The Gay and Lesbian Liberation Movement* (New York: Routledge, 1992).

"Customs We Could Do Without (Raids on Gay Bookstores)," *New Statesman*, 12 October 1984, 3.

Dahl, Robert. "Decision-Making in a Democracy: The Supreme Court as a National Policy-Maker," *Journal of Public Law* 6 (Fall 1957): 279-295.

Dean v. District of Columbia, DC SuperCt, No. 90-13892, 2 June, 1992 (on reconsideration of 18 FLR 1141), 18 FLR 1387, 23 June 1992.

DeBold, Kathleen. *Out for Office: Campaigning in the Gay 90's* (Washington, D.C.: Gay and Lesbian Victory Fund, 1994).

Defense of Marriage Act, Public Law No. 104-1909, sec. 3(a), 110 Stat. 2419 (1996).

Deitcher, David, ed. "Law and Desire," in David Deitcher, ed., *The Question of Equality* (New York: Scribner, 1995).

_____. *The Question of Equality* (New York: Scribner, 1995).

De La O, Maria. "The Fight for Same-Sex Marriage," *Human Rights* 12 (1994): 22-23.

D'Emilio, John. *Sexual Politics, Sexual Communities* (Chicago: University of Chicago Press, 1983).

De Santo v. Barnsley, 476 A.2d. 952 (Pa. Super. Ct 1984).

"Developments in the Law – Sexual Orientation and the Law," *Harvard Law Review* 102 (1989): 1508-1671.

"District of Columbia," *Family Law Reporter* (BNA) 18 (29 September 1992), 1552.

Dizon, Michael. "House Forwards to Edgar Bill on Same-Sex Unions," *Chicago Tribune*, 26 April 1996, 3.

Duberman, Martin. *Stonewall* (New York: Penguin, 1993).

Duke, Lynne. "25 Years after Landmark Decision, Still the Rarest of Wedding Bonds," *Washington Post*, 12 June 1992, A3.

Dworkin, Ronald. *Taking Rights Seriously* (Cambridge: Harvard University Press, 1977).

Eblin, Robert L. "Domestic Partnership Recognition in the Workplace: Equitable Employee Benefits for Gay Couples (and Others)," *Ohio State Law Journal* 51 (1990): 1067-1087.

Editorial. "Crime in the Bedroom," *New York Times*, 2 July 1986, A30.

Editorial. "GOP Plays the Gay Card," *St. Louis Post-Dispatch*, 16 April 1996, 28.

Editorial. "Let Employers Handle Benefits," *St. Petersburg Times*, 28 May 1997, 33.

Editorial. "Same-Sex Marriage Bill Teetering," *Omaha World-Herald*, 11 April 1997, 21.

Elsaser, Rick. Gay and Lesbian Victory Fund, Telephone interview by author, 19 October 1994, Washington, D.C.

Elshtain Jean Bethke. "Against Gay Marriage: Accepting Limits," *Commonweal*, 22 November 1991, 685-686.

Emanski, Robert A. "A Right to Privacy for Gay People under International Human Rights Law," *Boston College International & Comparative Law Review* 15 (1992): 141-164.

"End Victimless Crime, Hawaii Citizens Urge," *The Advocate*, 20 December 1972, 3.

Epstein, Stephen. "Politics, Ethnic Identity: The Limits of Social Constructionism," in Edward Stein, ed. *Forms of Desire* (1990).

Eskridge, William N., Jr. *The Case for Same-Sex Marriage* (New York: The Free Press, 1996).

──────. "Equality Practice: Liberal Reflections on the Jurisprudence of Civil Unions," *Albany Law Review* 64 (Spring 2001): 853.

Essoyan, Susan. "Hawaii Tries to Take a Stand against Same-Sex Marriages," *Los Angeles Times*, 26 April 1994, A5.

Essoyan, Susan, and Bettina Boxall. "Hawaii Ruling Lifts Ban on Marriage of Same-Sex Couples," *Los Angeles Times*, 4 December 1996, A1.

_____. "Gay Marriages on Hold while Ruling Is Appealed," *Los Angeles Times*, 5 December 1996, A3.

Ettlebrick, Paula, and Stoddard, Thomas. "Gay Marriage: A Must or a Bust?," *Out/Look* (Fall 1989): 8-19.

Fajer, Marc A. "Can Two Real Men Eat Quiche Together? Storytelling, Gender-Role Stereotypes, and Legal Protection for Lesbians and Gay Men," *University of Miami Law Review* 46 (1992): 511-651.

Farnsworth, Clyde H. "Argentine Homosexual Gets Refugee Status in Canada," *New York Times*, 14 January 1992, A5.

Freeman, J. "Defining Family in Mossop v. DDS," *University of Toronto Law Journal* 44 (1994): 41-96.

Fried, Charles. *Arguing the Reagan Revolution: A First-Hand Account* (New York: Simon & Schuster, 1991).

Friedman, Alissa. "The Necessity for State Recognition of Same-Sex Marriage: Constitutional Requirements and Evolving Notions of Family," *Berkeley Women's Law Journal* 3 (1987/88): 134-170.

Fulton, E. Kaye. "Gay and Proud," *MacClean's*, 16 May 1994, 36-39.

_____. "Storming the Ramparts," *MacClean's*, 28 November 1994, 31-34.

Galanter, Marc. "The Radiating Effects of Courts," in Keith D. Boyum and Lynn Mather, eds., *Empirical Theories of Courts* (New York: Longman, 1983), 117-142.

_____. "Why the 'Haves' Come out Ahead: Speculations on the Limits of Legal Change," *Law & Society Review* 9 (1974): 95-123.

Gallagher, John. "What America Thinks of You," *The Advocate*, 6 June 1992, 91-94.

_____. "Till Death Do Us Part," *The Advocate*, 15 June 1993, 24-27.

_____. "Love & War," *The Advocate*, 23 July 1996, 22-28.

"Gay Cleric Denounces Proposed Law on Marriages," UFMCC Press Release, 2 June 1977, on file with author.

"Gay Marriage" File, available at the International Gay and Lesbian Archives, West Hollywood, California.

"Gay Rights Step in Britain," *New York Times*, 22 February 1994, A6.

"Gays on the Continental March," *The Economist*, 5 July 1997, 52.

"Gay Unions in Denmark," *Frontiers*, 1 January 1993, 22.

"Georgia Senate OKs Ban on Same-Sex Marriage," Associated Press, 27 February 1996.

Glaberson, William. "Ruling Stretches Legal Concept of Family," *New York Times*, 8 July 1989, A25.

Goodman, Denise. "Maine Legislators Avoid Referendum," *Boston Globe*, 27 March 1997, 17.

Goreham, Richard A. "Comments on Legislation and Judicial Decisions: Human Rights Code of British Columbia," *Canadian Bar Review* 59 (1981): 165-179.

"Governor Signs Bill, Gays Plan Mass Wedding," *Bozeman Chronicle* (Montana), 1 May 1997, 7.

Greenberg, Larry M."Ontario Rights Panel Moves to Give Gay Partners Rights to Full Pensions," *New York Times*, 5 November 1990, A14.

Greenhouse, Linda. "Washington Talk; When Second Thoughts in Case Come Too Late," *New York Times*, 5 November 1990, A14.

Griswold v. Connecticut, 381 U.S. 479 (1965), (85 S.Ct. 1678, 14 L.Ed.2d 510).

Gross, Jane. "After a Ruling, Hawaii Weighs Gay Marriage," *New York Times*, 25 April 1994, A1.

Hadinger v. State, 573 N.E.2d 1191 (Ohio Ct. App. 1991).

Halley, Janet E. "The Construction of Heterosexuality," in Michael Warner, ed., *Fear of a Queer Planet* (Minneapolis: University of Minnesota Press, 1993), 82-102.

Hartinger, Brent. "A Case for Gay Marriage," *Commonweal*, 22 November 1991, 681-683.

"Hawaii" File, available at the International Gay and Lesbian Archives, West Hollywood, California.

Hay, Harry. "Birth of a Consciousness," *Harvard Gay and Lesbian Review*, Winter 1995, 11-14.

Healy, Melissa. "Clinton Signals He'd Sign Anti-Gay Marriage Bill," *Los Angeles Times*, 23 May 1996, A15.

_____. "House Backs Curbs on Gay Marriages," *Los Angeles Times*, 13 July 1996, A13.

Helfer, Laurence R. "Lesbian and Gay Rights as Human Rights: Strategies for a United Europe," *Virginia Journal of International Law* 32 (Fall 1991): 157- 207.

Henson, Deborah M. "A Comparative Analysis of Same-Sex Partnerships Protections: Recommendations for American Reform," *International Journal of Law and the Family* 7 (1993): 282-313.

Herman, Didi. *Rights of Passage: Struggles for Lesbian & Gay Legal Equality* (Toronto: University of Toronto Press, 1994).

Herman, Robin."New York High Court Voids Ban on Consensual Sodomy," *New York Times*, 19 December 1980, B2.

Hirsch, Stuart. "Ban on Gay Marriages Will Go to Governor," *Indianapolis Star*, 25 April 1997, 3.

"Homosexual Spousal Benefits Upheld," *Los Angeles Times*, 3 September 1992, A9.

"Homosexuals Stage Protest in Capital," *New York Times*, 30 May 1965, 42.

Horowitz, Donald L. *The Courts and Social Policy* (Washington, D.C., Brookings Institute, 1977).

Hosek, Linda. "Hawaii Considers Same-Sex Marriage," *Honolulu Star-Bulletin*, 11 May 1993, 3.

Howse, John. "Backyard Challenges," *MacClean's*, 22 March 1993, 20-21.

Hunt, Alan. "Rights and Social Movements:Counter-Hegemonic Strategies," *Journal of Law and Society* 17 (1990): 309-342.

In re Guardianship of Kowalski, 382 N.W. 2d 861 (Minn. App.), cert. denied sub. nom., Kowalski v. Kowalski et al., 475 U.S. 1085 (1986).

In the Matter of Alison D. v. Virginia M., 77 N.Y.2d 651, 572 N.E.2d 27, 569 N.Y.S.2d 586 (1991).

Isaacson, Walter. "Should Gays Have Marriage Rights?" *Time*, 20 November 1989, 98-101+.

Jacobs, Andrew M. "The Rhetorical Construction of Rights: The Case of the Gay Rights Movement, 1969-1991," *Nebraska Law Review* 72 (1993): 723-759.

Jeffery-Poulter, Stephen. *Peers, Queers & Commons* (London: Routledge, 1991).

Jenish, D'arcy. "A Clash of Values," *MacClean's*, 13 June 1994, 10-11.

Johnson, Charles A., and Bradley C. Canon. *Judicial Policies: Implementation and Impact* (Washington, D.C.: Congressional Quarterly Press, 1984).

Johnson, Greg. "Vermont Civil Unions: The New Language of Marriage," *Vermont Law Review* 25 (2000): 26.

Johnston, Michelle Dally. "Romer Kills Gay-Wedding Bill," *Denver Post*, 6 June 1997, 3.

Jones v. Hallahan, 501 S.W.2d 588 (Ky. App. 1973).

Kairys, David. ed. *The Politics of Law: A Progressive Critique* (New York: Pantheon, 1982).

Kane, Daniel J. "Homosexuality and the European Conventions on Human Rights: What Rights?" *Hastings International and Comparative Law Review* 11 (1988): 447-486.

Katz, Jonathan. *Gay American History* (New York: Harper & Row, 1976).

Keen, Lisa. "Virginia House, Senate Approve Anti-Marriage Bill," *Washington Blade*, 7 February 1997, 6.

_____. "Marriage Battle Erupts in Vermont," *Washington Blade*, 25 July 1997, 1.

Kelman, Mark. *A Guide to Critical Legal Studies* (Cambridge: Harvard University Press, 1987).

"Kenneth Baker's Weak Excuse (in Turning Down the Grant to the London Lesbian and Gay Centre)," editorial, *New Statesman*, 10 May 1985, 3.

Kepner, Jim. Interview, Los Angeles, Calif., 23 April 1995.

Kessler, Mark. "Legal Mobilization for Social Reform: Power and the Politics of Agenda Setting," *Law and Society Review* 24 (1990): 121-167.

Khayatt, Madiha Didi. "Proper Schooling for Teenage Lesbians in Canada," in Aart Hendriks, Rob Tielman, and Evert van der Veen, eds., *The Third Pink Book* (Buffalo, N.Y.: Prometheus Books, 1993), 123-139.

Koppelman, Andrew. "The Miscegenation Analogy: Sodomy Law as Sex Discrimination," *Yale Law Journal* 98 (November 1988): 145-164.

Kopyto, Harry. "The *Gay Alliance* Case Reconsidered," *Osgood Hall Law Journal* 18 (1980): 639-652.

Kujovich, Gil. "An Essay on the Passive Virtue of *Baker v. State*," *Vermont Law Review* 25 (2000): 134.

Labinski, Steve. "Session Ends in Standoff on Gay Issues," *Houston Voice*, 9 June 1997, 4.

Lambda Legal Defense and Education Fund, press release, 24 May 1996, on file with author.

Landau, Jack C. "Unspecific Charge of Homosexuality Held No Bar to Federal Employment," *Washington Post*, 29 August 1965, 3.

"Lawmakers' "Family Values" Vote Kills Gay-Marriage Ban," *Arizona Daily Star*, 2 April 1996, 33.

"Legal Briefs," *The Advocate*, 29 June 1993, 7.

Lesbian and Gay Immigration Rights Task Force, "World News in Brief," *Newsletter*, Spring 1997, 2.

"Lesbian Couple Sues Florida for Right to Wed," *Update*, 11 August 1993, 16.

"Lesbians and Gay Men," editorial, *New Statesman*, 11 October 1985, 4.

Lichtenstein, Grace. "Ruling on Homosexuality Seems to Have Little Effect," *New York Times*, 9 May 1976, 26.

Lindsey, Robert. "Homosexuals, Upset by Ruling, Plan Drive to Abolish Anti-Sodomy Laws," *New York Times*, 5 July 1986, 32.

Loving v. Virginia, 388 U.S. 1 (1967) (87 S.Ct. 1817, 18 L.Ed.2d. 1010).

Lucas, Greg. "Anti-Marriage Bill Killed in CA Senate," *San Francisco Chronicle*, 23 April 1997, 3.

Lumsden, Andrew. "Gayness Is Good for You," *New Statesman*, 31 August 1984, 13-16.

_____. "HMG Provides Cause Celebre for Gay Week," *New Statesman*, 21 June 1985, 4.

Macaulay, Stewart. "Non-Contractual Relations in Business: A Preliminary Study," *American Sociological Review* 28 (1963): 55-82.

"Male Couple Applies for Marriage License," *Los Angeles Times*, 24 February 1993, 21.

Marcus, Eric. *Making History: The Struggle for Gay and Lesbian Equal Rights 1945-1990* (1992).

Marotta, Toby. *The Politics of Homosexuality* (Boston: Houghton Mifflin Co., 1981).

Maynard v. Hill, 125 U.S. 190 (1888).

McCann, Michael W. *Taking Reform Seriously: Perspectives on Public Interest Liberalism* (Ithaca, N.Y.: Cornell University Press, 1986).

_____. "Legal Mobilization and Social Reform Movements," *Studies in Law, Politics, and Society* 11 (1991): 225-254, 228.

_____. "Reform Litigation on Trial," *Law and Social Inquiry* 17 (1992): 715-743, 731.

_____. "Reform Litigation on Trial," *Law and Social Inquiry* 18 (1993): 1101.

_____. *Rights at Work: Pay Equity Reform and the Politics of Legal Mobilization* (Chicago: University of Chicago Press, 1994).

_____. "How Does Law Matter for Social Movements?" unpublished paper, 1995.

McConnell v. Anderson, 451 F.2d 193 (8th Cir. 1971), cert. denied, 405 U.S. 1046 (1972).

McDonnell, Lynda. "Senate Rise to Occasion with Eloquent Debate," *St. Paul Pioneer Press*, 17 May 1997, 13.

McKinnon, John. *Wall Street Journal*, 12 June 1997, 13.

Merry, Sally Engle. *Getting Justice and Getting Even: Legal Consciousness among Working-Class Americans* (Chicago: University of Chicago Press, 1990).

"Men Challenge Laws Forbidding Same-Sex Marriage," *Frontiers*, 27 August 1993, 9.

Michaelson, Sherryl. "Religion and Morality Legislation: A Reexamination of Establishment Clause Analysis," *New York University Law Review* 51 (May 1984): 301-401.

Minow, Martha. *Making All the Difference: Inclusion, Exclusion, and American Law* (Ithaca, N.Y.: Cornell University Press, 1990).

Mohr, Richard D. "The Stakes in the Gay-Marriage Wars," in Robert M. Baird and Stuart E. Rosenbaum, eds. *Same-Sex Marriage: The Moral and Legal Debate* (Amherst, N.Y.: Prometheus Books, 1996): 106.

"Montgomery County Woman Challenges House to Weigh Same-Sex Unions," *Annapolis Daily Capital*, 13 March 1997, 13.

Moore v. City of East Cleveland, 431 U.S. 494, 503 (1977).

Morris, Robert J. "Aikane: Accounts of Hawaiian Same-Sex Relationships in the Journal of Captain Cook's Third Voyage (1776 - 80)," *Journal of Homosexuality* 29 (1990): 124-135.

Myers, Doug. "Homosexual Marriage Ban Delayed," *Baton Rouge Advocate*, 8 May 1997, 5.

Nemitz, Bill. "King's Stand Spoils Cosby's Celebration," *Portland Press-Herald*, 2 April 1997, 5.

Nicholson, John. "So Are Gay Rights A Vote Loser?," *New Statesman*, 4 October 1985, 8.

Nielsen, Linda. "Family Rights and the 'Registered Partnership' In Denmark," *International Journal of Law and the Family* 4 (1990): 297-307.

Norris v. Ireland, 142 Eur.Ct.H.R. (ser. A)(1988).

Note, "The Constitutional Status of Sexual Orientation:Homosexuality as a Suspect Class," *Harvard Law Review* 98 (1985): 1285-1309.

O'Brien, Dennis. "Against Gay Marriage: What Heterosexuality Means," *Commonweal*, 22 November 1991, 684-685.

O'Leary, Jean, and Bruce Voeller. "Implications of the Supreme Court Decision on Sodomy," *New York Times*, 15 May 1976, 25.

O'Neill, James M. "NJ Bill Opposing Same-Sex Marriages Passes First Hurdle," *Philadelphia Enquirer*, 24 January 1996, 7.

"Paper Includes Gay Couples on What Was Wedding Page," *New York Times*, 22 March 1991, A20.

Pedersen, Marianne Hojgaard. "Denmark:Homosexual Marriages and New Rules Regarding Separation and Divorce," *Journal of Family Law* 30 (1991/92): 289-293.

Perez v. Lippold, 32 Cal.2d 711, 198 P.2d 17 (1948).

Perry, Dan. "Israel Recognizes Gay Couples," *Boston Globe*, 1 December 1994, 2.

Petersen, C. "A Queer Response to Bashing: Legislating against Hate," *Queens Law Journal* 16 (1991): 237-260.

Pinkerton, James P. "A Conservative Argument for Gay Marriage," *Los Angeles Times*, 1 June 1993, B17.

Polikoff, Nancy. "We Will Get What We Ask for: Why Legalizing Gay and Lesbian Marriage Will Not 'Dismantle the Legal Structure of Gender In Every Marriage'," *Virginia Law Review* 79 (1993): 1535; Nan Hunter, "Marriage, Law, and Gender: A Feminist Legal Inquiry," *Law and Sexuality* 1 (1991): 9.

Power, Lisa, and Tim Barnett, "Gathering Strength and Gaining Power: How Lesbians and Gay Men Began to Change Their Fortunes in Britain in the Nineties, in Aart Hendriks, Rob Tielman, and Evert van der Veen, eds., *The Third Pink Book* (Buffalo, N.Y.: Prometheus Books, 1993), 171-180.

"Proposed Law Would Expand Rights of Registered Gay Couples," *Chicago Tribune*, 10 December 1996, 14.

"Public Opinion" File, available at the International Gay and Lesbian Archives, West Hollywood, California.

Rayside, David. "Gay Rights and Family Values: The Passage of Bill 7 in Ontario," *Studies in Political Economy* 26 (Summer 1988): 109-147.

_____. "Homophobia, Class and Party in England," *Canadian Journal of Political Science* 25 (March 1992): 121-149.

Richardson, Colin. "Homosexuality and the Judiciary," *New Law Review* 142 (31 January 1992): 130-131.

Richstone, Jeff, and J.Stuart Russell, "Shutting the Gate: Gay Civil Rights in the Supreme Court of Canada," *McGill Law Review* 27 (1981): 92-117.

Rivera, Rhonda R. "Our Straight-Laced Judges: The Legal Position of Homosexual Persons in the United States," *Hastings Law Journal* 30 (1979): 799-955.

_____. "Queer Law: Sexual Orientation Law in the Mid-Eighties," *University of Dayton Law Review* 11 (1987): 275-398.

Robinson, Svend. "Coming out as an MP in Canada," in Aart Hendriks, Rob Tielman, and Evert van der Veen, eds., *The Third Pink Book* (Buffalo, N.Y.: Prometheus Books, 1993), 181-183.

Roden, Robert. "Educating through the Law: The Los Angeles AIDS Dicrimination Ordinance," *UCLA Law Review* 33 (1986): 1410-1446.

Roe v. Wade, 410 U.S. 113.

Rosenberg, Gerald N. *The Hollow Hope: Can Courts Bring about Social Change?* (Chicago: University of Chicago Press, 1991).

Rubenstein, William B. "We Are Family: A Reflection on the Search for Legal Recognition of Lesbian and Gay Relationships," *Journal of Law & Politics* 8 (1991): 89-105.

———. "The Stonewall Anniversary: 25 Years of Gay Rights," *Human Rights*, Summer 1994, 18-23.

Rule, Sheila. "Rights for Gay Couples in Denmark," *New York Times*, 2 October 1989, 8.

Rwezaura, B. A. "The Legal Status of Woman-to-Woman Marriages in Tanzania," *East African Law Review* 7 (1974): 319-325.

Ryder, Bruce. "Equality Rights and Sexual Orientation: Confronting Heterosexual Family Privilege," *Canadian Journal of Family Law* 9 (1990): 39-97.

Sarat, Austin, and Thomas R. Kearns, eds. *Identities, Politics and Rights* (Ann Arbor, Mich.: University of Michigan Press, 1995): 13.

"Same-Sex Marriage Bill Easily Passes in the House," Associated Press, 21 February 1996.

Schattschneider, E.E. *The Semi-Sovereign People* (New York: Holt, Rinehart and Winston, 1960).

Schedler, Petra. "Two of a Kind, Two Different Kinds: Humanism, Homosexuality, and Emancipation in the Netherlands and Britain," in Aart Hendriks, Rob Tielman, and Evert van der Veen, eds., *The Third Pink Book* (Buffalo, N.Y.: Prometheus Books, 1993), 184-194.

Scheingold, Stuart A. *The Politics of Rights: Lawyers, Public Policy and Political Change* (New Haven, Conn.: Yale University Press, 1974).

Schmalz, Jeffrey. "Poll Finds an Even Split on Homosexuality's Cause," *New York Times*, 5 March 1993, C19.

_____. "In Hawaii, Step toward Legalized Gay Marriage," *New York Times*, 7 May 1993, A14.

Schmitt, Eric. "Senators Reject Both Job-Bias and Gay Marriage," *New York Times*, 11 September 1996, A1.

Schulte, Erin. "Debate Heard on Gay Unions," *Daily Nebraskan*, 19 March 1997, 14.

_____. "Same-Sex Marriage Bill Held up by 'Filibuster,'" *Daily Nebraskan*, 4 April 1997, 5.

_____. "Senators Try Amendments to Resolve Gay-Union Bill," *Daily Nebraskan*, 9 April 1997.

Schwarzschild, Hannah. "Same-Sex Marriage and Constitutional Privacy: Moral Threat and Legal Anomaly," *Berkeley Women's Law Journal* 4 (1988): 94-127.

Seabrook, Mike. "Homosexuality and the Police," *New Law Journal*, 6 March 1992, 325-326.

Shapiro, Joseph P. "Straight Talk about Gays," *U.S. News & World Report*, 5 July 1993, 42-48.

Shen, Fern. "A Same-Sex Couple Married to the Cause," *Washington Post*, 10 September 1996, A1.

Signorile, Michelangelo. "Bridal Wave," *Out*, December 1993/January 1994, 69-73+.

Silbey, Susan. "Making a Place for Cultural Analyses of Law," *Law and Social Inquiry* 17 (1992).

Singer v. Hara, 522 P.2d 1187, 11 Wash.App. 247 (1974).

Singer v. U.S. Civil Service Commission, 530 F.2d 247, 249 (9th Cir. 1976), vacated, 429 U.S. 103 (1977).

Skinner v. Oklahoma, 316 U.S. 535 (1942) (62 S.CT. 1110, 86 L.Ed. 1655).

Smith, Chris. "Coming out as an MP in the United Kingdom," in Aart Hendriks, Rob Tielman, and Evert van der Veen, eds., *The Third Pink Book* (Buffalo, N.Y.: Prometheus Books, 1993), 213-214.

Smith, Chris. "Not 'Out There'; the Hard Issue 1: Gay Rights," *New Statesman*, 5 June 1987, 20.

"A Solid Legislative Session," *Boulder Camera*, 13 May 1997, 23.

Steele, Scott. "Coming Out," *MacClean's*, 16 May 1994, 43.

Stevenson, Richard W. "British Gay Rights Groups Vow to Fight Consent Age," *New York Times*, 23 February 1994, 7.

Stone, Deborah. "Causal Stories and the Formation of Policy Agenda," *Political Science Quarterly* 104 (1989): 281-300.

Strasser, Mark. "Family, Definitions, and the Antimiscegenation Analogy," *Suffolk University Law Review* 25 (1991): 981-1034.

Sullivan, Andrew, ed. "The Politics of Homosexuality," *New Republic*, 10 May 1993, 24-27+.

_____. *Same-Sex Marriage: Pro and Con* (New York:Vintage Books, 1997).

Sunstein, Cass. "Foreword: Leaving Things Undecided," *Harvard Law Review* 110 (1996), 101

Swardson, Anne. "Ontario Turns down Gay Rights Measure," *Washington Post*, 10 June 1994, A26.

"Sweden Joins in Approving Partnership Law for Gay Couples," *Los Angeles Times*, 15 June 1994, E3.

"Swedish Law Allows Marriages for Gays," *Boston Globe*, 8 June 1994, 4.

Tatchell, Peter. *Out in Europe* (London:Channel Four Television, 1990).

_____. *Europe in the Pink* (London:GMP Publishers, 1992).

"Thousands Join in March for Homosexual Rights," *New York Times*, 28 June 1976, 31.

Tielman, Rob, and Hans Hammelburg, "World Survey of the Social and Legal Position of Gays and Lesbians," in Aart Hendriks, Rob Tielman and Evert van der Veen, eds., *The Third Pink Book* (Buffalo, N.Y.: Prometheus Books, 1993), 249-342.

Timmons, Stuart. *The Trouble with Harry Hay: Founder of the Modern Gay Movement* (Boston: Alyson Publications, 1990).

"Tradition Snags Gay Marriage Ban," *Austin American Statesman*, 14 May 1997, 8.

Treuthart, Mary Patricia. "Adopting a More Realistic Definition of Family," *Gonzaga Law Review* 26 (1990/91): 91-124.

Tribe, Laurence. "Toward a Less Perfect Union," *New York Times*, 26 May 1996, 32.

Trosino, James. "American Wedding: Same-Sex Marriage and the Miscegenation Analogy," *Boston University Law Review* 73 (1993): 93-120.

Tushnet, Marc. "An Essay on Rights," *Texas Law Review* 62 (1984): 1363-1412.

Tyler, Tracey. "Court Backs Gay Claims for Spousal Support," *Toronto Star*, 19 December 1996, 1.

Vaillancourt, Meg. "Hawaiian Marriages Will Hold-up in Bay State, Weld Says," *Boston Globe*, 5 December 1996, 7.

Veen, Evert van der, Aart Hendriks, and Astrid Mattijssen. "Lesbian and Gay Rights in Europe:Homosexuality and the Law," in Aart Hendriks, RobTielman, and Evert van der Veen, eds., *The Third Pink Book* (Buffalo, N.Y.: Prometheus Books, 1993), 225-248.

Waaldijk, Kees. "Standard Sequences in the Legal Recognition of Homosexuality–Europe's Past, Present and Future," *Australasian Gay and Lesbian Law Journal* 4 (1994): 50-72.

Waaldijk, Kees, and Andrew Clapham, eds. *Homosexuality: A European Community Issue* (Dordrecht, Netherlands: Martinus Nijhoff Publishers, 1993).

Wallsten, Peter. "Same-Sex Marriage Ban Raises Legal, Business Issues," *St. Petersburg Times*, 27 May 1997, 23.

Walsh, Mary William. "Canada Far Ahead of U.S. in Recognizing Gay Rights," *Los Angeles Times*, 29 December 1992, A1.

Weeks, Jeffrey. *Sex, Politics & Society*, 2d ed. (London: Longman, 1989), 96-121.

Wilkinson, J. Harvie, III, and G. Edward White. "Constitutional Protection of Personal Lifestyles," *Cornell Law Review* 62 (March 1977): 563-625.

Wilkowski, Mary A. "Rutherford Institute Challenges Fledgling Law–And Loses," *Island Lifestyle*, August 1992, 28-29.

Williams, Patricia. "Alchemical Notes: Reconstructing Ideals from Deconstructed Rights," *Harvard Civil Rights-Civil Liberties Law Review* 22 (1987): 410-33.

Williams, Walter L. *The Spirit and the Flesh* (Boston: Beacon Press, 1986)

Wilson, Adrienne K. "Same-Sex Marriage: A Review," *William Mitchell Law Review* 17 (1991): 539-562.

Wilson, James D. "Gays under Fire," *Newsweek*, 14 September 1992, 35-37+.

Wintemute, Robert. *Sexual Orientation and Human Rights* (Oxford:Clarendon Press, 1995).

Wockner, Rex. "Britain OKs Gay Partner Immigration," *Outlines*, 10 September 1997, 11.

Wolfson, Evan. "Crossing the Threshold: Equal Marriage Rights for Lesbians and Gay Men and the Intra-Community Critique," *Review of Law and Social Change* 21 (1994): 567 - 615.

_____. "The Freedom to Marry: Eyes on the Prize," *The Lamda Update*, Fall 1996, 1.

Wright, Jeff. "Anti-Gay Bill Passes Oregon Senate," *Eugene Register-Guard*, 24 May 1997, 12.

Zablocki v. Redhail, 434 U.S. 374, 98 S.CT. 673, 54 L.Ed.2d 618 (1978).

Zimmer, Lisa R. "Family, Marriage, and the Same-Sex Couple," *Cardozo Law Review* 12 (1990): 681-706.

Index

AIDS, 21, 25, 26, 60, 126–128, 157, 162
Alaska, 63–65, 74–76, 80, 81, 87–89, 105, 108, 110, 111, 113, 160, 161, 163, 167–169
American Civil Liberties Union, 23, 49, 73, 80, 84, 86, 93, 95
Amestoy, Jeffrey, 101–104, 107–109, 113
Baehr v. Lewin, 13, 49–62, 64, 71, 81, 88, 89, 97, 100, 110, 156, 162, 166, 167, 169
Baehr, Ninia, 50
Baker v. Nelson, 35–37, 40, 41
Baker v. Vermont, 51, 71, 99, 101, 102, 106–112, 115, 116, 166, 168–171
Beck, Nina, 99, 101
Belgium, 132
Brazil, 133, 136
Burger, Warren, 4
Burns, Kenneth, 18
Burns, James S., 52
Cain, Patricia, 16, 19, 20, 22, 26, 27
Cambodia, 145
Canada, 2, 122, 137–140, 155, 157, 159, 160
Casper, Jonathan, 3
Chang, Kevin S. C., 54, 55
Charter of Rights and Freedoms, 2, 137–139, 140, 157
Chayes, Abram, 3
China, 146
Civil Union Bill, 113, 114, 117, 163, 169
Clinton, Bill, 14, 90–92
Columbia, 156

Common Benefits Clause, 99, 101, 102, 104–107
Critical Legal Studies, 4, 5, 163
Czech Republic, 136
Dahl, Robert, 2, 3
Dancel, Genora, 49, 71
Dean, Craig, 42
Dean, Howard, 22, 88, 113, 115–117
Defense of Marriage Act, 14, 89, 90, 92, 173
Denmark, 121–129, 131, 133, 147, 156, 157, 159, 160
Dooley, John A., 104, 105, 107, 109
Dworkin, Ronald, 4, 7
D'Emilio, John, 14–18
Equal Protection Clause, 13, 39, 40, 51, 52, 56, 80, 84, 92, 99, 102, 105, 166
Equal Rights Amendment, 38, 39, 42, 56, 57, 100, 167
Eskridge, William, 158, 165, 171
European Convention on Human Rights, 2
European Court of Human Rights, 144, 145, 159
European Court of Justice, 144
Farnham, Lois, 99
Foley, Dan, 49, 50, 55–57, 59
France, 122, 133, 134, 145
Freedom to Marry Coalition, 88, 97, 172
Freedom to Marry Task Force, 101, 113, 118, 169
Full Faith and Credit Clause, 91, 92, 100, 102
Gay and Lesbian Advocates and Defenders, 53, 115, 172

Greenland, 131, 133
Gunderson, Steve, 33, 90
Halpern, Stephen, 4
Hamilton, Alexander, 2
Harrigan, Peter, 99
Hawaii, 13, 14, 44, 49–65, 71–77, 80–82, 88, 89, 92, 93, 97–99, 100, 101, 105, 108, 110–113, 156–170
Horowitz, Donald, 3–5
Human Rights Campaign Fund, 167
Hungary, 143
Hyde, Henry, 33
Iceland, 129, 131–133, 160
International Covenant on Civil and Political Rights, 144
Israel, 122, 140, 141, 156, 160
Johnson, Denise, 105–110, 168
Jolles, Stacy, 99, 101
Knight, William "Pete," 82
Kujovich, Gil, 166, 168–170
Lambda Legal Defense and Education Fund, 23, 49, 82, 88, 92, 97, 161
Levitt, Linda, 100, 101
Logan, Patrick, 49, 71
Mattachine Society, 14–18, 20–23
McCann, Michael, 5–8, 21, 27, 31, 165
Melillo, Joseph, 49, 71
Mohr, Richard, 165, 166
Moon, Ronald, 56
Mormon Church, 53, 74, 84, 92
Nakayama, Paul, 52
National Center for Lesbian Rights, 53
National Gay and Lesbian task Force, 24, 116
National Organization for Women, 53
Nepal, 147
Netherlands, 121, 129–133, 144
New Zealand, 122, 142, 143
Norway, 129, 131, 133, 160
Oregon, 80, 82, 83, 86–89, 92, 104, 109, 156
Pregil, Antoinette, 49, 71

Privacy, 22–24, 26, 33–37, 39, 43, 44, 49–51, 57, 62–64, 110, 111, 122, 145, 155, 162, 163
Puterbaugh, Holly, 99
Quakers, 53
Rodrigues, Tammy, 49, 71
Roman Catholic Church, 84, 136
Rosenberg, Gerald, 4, 6, 139, 161–163
Scheingold, Stuart, 4
Sex discrimination, 13, 44, 52, 53, 105, 107, 111, 112, 140–142, 144, 155, 163, 170
Sodomy, 17, 21–27, 42, 43, 61, 121, 146, 159, 160, 167, 168
South Africa, 2, 122, 147, 148
Spain, 122, 135, 136
Sullivan, Andrew, 34, 40
Suspect classification, 39, 43, 44, 52, 104
Sweden, 122, 129, 131, 133, 160
Taiwan, 146
Traditional Values Coalition, 53, 114
United Kingdom, 132, 157
Universal Declaration of Human Rights, 2
Universal Fellowship of Metropolitan Community Churches, 85
Vermont, 14, 62, 75, 80, 82, 87–89, 92, 99–104, 106, 108–118, 156–173
Warren, Earl, 3, 4, 36
Wolfson, Evan, 34, 62, 69, 70, 88, 92
Woods, Bill, 49

TEACHING TEXTS IN LAW AND POLITICS

David Schultz, *General Editor*

The new series Teaching Texts in Law and Politics is devoted to textbooks that explore the multidimensional and multidisciplinary areas of law and politics. Special emphasis will be given to textbooks written for the undergraduate classroom. Subject matters to be addressed in this series include, but will not be limited to: constitutional law; civil rights and liberties issues; law, race, gender, and gender orientation studies; law and ethics; women and the law; judicial behavior and decision-making; legal theory; comparative legal systems; criminal justice; courts and the political process; and other topics on the law and the political process that would be of interest to undergraduate curriculum and education. Submission of single-author and collaborative studies, as well as collections of essays are invited.

Authors wishing to have works considered for this series should contact:
> Peter Lang Publishing
> Acquisitions Department
> 275 Seventh Avenue, 28th floor
> New York, New York 10001

To order other books in this series, please contact our Customer Service Department at:
> 800-770-LANG (within the U.S.)
> (212) 647-7706 (outside the U.S.)
> (212) 647-7707 FAX

or browse online by series at:
> WWW.PETERLANGUSA.COM